THE
ARCHITECT
of
DESIRE

THE
ARCHITECT
of
DESIRE

BEAUTY AND DANGER
in the
STANFORD WHITE
FAMILY

SUZANNAH LESSARD

THE DIAL PRESS

Published by
THE DIAL PRESS
Bantam Doubleday Dell Publishing Group, Inc.
1540 Broadway
New York, New York 10036

The lines from "Diving into the Wreck," from DIVING INTO THE WRECK: Poems 1971–1972 by Adrienne Rich. Copyright 1973 by W.W. Norton & Company, Inc. Reprinted by permission of the author and W.W. Norton & Company, Inc.

Excerpts from STANNY: The Gilded Life of Stanford White by Paul R. Baker are reprinted with permission of The Free Press, a division of Simon & Schuster. Copyright 1989 by Paul R. Baker.

Quotations by Charles McKim are from The Life and Times of Charles Follen McKim by Charles Moore; Houghton Mifflin 1929.

Quotations by Edward Simmons are from From Seven to Seventy by Edward Simmons. Harper & Brothers, New York, 1922.

Quotations by H. Van Buren Magonigle are from "A Half-Century of Architecture: A Biographical Review," by H. Van Buren Magonigle; Pencil Points, 15 (March 1934).

Quotations by Evelyn Nesbit are from Prodigal Days: The Untold Story by Evelyn Nesbit; Julian Messner, Inc., New York, 1934.

The quotation by Brendan Gill is reprinted by permission of the author. Copyright 1990 by Brendan Gill. Originally in The New Yorker. All rights reserved.

Excerpts from the personal memoirs and correspondence of Bessie Smith White, Lawrence Grant White and Laura Chanler White appear courtesy of Guy G. Rutherfurd, Morris & McVeigh.

Excerpts from Family Vista by Margaret Chanler Aldrich and the correspondence of Margaret Chanler Aldrich and J. Armstrong Aldrich appear courtesy of the Rokeby Archives.

Excerpts from poems by Claire Nicolas White appear courtesy of the author.

Endpapers: Freehand rendering by Stanford White on sepia print construction document for Box Hill and surroundings. Courtesy Avery Architectural Fine Arts Library, Columbia University in the City of New York.

Photo editor: Vincent Virga

Copyright © 1996 by Suzannah Lessard

Library of Congress Cataloging in Publication Data
Lessard, Suzannah.
The architect of desire : beauty and danger in the Stanford White family / by Suzannah Lessard.
p.   cm.
ISBN 0-385-31445-0
1. Murder—New York (N.Y.)   2. White, Stanford, 1853–1906.   3. Nesbit, Evelyn, 1884–1967.
4. Thaw, Harry Kendall, 1871–1947.   I. Title.
HV6534.N5L395   1996
364.1'523'09227471—dc20   96-17159
                                                                                  CIP

Book design by Julie Duquet
Manufactured in the United States of America
Published simultaneously in Canada
November 1996
10   9   8   7   6   5   4   3   2
BVG

for
William Shawn

I came to see the damage that was done
And the treasures that prevail.

—ADRIENNE RICH,

"DIVING INTO THE WRECK"

THE FAMILY

Richard Grant White-*m*-Alexina Black Mease
1826–1885   1830–1921

Richard Mansfield
(1851–unknown)

John Lawrence Smith-*m*-Sarah Clinch
1816–1889   1823–1890

The Smiths
Nellie, Ella, Kate, Louise,
James, Lawrence, May

John Winthrop Chanler-*m*-Margaret Astor Ward
1826–1877   1838–1875

"The Astor Orphans"
J. Armstrong ("Archie"), Emily, Elizabeth, William,
Marion, Lewis, Margaret, Robert, Alida, Egerton

Winthrop ("Wintie")-*m*-Margaret Terry ("Daisy")
1863–1926   1861–1952

Hester, Gabrielle, Marion, Theodore,
Beatrice, Hubert, John

Stanford —*m*— Bessie ("Grandma White")
1853–1906   1862–1950

Lawrence ("Papa") —*m*— Laura ("Mama")
1887–1956   1887–1984

Peter   Elizabeth   **Bobby**   **Johnny**   Cynthia   Sarah   Ann
1920–   1925–1989

Sebastian, Stephanie,   **Pamela**
Christian, Natalie

Mary-*m*-**Frank Rousseau**
1923–   1920–

Suzannah   Beatrice   Felicity   Madeleine   Isabella   Gertrude
1944–   1948–   1950–   1951–   1955–   1963–

(The names of some of the individuals in this family tree have been changed to protect their privacy or the privacy of their families.)

CONTENTS

❧

THE
ARCHITECT
of
DESIRE

THE PLACE

Collection of The New-York Historical Society

WHEN I WAS a little girl, I liked to go into a formal garden of box bushes that lay just to the west of my grandparents' house. The box garden, as it was called, was on a terrace that was significantly lower than the house and thus apart, in a zone of its own. The hedges that lined the paths had grown high and billowy, so that they were over my head, and in some places had grown so close together that I had to push my way through. The bushes would then spray me with their gritty dust, and I'd smell the sharp-smelling box-bush decay rising from the damp ground where no sun reached, and see up close the way the leaves were bunched in kernels like tiny loose cabbages. It seems to me now that my family story was all there always, everywhere, layered away, as in the kernels of box, and that I absorbed it somatically—took it in through my pores with the gritty box dust.

At the center of the garden was a circular space, also hedged by box, in which there was a shallow, round pool, with a crouching marble statue of Venus in the middle, her nude back roughened with exposure. The weedy gravel around the pool was also spongy with yew needles, and in one spot there was a bronze flower-shaped lid, light-catching with verdigris, that covered a small well. Removing this cover, I would then reach down till my armpit was crushed against the edge, through dampness and maybe bugs, to turn a rusty wheel at the bottom. Then water would spurt from four jets around the statue into the sky.

Beyond the box garden was the estate that my great-grandfather Stanford White had designed—the Place, as we called it in the family. That Stanford was a famous Beaux-Arts architect, notorious for being murdered in scandalous circumstances, was part of the environment too. He was, however, rarely mentioned on the Place. He was latent. The silence about him was something dark right there in the light. When I was a child, the Place was very bright. In that brightness, silence extended to the horizon like the sea, or like his fame: it was everywhere so that you didn't notice it, like the air.

The Place was sixty miles from New York on the North Shore of Long Island, in the village of St. James, which was part of the town of Smithtown. It consisted of sixty acres—a plateau on which the dwellings stood, and steep wooded hills that fell to Stony Brook Harbor. The principal feature of the Place was the main house called Box Hill—occupied by my grandparents in my girlhood. There was also a cluster of barns, also designed by Stanford, plus some older barns and farmhouses from earlier times. There were nodes on the Place—a temple in a laurel wood, a statue among pines on a hill—connected, either explicitly, by roads and pathways, or implicitly, by the way they were placed in relation to each other. The harmony and symmetry and the balanced interrelation of spots created an atmosphere of providential protection. This rationality and integration is typical of Beaux-Arts design, in which the landscape is an extension of the architecture and the smallest detail is connected to the vision of the whole. Thus, the silence notwithstanding, there was hardly a spot on the Place in which Stanford was not present.

It's not true that Stanford was *never* mentioned, however. I remember times in the Box Hill library, way, way back—winter scenes, with the sun pouring in, with sherry for the grown-ups and cheddar spread on Ritz crackers, and a fire on the hearth in sunlight—when my grandmother would mention Stanford in a happy way, having to do with his hair, which was red: intimate allusions, in which she would point out how Stanford's hair had turned up in my grandfather's red mustache, disappeared for a generation, and then popped up on me.

As I grew I gradually went farther and farther afield, establishing an emotional residence in the landscape which for a long time would be what I remembered of my childhood—would become what I thought of as my real life. Eventually I found my way down through the woods to the harbor. Sometimes the water in the harbor was a feral blue and choppy in a way that made it look like fur roughed backward, while the trees on the far shores glowed. Or the water might be pewter and as flat as a mirror and the shores slate. Or there could be mists rising off the water with swans swimming out of them under a pink sky.

A short way along the shore, to the west, standing on a high bank above the beach there was a windmill, designed by Stanford, shingled and very tall in order to catch the prevailing south wind. Its petal-like vanes were like a halo. The windmill had been built to pump spring water to the houses on top of the hill. Indeed, springs ran out from under the bank all along the beach there, the water so cold that the sensation would shoot up my legs like the notes of a trumpet. As I neared it the windmill's dark mass loomed upward, too close to see whole—an enormous, moldy derelict in a sunless place. Inside, the stairs zigzagged upward to infinity in a gray light that came in through holes in the sides where storms had blown shingles away. Inside, was a creaking sound—the vanes, connected to the pumping mechanism, changing direction with slight shifts in the wind.

I have come to see family history as similar to architecture in certain ways. Like architecture, it is quiet. It encompasses, but does not necessarily demand attention. You might not even notice that it's there. Like architecture, too, family history can suddenly loom into consciousness. For example, you can sit in the New York Public Library at Forty-second Street—designed by Carrère & Hastings, and perhaps the greatest building in New York—with your nose in a book, or busy with the catalogue and transactions with clerks, all the while oblivious of the splendid interior around you. You can forget it utterly, or perhaps not have noticed it at all that day, and then, casually looking up, be astonished, even momentarily disoriented by what you see. So it is with family history. One can go about one's life with no thought of the past, and then, as if waking from a dream, be astonished to see that you are living within its enclosure. I was in my thirties when I began to perceive that my own life was encompassed in this way. At first this seemed to be a form of bondage, but it turned out to be a gift, and all family history, it seems to me, must be a gift in a similar way.

The legacy of real architecture is that it can affirm aspects of sensibility that otherwise might lie fallow, unsuspected. Chartres draws into salience the faculty of awe that in our secular age might never be awakened. An eighteenth-century drawing room makes one aware of one's innate dignity, which might easily be forgotten in the age of the mall. The correlation between architecture and interior life allows us to relive past visions by simply entering the architecture those visions produced.

In a similar way, there was for me a correlation between the architecture of my family history and my inner life. In both something was hidden. In the beautiful environment of the family past, there was a magnificent figure who had gone out of control in ways destructive to those on his course—including his family—and ultimately to himself. Behind my memories of a blissful childhood in a beautiful place, there were also destructive forces that were blind and out of control, but unacknowledged. Yet to this inner truth and all its ramifications I had no access. This was the great role of family history to me. It made my hidden experience resonate, and by so doing delivered to me a whole self.

The family architecture also taught me how short time is, how close the generations are, how powerfully lives reverberate down through the structure of family, deeply affecting each other. This is the other part of the imperative to go back into the architecture of time, for with our response to those reverberations, whether witting or unwitting, we in turn create the unseen structure within which our children must live.

Opals

F or seventeen years, between the ages of twenty-eight and forty-five, I lived on Lower Fifth Avenue in New York City. The atmosphere of this neighborhood had drawn me in an uncanny way. The traffic slowed, anticipating the end of the Avenue, and the broadness of the sidewalks encouraged a promenade pace. Two churches, one red, one black, both set back in yards, opened the Avenue with their towers to the sky, and on breezy days the boughs of the trees in the yard of the black church curtsied and whispered. At the foot of the Avenue was Washington Square Arch, and beyond was the park, with its wide, shallow fountain, and the radial design of its walks. That the arch and the park had been designed by Stanford White was known to me, yet I usually pushed my knowl-

edge aside as if to protect my life from encroaching family associations. I loved the way the deep red of the old brick of the houses
that still lined one side of the Square flashed through the trees,
giving the park a feeling of enclosure without confinement. Even
along the Avenue, there was a feeling of brownstone scale, though
only one brownstone, 49 Fifth Avenue, remained. Number 49 stood
just opposite the black church and right next door to my apartment
building on the corner of Twelfth Street. This brownstone was a
majestic specimen with a sweeping stoop, double the normal width,
which led up to a pedimented and deeply inset door flanked by three
French windows and delicate ironwork balconies. Especially around
its windows, there was a feeling of novels.

One day my maternal grandmother—Laura Chanler White,
whom we called Mama in the family—telephoned from the country
and in the course of our conversation reminded me that when she
was a girl she had lived with her parents at number 49. She had had
her coming-out party there, in 1904, she said. I realized that I'd
known this all along. Then Mama remembered—and in her old age
her remembering state could be almost trancelike—that in that
same year there had been a scandal in the neighborhood. One of the
parishioners of the church across the street—the black church—was
rumored to be having an affair with the minister, and, indeed,
Mama had often noticed that parishioner's well-known crimson
coupe flagrantly parked on Fifth Avenue right in front of the church,
for all to see. Then she remembered she had in that same period
been sitting in the parlor looking out the window at the passing
traffic—still mostly horse-drawn—and had seen Stanford White in a
little red car. The car was driven by a chauffeur, but Stanford was in
the front seat, and though the car was already going very fast for
those times—faster than anyone else—he was leaning forward, as if
to make it go faster. He was a big man, Mama said, and he looked
almost too big for the little car.

Mama knew Stanford because he was a friend of her parents,
Winthrop and Daisy Chanler, who knew all the choicest people—
among them Henry James, Bernard Berenson, Edith Wharton, and

even Theodore Roosevelt, the President of the United States at the time. The idea of "the choicest people" is a quintessentially Daisy Chanler idea, to which might be added her suggestion that "bore insurance" be issued, against the danger of being seated next to a boring person at a dinner party. Stanford was fifty years old and a social lion himself—a far from boring one—when Mama met him, and she was sixteen, but he had befriended her in her own right. That year, at a dance, to Mama's wonder, Stanford sat next to her for the entire evening. He made a connection with her that remained vivid for the rest of her life.

On another occasion, Mama arranged a dinner to honor her parents, inviting luminaries—including Stanford—whom at sixteen she would never have dared approach were it not for her parents' auspices. Then, at the last minute, just before the guests were about to arrive, her parents swept down the stairs in evening clothes. They told Mama that they had other plans—that they were going out for the evening and she was on her own with her fancy guests. And out they went. Mama always told the story as if her parents had turned the tables on her in a witty manner. They had tossed her a challenge, the idea was, that Mama roundly deserved for having such big ideas. As a child I of course assumed that Mama's parents were right, because that was the way Mama told the story, laughing at the fact that she had been terrified and humiliated because she was totally at a loss about how to care for such guests.

Then Stanford arrived. Immediately he gathered what had happened, assumed the role of host, and made the evening a success. It is always a great occasion when another person perceives one's predicament, for not only does this mean help but it means that one has been *seen*. Even when she told this story in great old age, Mama was grateful to Stanford for seeing her. She laughed, but her feelings—gasping fear, followed by relief—were still fresh, as if the incident had just happened. Always when Mama mentioned Stanford there was something in her voice that was womanly and deeply feeling, though also the tone of one puzzling something out, weighing and parsing, yet keeping her counsel.

At the time my grandmother caught sight of Stanford White driving on Lower Fifth Avenue he was a major figure in society, and in civic affairs in New York, and he was at the peak of his career as an architect. He had built many city landmarks: he had designed Washington Square Arch, the layout of the park beyond it, and Judson Memorial Church, with its Italianate tower of loggias overlooking the south side of the park. The arch had its origin as a temporary wooden structure for a blowout celebration of the centennial of Washington's Inauguration, in 1889—Stanford was the impresario of the whole affair which was just one of many civic extravaganzas that he had been called upon to produce. His wooden arch had been so popular that it was replaced with a marble one. Stanford had by that time also designed many palaces for the Gilded Age rich, and many clubs—for the Gilded Agers and for the old New Yorkers who snubbed them. He had designed New York University (the uptown campus in the Bronx) and a number of banks and government buildings, and he had significantly expanded and refurbished Thomas Jefferson's campus at the University of Virginia. But his most famous building, the one that most fully reflected his extravagance and his ebullience, was Madison Square Garden, just a few blocks up Fifth Avenue from where Mama saw him in his little red car.

Madison Square Garden stood on Twenty-sixth Street where Fifth Avenue and Broadway—or High Society and Café Society—crossed, the right location for Stanford, who moved in both worlds. Completed in 1890, it was a joyously ornamented, imperial edifice of yellow brick, white tile, and terra-cotta. The main arena could accommodate fourteen thousand people, had a floor that could be flooded for aquatic spectacles, was bright with hundreds of electric lights—a novelty—and had a huge skylight that could be opened to the air. There was also a theatre that could seat twelve hundred, a fifteen-hundred-seat concert hall, and the Roof Garden, which was a partly outdoor restaurant, its terrace surrounded by a colonnade, and with a stage for light entertainment—all beneath a tower that soared to three hundred and forty-one feet. The tower, completed a year later, was modelled on a Spanish cathedral tower that was partly Moorish and partly late Spanish Renaissance, a flamboyant period, and Stanford's tower was higher than its model. It had seven stories, then an upper loggia, from which a winding staircase led to a chamber enclosed by columns, and from the chamber rose a ladder to a small balcony around a cupola that supported a large bronze statue of the goddess Diana, balancing on one foot, with her bow drawn.

It was not just the architecture of Madison Square Garden that reflected Stanford, it was the way he had impelled it into being, working on it night and day from mid-1887 until mid-1890, raising funds as well as seeing that the design was executed properly, pouring money into it himself, negotiating with strikers, badgering the directors, and then mercilessly pressuring them when they began to balk at runaway costs. The directors wanted to eliminate the tower, for example, but under unrelenting pressure from Stanford their resolve collapsed. Stanford pressured the contractor too, something that, of course, an architect is supposed to do, but not to the extent that Stanford did it: "White is . . . hounding me into the ground," the contractor complained. Stanford designed every detail of the building that became known as the Palace of Pleasures, right down to the ushers' orange swallowtail coats, red waistcoats, and silver buttons. He subsequently produced many extravaganzas there, including, in the flooded arena, a miniature Venice that patrons could explore in gondolas, and a Caribbean show in which small-scale ships refought the Battle of Santiago.

But the aspect on which he lavished the most effort and expense was the statue of Diana. With the contractor and the directors in rebellion, he persuaded his friend the sculptor Augustus Saint-Gaudens to create the statue free of charge, while he himself picked up the considerable cost of materials and of the statue's installation on top of the tower. On the night of the unveiling of Diana, eight thousand lights outlined Madison Square Garden, and she stood at its apex, eighteen feet high and a thousand eight hundred pounds, in the curve of a plate-glass crescent moon that was twelve feet wide and lit from within by sixty-six bulbs. The moon was balanced on a rotating ball so that the statue would respond like a weathervane—and it did, even to very light puffs of air. Two searchlights lit up her gilded figure as she turned, shocking New Yorkers with her nudity, just as Saint-Gaudens and Stanford had hoped. A man in Greenwich, Connecticut, picked her out with his telescope.

Alas, once she was up there both Stanford and Saint-Gaudens thought she was too big for the tower, and so—here is the obsessive perfectionism that characterized Stanford throughout his life—they had her taken down. A to-do arose when the statue was accepted for the Women's Pavilion at the Columbian Exposition in Chicago, because the Women's Christian Temperance Union insisted that she be clothed; she ended up on top of the Agriculture Building, designed by Stanford's partner Charles McKim. A replacement Diana for the Madison Square Garden tower was five feet shorter, smaller breasted, and had a slimmer figure, and was made in part from plaster casts taken by Saint-Gaudens from a model's living body and then enlarged. There was no moon this time. The new Diana stood directly on the swivelling orb, balancing—almost leaping—on the ball of one foot, with the other foot outstretched behind, about to absorb the powerful recoil of her fully drawn bow. At the top of the tower that itself leapt upward vertiginously, she turned lightly in the wind.

There were seven small apartments in the tower above the Roof Garden, and Stanford took one for private parties and rendezvous. He had its small studio painted umber, sienna, vermillion, and chrome yellow. One cannot tell the story of Stanford White without litanies of this sort. The studio was furnished with carved chairs and divans, paintings, tapestries, Oriental rugs, leopard and tiger skins, a crystal globe, a Japanese fish in a fishbowl, a cardinal's hat that served as a lampshade, and a copy of the MacMonnies' "Bacchante"—a bronze nude of a young woman leaping ecstatically, balanced on one foot, effortlessly carrying an infant who reaches for grapes she holds above him. The statue had been commissioned for the courtyard of the Boston Public Library—one of McKim, Mead

& White's great successes—but a scandalized public had insisted that it be withdrawn. There was also a bed in the studio; some social occasions in Stanford's tower apartment were more intimate than others.

Another Stanford occasion was a gala festivity that took place at the photography studio of his friend James Breese on May 20, 1895, and came to be known as the Pie Girl Dinner. It was a stag event at which scarcely nubile and nearly nude young women served the wine—a blonde for the white and a brunette for the red—and a young woman called Susie Johnson jumped naked or clad in gauze (accounts differ) out of a pie, accompanied by canaries. Word of this dinner reached the newspapers, and the publicity dogged Stanford. By 1904, when Mama saw Stanford in his car on Lower Fifth Avenue, there had come to be a penumbra of depravity around the gregarious, dynamic, much loved and celebrated architect.

In 1904 Mama knew and was courted by Lawrence Grant White, Stanford's only child, known to his friends as Larry. They had met at a dance class, and were the same age almost to the day. On the weekend of June 23, 1906, she went out with Larry to Box Hill. On Sunday night they dined with Stanford and Bessie, Larry's mother. Stanford had bought an opal necklace for Bessie, but she had said she couldn't possibly accept it, because opals brought bad luck. Sometime that evening he also offered it to Mama, but, though she thought it beautiful, she too turned it down on the ground that opals brought bad luck. Mama wasn't superstitious: perhaps she felt uncomfortable at the thought of accepting such a gift from her host, who was three times her age and the father of her beau, yet was also a man to whom she was powerfully attracted. In a gesture that Mama never forgot, Stanford put the opals back in his jacket pocket.

Mama later described Larry in this period as a "callow youth" and Stanford as "bristling with life." Callow or not, Larry was a handsome, polished young man, and he and his father—who was not so polished, and who had not had the kind of privileged upbringing that his son had enjoyed—tended to become irritable with each other. Stanford was in an enthusiastic mood that night at Box

Hill, as he often was, and Larry was in a negative mood, as he often could be: he contradicted nearly everything that his father said, until, exasperated, Stanford poked Mama in the ribs with his elbow and said to his son, "Well, you like *this,* don't you?" The remark mortified Larry; he fell silent, and remained so for the rest of the meal. Mama did not say how she herself felt about it.

On Monday Mama returned to New York with Larry in the afternoon. Stanford, who had returned in the morning, wanted to take them to dinner and a show, but they couldn't join him because Mama had to catch the Lackawanna night train for her parents' home in the Genesee Valley, in upstate New York. So Larry and Mama had sandwiches with friends instead, then he accompanied her on the ferry across the Hudson to the Lackawanna station in New Jersey, and saw her off. The next day, Mama and everyone else in America who read the newspapers learned that Stanford had gone the previous evening to see "Mamzelle Champagne," a musical that was being put on at the Roof Garden. He had been seated at a front table that was always reserved for him and, while listening to a song entitled "I Could Love a Million Girls," had been approached by Harry K. Thaw, a millionaire from Pittsburgh, who was very pale and seemed to be in an agitated state. Stanford had looked at Thaw "without moving," according to the New York *Times,* as Thaw had pulled out a pistol and fired from a range of three inches into Stanford's face.

The New York *Times* quoted Thaw as having said, after Stanford tumbled to the floor, "You'll never go out with that woman again." The paper said that Thaw's wife was the former Evelyn Nesbit, whom White had put on the stage when she was fifteen or sixteen, and that Lawrence White, who had been informed of the death of his father by reporters when he came home that evening, told the reporters he had never heard of Evelyn Nesbit. Larry also told the reporters that he and a "college friend" had dined with his father that evening and then gone their separate ways. Mama, who had had supper with Larry, always regarded this as a fib that Larry told to keep her name out of the newspapers.

The murder and the circumstances surrounding it became a sensational ongoing newspaper story with Stanford White's sex life at the center of it. Even allowing for sensationalism, it became evident that Stanford had loved, if not a million girls, then, perhaps a thousand. The scandal exploded so fast that Stanford's funeral, scheduled to be held in St. Bartholomew's Church, had to be cancelled because crowds of sensation seekers threatened to overwhelm it; instead a small service took place at the Episcopal church in St. James. Stanford's numerous friends were in a state of shock over the revelations, some because they were horrified, others because they had participated in Stanford's secret life and were scared. Allan Evarts, a lawyer whom Larry hired to represent the family, spoke for them when he said to the press, "Many charges have been made as to the private life of Mr. White and so far not a single person has come forward to clear his name. The time has not come." Until then, he said, the family would be silent on the matter. But there were only more and more scandalous revelations. The time never came.

In January 1907, Thaw was tried for murder. The first witness was Larry, who was described by the *Times* as "a tall well-built young man," and as testifying "without emotion" and "without straining for effect." Larry's testimony concerned the evening of the murder. He repeated the story of having had supper with his father and a college friend and of going their separate ways. He thereupon left the courtroom and never returned: indeed, with one exception, he never made another public comment about his father's death, and the only private one that I know of was to Mama. To her he said that he realized that because of the scandals it would be impossible for her to consider marrying him. She said, "Don't be silly"—not that Mama was ready to marry anyone yet. She was about to leave for Paris, to study painting.

The defense sought sympathy for Thaw by portraying Stanford as someone whose morals were so bad that he deserved to be shot. Thus the trial became, in effect, a trial of Stanford White. The only stroke of good luck from the point of view of the family—and of the prosecution—was the judge's ruling that material concerning Stanford's life apart from his relationship to Evelyn Nesbit Thaw was irrelevant. Still, the revelations were quite bad enough even then. Largely because Evelyn gave an explicit and lengthy testimony of her seduction by Stanford, President Roosevelt, who moved in the Whites' social circle, asked the Postmaster General to ban accounts of the trial from the mails on the ground that they were pornography. The ban was not imposed, nor did Congress pass a resolution condemning Stanford, although, as the *Times* reported, Congress seemed to do little else but discuss the scandal.

Stanford White became a staple of church sermons on the Biblical text about sowing the wind and reaping the whirlwind. "He was the architect of his own ruin," a preacher from Philadelphia wrote in a letter to the *Times*. "Hundreds of Whites exist in this country but their wealth protects them from exposure," another wrote, voicing the groundswell of anger at the conspicuous rich and their ways which found an outlet in the Stanford White affair. That set had deserted Stanford in death, however, as had even close friends, most of whom continued to absent themselves during the trial: "Will no one say a word for Stanford White?" the prosecutor, William Travers Jerome, pleaded.

The January trial ended in a hung jury on April 12th, so the process had to be repeated the following year. On February 1, 1908, Thaw was acquitted by reason of insanity and sent to a mental institution. On June 16, 1916, ten years after Stanford's death, Laura Chanler and Larry White married. A family friend once told me that *her* mother, who had been a member of the New York society of the time, said that because of the scandals it took great social courage for Mama to marry Papa—as Larry became known in the family. Mama never implied anything of the sort, however, and I don't believe she saw her choice that way. Far from portraying her marriage to Papa as heroic, she tended to describe it as a kind of last-minute, "Why not?" decision on her part: and she was twenty-eight: for her it was time to be married. Papa had been away in training for the war and had lost weight and looked handsome, so why not?

My grandmother and grandfather made a most respectable couple with charming manners and well-made clothes and good shoes. They had three boys and five girls: my mother, Mary, was their fourth child. At first the family lived in New York, but then they moved to Box Hill. They were married for forty years, and in that lifetime together, according to Mama, the one discussion they ever had about the murder of Stanford was in that conversation shortly after the murder when Mama had said "Don't be silly."

I know of only one time that the trauma of the murder overtly registered in family life on the Place. When my younger sister Madeleine was twelve she was given a star opal by her godfather. She showed it to Mama, who blanched—the only instance I know of in which my grandmother showed fear. She conveyed such alarm that Madeleine ran off the Place, and across the public road, and threw the opal as far as she could into some brambles and vines on the edge of the potato field there.

THE RED COTTAGE

THE DINING ROOM in the Red Cottage had a wavy wooden floor that pitched down, with a twist in it, like a swaying field. Patched and repatched, the plaster walls were wavy too. The ceiling was low. There were two windows facing west, one of them partly obscured by a rosebush. Beyond the rosebush was a bit of garden, and then a barrier of trees. In the evening, beams from the setting sun would shoot through the trees into the dining room, filling it with radiance, and then dim to skewed rectangles of light on the wall. The light looked as if it were shining through mottled water, but the mottles on the wall were still. Sometimes when the rosebush was in bloom, the gray shadow of a rose would quiver and bob in the mottled light. One evening when I was a child my mother said of a rose-shadow: "That is the signature of this place."

I grew up in the Red Cottage with my parents, Frank and Mary Rousseau, and my sisters Beatrice, Felicity, Madeleine, Isabella, and Gertrude, whom we called Trudi. My father was a composer in the neoclassical style, and my mother was a singer. The Red Cottage was a nineteenth-century farmhouse on the Place that had been built by a craftsman—because a house was needed, that's all. On the outside it was unconcerned with its appearance and, on the inside, was without expectation that people be special or events be memorable. Yet when I was thinking of designing my own house, and cast about in my mind for rooms I'd known with pleasurable proportions, the Red Cottage dining room was one of them. What the dining room had in common with other rooms I liked was that it was almost but not quite square. The other rooms had been designed by architects, however, and there was about them a sense of knowing choice that gave one the feeling of being solidly positioned in an evolved society. The Red Cottage dining room, in contrast, had been built by a carpenter moving right along, and then had matured into waviness. Its rightness was a fluke: beyond choice— beyond luck, even. The flukiness could make you feel as if you were floating in a painting by Chagall, or could precipitate you into a long complicated train of thought that ran its course in an instant in the middle of a conversation about something else. Rooms conceived by architects usually convey a sense of relations between people, but the Red Cottage dining room was about internal experiences. At supper the wind would blow up through the floorboards and lift our dresses and gently blow our hair.

The context of the Red Cottage was different from the context of other houses. For other houses, the context might be society, or history, or the present day, or, as with Box Hill, the context might be fantasy. But the context of my childhood home was none of these things. It can happen anywhere that an abrupt silence can develop for no discernible reason—the crickets stop chirping or the traffic ceases—and in that silence your ears seem to pop and you momentarily forget not just the date but even what your name is. The Red Cottage was in such an unmoored stillness all the time.

The Red Cottage garden took its character from the traces of its varied uses in the days when it was a little farm. Around the house the terrain was stubbornly hummocky and, where the grassy places ran into the woods, wayward. There were some tumbledown barns in the woods, and a deep foundation where a larger barn had once stood: indeed the woods themselves were grown-up pasture with old fence posts running through under the trees. The anonymous presence of those who had lived and worked there lingered low on the ground like smoke, and in this there was a kind of cozy companionship. But it was wild there too. The birds racketed in the trees as if there were no people around. In midsummer a leafiness could seem to liquefy, almost to pulse. Even the most formal gardens have an animistic quality that comes out in the dark and belongs purely to nature. The Red Cottage garden had the quality of a garden in darkness even at noon.

For a long time, it seemed to me that the only way to describe my experience as a child in the Red Cottage was to describe the rooms. For a long time my experience was out of sight and reach; it was something there, but not in the picture, with the result that the physical character of the house seemed to me to be the telling thing.

The dining room was the piano room for a while when I was a tiny girl. The piano was a Steinway parlor grand, just one grade below the biggest made, "a foot longer than a regular grand," my mother would say, adding, "nearly a concert grand." The piano had been Stanford White's and had come from Box Hill, but its enormous importance in the household stemmed not from its dynastic provenance, or even from its sheer size, but from the importance of the force of music in our family life. My father's musical gift generated a sense of purpose that enveloped us. There was nothing my sisters and I might do that could compare in importance to that gift and the fulfillment of its promise.

My father was tall and lanky and had narrow, rounded shoulders and a big head with a winged jaw, a mischievous, catlike expression, and curly dark hair that receded to make inlets near the temples. His ears were comely and large, with acoustical convolutions that were more complex than usual. My sense of his presence in the Red Cottage is encompassing, but in many of my childhood memories of Dad he appears in a visually incomplete form: a set to his mouth, a look in his eye, knuckles, the piece of foot with a brown birthmark on it. I remember the piano in the same disjunctive, cubist way—the amber insides of the hammers, the rigid parallel strings, the cracked and yellowing keys—the architecture around these fractured images is the Red Cottage, but it too is incomplete and often wildly skewed, as if from a perspective on the floor, or from the changing positions of tumbling. Always most vivid in these memories is the sense of my father's presence which is almost apart from his physical features, so that my memories are like perceptions of one's own body without mirrors: one is *in* it yet sees it in bits.

Sometimes Dad would jump up in the middle of the night and rush down to the piano to compose some music that had come into his head. Sometimes during the day he would sit at a drawing board near the piano and copy out his music for hours with a tiny quill pen and India ink as we tried not to run and jiggle the floor. Sometimes he would play the teeth of the leviathan, and an ocean of glory would roll through our matchstick house.

My father changed when he sat at the piano. He played effortlessly, his body still and relaxed, looking all the while around the room in an abstracted way—this is a whole image—and smiling occasionally at the music as if it were independent of his playing and had surprised him. At the piano, my father seemed supernally calm. He was at home with music and the Steinway, but he was not at home with his girls. Dad had an infectious laugh that conveyed the absurdity of life, and he would laugh at the fact that—one, two, three, four, five, six—we had all turned out to be girls. This great quantity of femininity pitching around one unit of gifted masculine force magnificently amplified by the Steinway was the overt structure of life in the Red Cottage when I was young.

My mother was beautiful, and famous for her beauty on the Place and in our house and in the world. She had black unmanageable hair, fair skin with high color, and greenish eyes. Her teeth were white and slightly transparent, and her smile was fresh and unreserved. I remember her hips swaying in a straight skirt—she was wearing stockings and heels, and a silk blouse, and a necklace and perfume—as she went up the stairs.

My father was a person of clefs and measures, sharps and flats, who advocated discipline and boundaries—especially the boundaries between children and grown-ups. In contrast my mother was a person of the inspiration of the moment, and of a mysticism that did not recognize borders or limits. She identified with aboriginal peoples—our local Indians, the Setaukets, for example, who had led a woebegone life of subsistence on clams. She was spontaneous, and her moods had a global quality. If she was sad, there was no space in which to stand outside her sadness. If it was raining in February, she would be thinking aloud about how dismal it must have been in February for the Setaukets and then we would all be sad. Her moods could have unexpected causes. When we went to the circus a woman wearing a pink tutu and riding on top of an elephant made her cry. Her crying, then, became my memory of the circus.

My mother was whimsical. Once at supper she drew her black hair around her face so that it looked like a beard. One night when I was six or so, she put autumn leaves in her hair and blackened her face with burnt cork. Some years later she followed our dog into the woods on all fours, smelling the ground, trying to pick up the scent that had the dog so excited. (She couldn't.) We little girls were, of course, accustomed to our mother, but when others were amazed by the surprising things that she did we felt special, as we did because our house with the wind blowing through was not like the ordinary houses of children we knew in school.

My sister Beatrice was four years younger than I; a boy born in between had not survived. Two years after Beatrice, Felicity arrived and, a year after her, Madeleine. For a while, Mama provided what we called a "Scotch nanny" when my mother had a baby. When she had Beatrice, my mother recuperated at Box Hill, but thereafter she came home to the Red Cottage, and, for Felicity and Madeleine, the nanny came there too and had to take care of the rest of us as well as of the baby. A nanny, dressed all in white—including cap, stockings, and shoes—looked odd in the Red Cottage. The nannies (used to better) thought so too.

Isabella was born when I was twelve and was about to go off to boarding school, and Trudi came when I was in college. I remember Isabella and Trudi as infants vividly, because by the time they came I could care for them like a mother, and did. I can still feel Isabella's little back fitting in my hand as I burped her, and the way Trudi would cling as I walked her to quiet her down.

But it was Beatrice, Felicity, and Madeleine with whom I experienced a shared fate, whose personalities are embedded in my soul like no others in the world. Still, I felt different from them and apart, as skinny and long when they were roly-poly, as made to do the dishes when they were not, as put in charge. As the oldest, I was exposed. They in contrast had protection in numbers, or so it seemed to me. There was in any event a feeling of numbers in the Red Cottage; of babies coming one after another and later of knees and shins and feet of different sizes: I know my sisters' bodies nearly as well as I know my own. Our mother bought us dresses that were long, so that we would have room to grow into them, and after we grew out of them they were handed down. I have an impression of us barefoot in our long dresses, of an unruliness, of the problem of combing hair. Beatrice had thick, dark-brown straight hair, whereas mine was red and curly. I was powerful and tyrannized Beatrice. The famous funny story of her retaliation was that by calling me a teacup she made me cry.

As musicians, both my parents were fanatical about sounds. Quite ordinary sounds hurt them—a radio on the beach, or a truck rattling on the road, or we children getting raucous. I wanted to protect my parents from being hurt by sounds, particularly my father who was especially hurt by popular music. (My mother had an iconoclastic taste for Elvis and Cole Porter.) My father found it difficult to go to movies, because of soundtracks, or to shops where Muzak played. The incidental use of classical music in restaurants was trying for him too. With the exception of those times when my parents were working on a performance, we did not hear much classical music at home either. My father said that he never heard in actual life what he heard in his head. As a result we experienced music largely through its absence. Even the phonograph was silent since Dad preferred to read the contemporary music that he admired from scores. As she approached adolescence Beatrice surreptitiously listened to Elvis on the radio, and Felicity, in turn, played the Beatles on the phonograph, eliciting from our furious father the statement that this could ruin the machine. I, however, never dared violate the silence in this way. I was the defiant, confrontational one of us sisters, but when I was small the force of that silence was such that even the thought of challenging it never crossed my mind.

It was in that charged quiet that my father would occasionally sit at the Steinway and play. Then notes would roll through the house and up the stairs and out the windows, and we would all be awash, yet awash not in something abundant, exactly, but in something breathtaking that we knew might, at any moment, stop. Once, when I was seven, Dad played a boogie-woogie on the piano and I thought I would pass out with joy. Once or twice, he took out his trumpet and played a few measures. I remember the concentration on his face as he lifted the silver trumpet to his lips. I remember the trumpet itself, its silveriness, the flared bell, the valves, and the looping tube. Then came a sound that sliced me vertically, effortlessly, like a blade.

Yet there were also times when music was folded into our daily life. My mother's mezzo-soprano voice was crystalline and the most beautiful thing. She might sing through her exercises in the morning. She might practice with my father on a cycle of songs in the afternoon. She sang French, German, and Italian as well as English, with every word clear and rich in linguistic pleasure. When they had perfected a cycle they would perform it, usually before a high-level musical crowd in a rich person's home in New York (and those of us children who were old enough would go), but sometimes in the Red Cottage too.

My mother's musicality was intuitive and responsive, bridging the separation between herself and her listeners. My father's art manifested itself as mastery and musical intelligence, and accentuated the division between himself and his listeners. My father's majestic casualness at the piano was the underpinning of these performances. He would bear my mother along in a net of notes and then the net would pop her up, and she would soar. My father's precision on the keyboard was infused with an almost aromatic masculinity. He was powerful in his ease, his solid privilege in the musical dimension: a kind of heaven on earth that he just naturally inhabited, glorious as an athlete, as he played with the seductive femininity of the artistic male.

My parents also performed songs written by my father, settings of poems by Robert Herrick, Ezra Pound, Mother Goose, William Shakespeare, and Claire Nicolas White, my uncle Bobby's wife and my aunt, among others. Back then, Dad composed in a style which was lyrical yet disjunctive, melodic yet modernist. The neoclassical style presumes a familiarity with the classical tradition and then defies expectation by breaking the classical rules. It is a style of staircases that go nowhere, vaults that support nothing, a breaking-out-of-conventions music whose materials are nevertheless conventions; a music of ruins; a music that was decorous yet revolutionary, that paid homage to the past yet also, in an insouciant way, destroyed it.

My father didn't see music as in any way related to the heart, or the soul, to life, to meaning, to anything other than itself. He felt that music ought to be only about the musical materials themselves. It ought to be *only* aesthetic. This was a view that many—Stravinsky included—shared at that time. Certainly it was the view of the

French neoclassical school, the group that had the greatest influence on my father. That school affirmed my father's belief that music should be a quest for beauty, originality, and the expression of musical thoughts entirely independent of feeling or narrative. This belief was, in many ways, a natural, generational reaction against the excesses of late romanticism—a return to the astringent classicism of the eighteenth century. It is the most respectable aesthetic ideology, in that it is purely aesthetic, undiluted by what my father calls Soap Operas, meaning our real lives.

My father was charged and masterful and magnificent and yet he was also, in my perceptions, blanked out. Sex was everywhere in the Red Cottage—Daddy kissing Mummy at the bottom of the stairs, grazing, grazing—and yet the feeling of sex there largely hid behind blankness, as if there were no sex at all. There was a cloistered part of our experience in the Red Cottage that didn't show up on the mental blueprint of our lives. I might, for example, have a memory without any emotion attached, so that it had no significance, or I might simply seal it off in the cloister. There was also a part of our father that was cloistered from himself, a domain that belonged to the jewel-like amber in the bottle of Heaven Hill bourbon on the kitchen sideboard, the gallon jug of purple-black wine on the floor.

The parlor was the only part of the house that had a cellar underneath. This was a dirt-floored cellar, walled with a foundation of boulders cemented together, and gloomy too, with cobwebs and mildew and a moldy smell of old earth. In winter my father would go there twice a day to feed the furnace with coal. When he opened the door of the furnace the light inside was a deep, pulsing orange—a dark kind of light which flickered but could also roar and become bright. Through a vent in the door I could see the coals pulsing. Sometimes I would sit on the cellar stairs while Dad took care of the furnace: this was before Beatrice was born and just my parents and I were in the Red Cottage. In adulthood a kind of memory came to me of a small violent scene that seemed to be less the recollection of something outward in history than a kind of waking dream image that led downward into a cave—a neolithic past. Here I am on the stairs, a pretty little girl with curly hair wearing a pretty little dress with my daddy shovelling coal, and I am happy in the femininity of me and the masculinity of him. Then my Daddy comes around from the furnace with a change in his eyes that makes him strange. Then, with the dispassionate objectivity of children, I note that strangeness. Then my Daddy reaches up and pokes me between the legs. At this point in the sequence I always wince and often experience an impulse to kick viciously, as if my body itself were remembering in a way that brought the event into the present.

I have come to believe that there are mind memories and body memories. Mind memories are documentary, grounded in who, what, when, where. Body memories are a reliving of sensations and have a tendency to blot out the documentary factors. Another recollection—half-solid, half-unsolid—in which the two are mixed is a memory of lying in bed in the corner room that had one window overlooking the potato fields to the south. The first part of the memory is of seeing the brown glass doorknob turning. This is documentary—very vivid and almost in slow motion. Then I saw my father's brown wool wrapper, and his foot with the brown birthmark coming in. This too is documentary. It was daytime, I saw the doorknob turn from the perspective of lying in bed; from the sense of my length and skinniness I would guess that I was about six. While the doorknob is turning, the room is squared off properly, but, as he comes in, the room, in my mind, becomes skewed, like a partially collapsed box. In adulthood the documentary memory was followed by unstable images that escaped the cloister. First there was a picture, observed without emotion, of a plane exploding in air, and body parts, the foot with the birthmark among them, flying. As I never saw a plane exploding, this picture is not a memory in the documentary sense at all. I think it was a displaced body memory, because as I began to come to terms with my childhood, instead of seeing the silent explosion of the plane in the sky I would experience a sense of interior exploding, an overload of mixed feelings, including rage (again a wish to kick viciously), all of this in chaos, as if blowing out a nervous system too small-gauged to contain it.

Body memory has a visceral density that is like bedrock beneath the shifting sands of narrative memory. Yet its connection to factual narrative is at best intuitive. Nevertheless body memory is also the most primitive reality, the inchoate realm out of which narrative arises. Within the mute dark realm of my body-life where the explosion took place, I have come to understand that, with the explosion—whatever it was, for it was something: it was not nothing—a long, slow shattering was initiated that would extend outward through the years, fracturing both the little things in my life—a household task, a wish to read a book from start to finish—and the large.

For a time I shared a room with my sister Beatrice, a room that also served as a passage to the corner room with the brown glass doorknob, that was taken over by my father in this period for sleepless nights. Dad would read in bed there and late at night Beatrice and I would hear him laugh. The titles of the books that made him laugh joined the bits of information that circulated in the house. Three titles that I remember are "Tristram Shandy," "Jacques le Fataliste," and "Don Quixote." Dad read "Don Quixote" in French, and he pronounced it in the French way, "Dawn Keyshut." Indeed I grew up with the idea that somehow Dad *was* French—Parisian in particular—even though another bit of information circulating in the Red Cottage was "310 Donohoe Street," the address of my father's childhood home in Palo Alto, California. When Dad spoke French, or of France, he became elegant and intellectual in a sensual way, and projected an impression of an inner circle of cosmopolitanism beyond the ken of Americans. When he said "310 Donohoe Street" his Western accent got stronger, and a quality of masculine practicality and immediacy became dominant. At these times he spoke from a dusty and obscure place, where people said "wahta" and "awringes" and where the weather, at least, was a comfort.

Dad shared 310 Donohoe Street with us in the upstairs rooms at bedtime, occasions that had a clandestine quality of being apart from my mother but were not cloistered. They were, rather, good times in which Dad seemed to enjoy us and we felt close. Incantatory phrases of this world were "Bethlehem Steel," the name of the company where Dad's father had worked, and "machinist." Another was "all his life." Dad's father had "worked as a machinist for Bethlehem Steel all his life." Dad said "Bethlehem Steel" with a deference that he accorded no other entity. "The Depression" was another term of the upstairs rooms. Dad's father had been "laid off" in "the Depression." This brought up "squabs," the word for the pigeons that his family had raised on three acres behind 310 Donohoe Street and that, together with the fruit trees there, had fed the family during "the Depression." The word "squabs" was new to me, and to my girlhood ear cut through the mystique of Box Hill like a buzz saw. I heard it as a flat word of brute survival—of what's left when all mystique, even that of Bethlehem Steel, fails.

Dad had warm hands, and smoked a pipe, and wore a workman's cap at a slight angle. Often he had on a rough wool jacket and he smelled of tobacco and fresh air. His cheeks were like sandpaper. He had a sensitivity about him, a flexible artistic precision like that of the quill pens with which he wrote his music. He liked to swim. He taught me to swim. When the family went to the beach he'd swim so far out into the Sound that we, on the shore, couldn't see him. Sometimes there were schools of dolphins out there, from the shore a frolicking disturbance on the surface of the water. When Dad came back, he'd tell us that he'd been swimming with the dolphins, that they'd bumped him and nudged him in a joshing way, that they'd been playing with him. He'd say it casually, but there was awe in his face, an expression of speechlessness, of emotion.

The spankings started early, though not, I think, right away. I think there was time to fall in love, time to feel safety in my femininity as I was encircled in the masculinity of him. I didn't know why Dad came at me as he did—he did not spank my sisters in this way. I can speculate now that perhaps it was the result of tensions generated by his experience in the Second World War—he was overseas when I was born—or perhaps it was that he identified me with my mother's family. I was almost two when he first saw me and was ensconced in the world of Box Hill, spoiled rotten, he said later: "They thought you were the reincarnation of Stanford White." The spankings were formal, but my recollection of the experience is of something like a gale coming at me, and of my eyes squinched closed: I don't want to see.

My mother was a flicker, an inflection, a summer dress. She was gifted with the accessories of love: a smile, a hand cupping a head, a way of saying "darling." I'd lunge for these flickers. But then if I did something bad, she'd say, "You'll get a spanking when Daddy comes in from the studio." Cold, unreachable, she would hand me over. Or sometimes the sentence came directly from him.

When I was six or seven, my father fashioned a spanking stick. It was made of a board, three to four inches wide perhaps, and half an inch thick, two to three feet long with one end whittled into a handle. If he was using the stick, the spanking would be outside, behind the lilacs in the Red Cottage garden. If he used his hand, which often hurt more, he'd do it upstairs in the bathroom or downstairs in the laundry. The laundry, off the usual track of our lives, was disorderly in an especially uncontrolled distraught-seeming way that was also static. Dad would spank me there amidst the wild, stale piles, and the old-fashioned washing machine with a hand wringer and the potbellied stove. When he was done he would hug and kiss me in a false, lizardy way, telling me how he loved me, and I would submit because my convulsive crying would leave me without the psychic muscle tone to resist.

Music lessons started when I was three or four. They consisted of ear training and finger exercises and simple pieces to learn, but our lessons were not a simple matter for me. Dad, beside me, was an overwhelming presence. Even today the thought of those lessons can disassemble my body, so that I feel as if my chest were caving in till my torso disappears, my head becomes big, and my tongue lolls without my knowing it; as if I have an enormous bottom and thighs, and long shins, and skinny, pigeon-toed feet, but, above all, tiny, palsied arms with shrivelled hands that cannot play.

I strove to play anyway, through the frozenness. We were both frozen, I think, our individual coastlines submerged in a Gondwanaland of rage. Playing like a little robot yet full of strain, I would inevitably fail, and when I failed Dad would sometimes recall, with puzzlement, that before I could talk he had heard me in my crib in Box Hill singing the melody of "Speed Bonnie Boat"—a complex, difficult melody, he would always point out—perfectly. This gave me the idea that there had been a golden time when I was musical, and then my body had gone bad. This is my idea now: my father discharged rage into my body, making it radioactive in a way that rendered it deformed as I experienced it from the inside. Sometimes I think that, as a result, I hid my musicality so deep within me that it became lost.

Music drew me like a moth to the flame. It attracted me urgently, yet was a torture because it stirred my deepest being and at the same time caused great pain. Despite my father's aesthetic of detachment from feeling, the music my parents performed often seemed highly expressive and deeply felt. My mother sang Schubert: *"Mein Herz! Mein Herz!"* "La Bonne Chanson," a setting by Fauré of poems by Verlaine, was lyrical in a way that made me swoon even before I understood French. For me the actual music that I heard in the Red Cottage was almost too stimulating of emotions. It invaded me with feelings, or, in a way, it invaded me with the feelings that it felt *for* me, materializing grief and love, despair and ecstasy, flooding the room with that which was forbidden: leaving me like a delta—splayed, silted, and defenseless.

As a girl at concerts, I could see in the eyes of the audience how much they liked the way my parents were so young and handsome, so much in love. That my mother and father were in love was as important a part of our idea of life in the Red Cottage as my father's musical gift. Our poverty was a part of the romance of my parents, along with their extreme youth, their art, their in-loveness, my mother's beauty and sensitivity, my father's gift and future as a great composer. We children were a part of the romance in that there were a lot of us. My mother was in fact exhausted often. We knew that as a Chanler she was meant to live in a big house with a long driveway, that it was hard for her to be with us in the Red Cottage without help. As soon as possible I was put in charge. Thrashed, I thrashed my sisters, though with less formality. Thus my life careened out of control too. Thus I too became the agent of unfeeling, unaccountable violence. There was conscience—a glimmer— but helplessness. I had no idea how to become responsible for the force in me that arose out of nowhere, overwhelming; and so there was despair. There were only children in the Red Cottage—orphans. And it was not safe for children there.

In the gale of Daddy coming at me there was no twoness, no sense of constellation: no him *and* me. How was I to get a purchase on myself? I was a nobody, flattened, dispassionately degraded, and that's the way it was. Just so, when I spiralled out of control with my sisters—and this I did recognize as violence—there was in turn just me discharging force and my sisters were nobodies. My selfhood was lost with the annihilation of theirs, and my place in the constellation with my sisters was lost too. It was a paradox of my situation in my family and on the Place that in that complex network of people, there was, at the core, no relatedness. Rather, within that dense, rich tapestry there was isolation. This was more than I could have borne to register at the time, or for many years. Even now it is the part of my life that I am least able to open, the saddest thing.

COMFORT

BESSIE SMITH WHITE, my great-grandmother, was a handsome, big-boned woman, with thick white hair, parted on the side and drawn back loosely into a bun, so that it crested hand-somely over her forehead. Her jaw was strong, and there was an aspect to her expression that was both imperious and elfin, albeit much softened by age. Time had also burnished and articulated her large, capable hands to a point of radiance. From the time I was two and a half I went to visit her every day. Sometimes she wore satin and pearls, and sometimes she wore raggedy things; often her dresses were of other decades; three-quarter length or long. The White Cottage, where she lived, had a porch on two sides where we would often sit in warm weather and have ginger ale and gingersnaps. As she got older, she would sometimes be in bed upstairs when I visited and on those occasions she would invite me to go down to the kitchen to get my ginger ale and gingersnaps myself.

In the middle of Grandma White's lawn there was an ancient apple tree. It was so old that it bore only runty apples, but Grandma was interested in those miserable little apples, simply because they had appeared. She also loved Queen Anne's lace, which seemed to me too plain for up-close attention—unlike, say, acorns or shells which she also liked. In winter she wore a black felt hat that fitted her perfectly—a lady's hat, a hat that goes with the word ''milliner''; and she had a red one exactly like it which she wore for fancier occasions. Her wool coat stretched flat across her back like a man's. Sometimes she sent me out to pick dandelions for her, which she'd put in a glass with some water; but they'd wilt soon, though she didn't mind. A statue of a boy taking a splinter out of his foot stood at the eastern end of her lawn—the end near the Red Cottage; wild violets grew all around it and when they were in bloom I picked them too.

Our hearts touched across an abyss of time—an abyss that was structured in that I was a very little girl in relation to a very old woman, in an almost archetypal way. Our relationship was reliable and without ambiguity of any kind, the fact that in her sheltering lap I was enveloped in an avoided history notwithstanding. There we are taking a walk in the woods, her large hand holding mine. We are wearing coats. The path is broad and covered with brown leaves. The leafless trees hold the light as if it were amber: there I am with Grandma in an amber of time where nothing moves on the emotional plane.

Stanford remained a living part of our history through the large presence on the Place of Grandma. Stanford was murdered in 1906, and I was born in 1944, but Grandma White lived on until 1950; we overlapped for six years. I can feel even now that my great-grandmother loved me.

It is, perhaps, indicative of how deeply that history was muffled in silence that Grandma, who embodied the history, was oddly without narrative in our family life. If she had had a "story"—even a girlhood story—it would have led too easily to the story of Stanford, in an unravelling way. The relationship between Stanford and Grandma was the primary one that defined and enclosed us as an extended family. Yet nowhere in the family picture of Grandma White that I received, or in my direct association with her, was there an intimation of disaster in her life and especially not in the areas of love and family. Grandma was, above all, placid. Certainly there was nothing in her demeanor that suggested an experience of murder in her family life.

The story about Grandma that had currency in the family was an ahistorical one: of her rootedness in the locality, of how she was sustained—and perhaps consoled, if the need for consolation can be floated free of a cause—by networks of kin and the small pleasures of the countryside with which she was so deeply familiar. She had dowager grandeur, but the story of Grandma in the family was the story of the thatch meadows and the clam flats, the berries and the beach.

Inside, Grandma's house was sad. The wallpaper had lost its life. There were sparks of merriment in Grandma and a groundswell of affection, but there was also an atmosphere about her of huge passivity, of stubborn innocence, of surviving to great old age in a historyless way. She was there on the Place like an oak, like a rock, like a very large girl. She and I created a tie from farthest reach to farthest reach of the family as it existed then, and there was a special cozy tone in which our relationship was mentioned in the family—a tone that after I had grown up almost excluded me: "You don't remember, do you," my mother or my aunts were likely to say of the closeness between me and Grandma, and, when I said that I did remember, they didn't notice, as if they were possessive of the memory, as if I had been a different person then and the memory belonged more to them than to me. Indeed, it is not easy for me to extricate my experience with Grandma from what our relationship means to others—to sense what it was, specifically and independently, for me to be engulfed lovingly in an innocence of that stupendous endurance, in that passivity, in a sadness that showed only in the wallpaper and in a certain deadness in the interior of a house.

You could get to Box Hill from Grandma's by crossing a subsidiary driveway to Box Hill just west of her house and proceeding up a long, undulating path: a secondary axis, hedged with privet that had grown so high that in many places it joined overhead, funnelling you through shade toward a round opening of sunlight. At the end you were in a slightly elevated spot, with some barns and my uncle Bobby's house on the left. Ahead and a little to the right across the fields, Box Hill nestled in its trees and snuggled into the land just below a hilltop. The hill crested just to the right of Box Hill, and there were pine trees on the crest. From the end of the Privet Path you could see through the pines to a bronze statue of Diana.

From the top of the Privet Path one noticed clouds, the reddish grass of the fields, and the real lay of the land—the falling off behind Box Hill, the swooping topography of an orchard to the right of Diana—in contrast to the molded planes of the grounds around the house, the long, evenly graded drive. This was Grandma's landscape, something firm underneath, where I did not lose my edges as I could in the landscape that Stanford had superimposed on it. I have an image of how, when I was with Grandma White, the countryside steadied out around her, extending solidly and seamlessly to the horizon. In that steadied landscape Box Hill and the gardens dissolve, and so do Diana and the pines, until I see only a bare hilltop with a robin, a mulberry tree, a dandelion puff to blow.

Past Diana, the seamless landscape of the clouds and the swooping lines of the orchard continued down steep, wooded hills to the harbor. When I was a girl I had no idea that the windmill standing a little way to the west along the shore had been designed by Stanford—I saw it more as a feature of the natural landscape than as architecture. Indeed, it was the axle of the countryside of my childhood. The landscape of the windmill, so to speak, continued west-

ward from the harbor, through woods and meadows to the Nissequogue River, a marshy, estuarial body of water that moseyed inland
about three miles away. This was a landscape of special meaning and
feeling that was charismatic and circumscribed. Across the Nissequogue River, for example, you were definitely no longer in it.

One factor that defined the boundaries of this landscape of tenderness and depth was the presence of Grandma's branch of the
Smith clan, a very large and old farming family that had founded
Smithtown and had lived there in large numbers ever since. After
ten generations, Smith kin extended to so many removes that they
blurred, like trees across fields on a hazy day. As a child I sublimi-
nally "knew" that this landscape was ancestral, because my mother
kept up the habit of visiting Smith cousins—a way of staying connected to Grandma, perhaps. More and more, though, as I got older
she would just invoke their names as we passed their houses, with
the result that I came to associate people with features of the landscape, rather than the other way around. From the time I was a very
small child, perhaps four or five, it seemed to me that people *became*
the landscape, in a way. Cousins Mildred and Josephine Smith, two
elderly spinsters, were the big trees in their front yard as much as
they were themselves. Cousin Dorothy Smith, whom I don't remember ever meeting, was a gable peeking over the crest of a Smith
truck-farming field that in summer was streaked with the greens,
purples, and aquamarines of vegetable crops that rolled to the road
like an ocean.

In this atmosphere it didn't matter as much as it usually does
whether a person had died or not. Since people were embodied in
the landscape, it was easy to forget that a person had actually gone,
and sometimes it seemed that people who were still alive had died
long ago, because they had passed so completely into the landscape
that actually seeing them would have been a shock. It was an easy
step further—almost a matter of course—for me as a child to
experience the presence of people in the landscape who had died
before I was born. In a sense, everybody in the community—dead
or alive—was both there in the landscape and not there, and it was

perhaps this mixture of presence and absence that made the landscape susceptible to suddenly slipping out of ordinary time so that,
for a moment, you would have no idea what the date or the year
was: for a moment it could be very long ago. Anything could do it:
a coincidence of angles, the light on a field, an unexpected glimpse
of the harbor through a scrim of oaks, and especially a shift in
sound, like wind rising—or falling—or crickets or birds falling
silent. In that slippage, it would seem that something was uncovered
that was always present but only out of mind.

As a very little girl I didn't associate this subtexted countryside
explicitly with Grandma—Grandma was there herself next door—
but somewhere along the line Grandma too became a part of the
countryside: not in a specific spot, as with her relatives, but at large,
like a pressure in the atmosphere or like a sound. Grandma was
present in the countryside like the sound of rainfall or wind in the
trees: Grandma, with her dumb-beast entrapment in the physical
body, her righteousness, her complacency, her simple love of me.

The wind-in-the-trees ancestral atmosphere that I sensed as a
child was real; to a large degree the unusual aspects of Grandma's
character can be attributed to the encompassing Smith milieu in
which she was raised. She had a simplicity, combined with a sense of
belonging that was so settled and assured that not even association
with the meteoric, catastrophic trajectory of Stanford White could
shake it.

The history of the Smiths on Long Island began in 1640 when a
yeoman from Yorkshire called Richard Bull Smith received the pa-
tent to the land that became the Town of Smithtown, and that he
was a mere yeoman—unlike other recipients of large land grants—
is the key to the simplicity of the Smiths, who never became pretentious. That he left all his land to his nine children, who in turn left it
to their children, thus locking up the township for three generations, is the key to the Smith sense of entitlement and settledness
without the attachment to status that one would expect to go with
it. By that third generation Smiths were occupying all class levels in
the township, and this pattern held right down to Grandma's time,

when, without self-consciousness or strain, her cousin Stanley Smith served as her chauffeur. To the Smiths wealth, fortune, and fashion had an unusually weak valence. A typical story is of Caleb Smith, who would go to Gilded Age dinners at a mansion near his farm where a hundred guests would be attended by a hundred liveried footmen: the next morning, without embarrassment, he would hitch up his team and go around to the mansion kitchen to pick up the slops for his hogs—the slops from the very dinner he had attended the night before.

Grandma grew up with her parents and eight siblings in the village of Smithtown, about four miles away from the Place, in the house that we later called the Smithtown House in the family. When I was a girl my uncle Peter (my mother's oldest brother) and aunt Jehanne were raising their eleven children there. By the nineteen-fifties, the village of Smithtown had grown up around the house into a good-sized town, and the road in front had turned into a highway, but the house itself, and the land attached to it, belonged to a rural world. Built in Colonial times, the house was of substantial size, with several barns and farm outbuildings behind it: cribs, stalls, a carriage barn, a smokehouse, and an icehouse in which chunks of ice cut from a pond on the property were deposited in winter. Above the kitchen there was a slave quarters. It was the kind of farm designed not for cash crops but to sustain a family.

Grandma's father, Judge John Lawrence Smith, was the farmer and he had his law offices in the house too, in a small wing with a separate entrance. He was the county judge, and when he grew too old to travel to Riverhead, the county seat, he turned his office into Judge's Chambers and held court right there. "Judge Smith's office was the real judgement seat for the townspeople, a place to be feared and revered," Grandma wrote in a memoir of her childhood. Indeed Judge Smith was the most important man in both the family and the township.

Grandma's father had been educated at Yale and Princeton and, as a young man, had worked in New York as a lawyer. There he had met and married Sarah Clinch, a socialite from a prominent family that was intertwined with the Nicolls, the Van Cortlandts, and the Van Rensselaers, all families of high status in the social and political establishment of the region. The couple lived in New York at first and then, after a few years, moved to Smithtown. Of their children five daughters and two sons lived to adulthood. Grandma was the youngest.

The Judge was a Victorian colossus of a father who reigned over his children like a god. He pulled their teeth; he made them memorize long passages of the Bible; he cured them of defects, such as stuttering (Grandma's failing); he taught them how to carve a turkey, smoke a ham, make sausage—to do whatever he did himself about the farm. He gave them swimming instructions by pushing them into water over their heads from a flatboat on the Nissequogue River and, when the minister was away, he preached to them in church on Sundays too. While still a girl, Grandma regularly drove her father in a carriage fifteen miles to the railroad station at Islip where he would get a train to Riverhead. One day, they were overtaken by a cloud of locusts which flew into Grandma's face and got stuck in her hair and her clothes, but the Judge would not let her protect her face or brush them away: he made her keep the reins in both hands, made her concentrate, throughout the ordeal, on controlling the horses. "I *worshipped* my father," Grandma wrote in her memoir (the italics are hers), "who, I know now, must have been a very remarkable man."

John Lawrence replaced the plain wooden mantels in the Smithtown house with marble ones and had the windows in the parlor transformed into French doors. When his fashionable mother-in-law became widowed, and came to live with them, he added a wing in the Palladian style to the east side of the house to serve as her quarters. Along the way, he also had a sturdy cage built in the attic. The purpose of the cage was to incarcerate Grandma's sister Ella when she wanted to marry Charles Nicoll Clinch, a young army officer and a cousin on both sides. As a modern educated man, the Judge knew that too much intermarriage wasn't good. The cage was made of sturdy planks: it was of a kind that had been used

earlier in the century to imprison recalcitrant slaves. The story is
that Ella was locked in the cage for a month, during which she was
fed on bread and water. The engagement was broken.

Like the house, Grandma was both fancy and plain. She went to
the one-room village school—the path to it would flood, and sometimes in winter she would skate there—and though she was the
daughter of Judge John Lawrence Smith she swept the school floor
in her turn. In her memoir, she tells of a countrified way of life, and
there is something countrified about the telling too, in that the time
the dog's tail got stuck to the ice and the death of a sister are
recounted in exactly the same tone. Her mandate as the youngest,
she wrote, was to make her aging parents merry, and that she did
this by skipping about and singing. (Her principal talent, it has come
down in the family, was that she could whistle and sing at the same
time.) She also writes:

> Pig killing time was the most exciting time of the year. The
> kitchen laundry and all the outhouses were given up to sausage
> making, and head cheese, and the pigs were brought out and
> killed right there in the yard and hung up for two days in the
> cold air. I adored the sausage machine and used to love to
> grind the sausage meat and see it filling the skins while Lizzie
> tied it at intervals making it into "links" which were hung up
> in the attic, with dried catnip and all kinds of herbs! The old
> attic still smells of them, and I often think I can hear the pigs
> squealing as their throats were cut.

Grandma's socialite mother, Sarah Clinch Smith, fled to the city at
pig-killing time.

A kind of daffy delirium about the virtues of Smithtown is a
Smith characteristic. Even the Judge was susceptible: in his otherwise detached and mildly ironic "History of Smithtown" he raves
about the superiority of the breezes of Smithtown and the trout in
the Nissequogue River. Grandma had that passion for the location
too: in her case it was focussed with a special intensity on Carman

Hill, the spot where Diana eventually stood. In Grandma's time Carman Hill was not, as I had always imagined, a bare crest: there was a huge barn there, "a landmark for mariners for miles around," she wrote in a memoir. There was a farmhouse where Box Hill later stood—indeed, in a sense, Box Hill grew out of it— and the land that in my time had grown up into woods was clear right down to the harbor. The Judge John Lawrence Smith family liked to swim at a small beach at the bottom of the hill, and when they passed Carman Hill Farm on the way to the beach, Grandma would jump out of the cart and run to the high spot where the big barn was to look at the view—it was the view that she loved— before running down, a distance of more than half a mile, to join the family on the shore below. When Grandma married, Judge Smith told Stanford that if he wanted his wife to be happy he had better buy Carman Hill Farm.

A dimension to Grandma's life about which I heard absolutely nothing as a child, but without which her marriage to Stanford makes no sense, is that she had a great-aunt on her mother's side, who had inherited from her husband, department store magnate A. T. Stewart, a fortune second only to that of John Jacob Astor. Aunt Cornelia took an active interest in her grandnieces in Smithtown. As each neared womanhood, an invitation was issued to live with Aunt Cornelia in the white marble palace in New York that A. T. Stewart had built at Thirty-fourth Street and Fifth Avenue. She sent her nieces to finishing school and introduced them to society: this is when the satin-and-pearls side of Grandma evolved. It was, despite her fondness for pig-killing time, a strong part of her aura. Grandma was both rustic and fancy. She was also an heiress: Aunt Cornelia's Smithtown nieces knew that, along with other nieces and nephews, they would be included amply in her will.

Thus when Stanford met Grandma she knew how to make sausage and how to drive a buggy through a cloud of locusts, but she had also been to finishing school and had been around in New York society and, furthermore, stood to inherit a nice sum of money. The two aspects of her life were not in conflict, exactly, but they were not a conventional blend either: they were like an unusual chord. I have a little watch of Grandma's, a Tiffany pocket watch, gold, with a cover on which her initials are monogrammed in tiny diamonds. This is the fancy side of Grandma, solid, conventional, ladylike. The other side could be represented by an acorn, or a clamshell. You could put an acorn and a clamshell, and perhaps a runty little apple as well, on a table next to the watch, and you would have the chord.

Grandma told my aunt Claire that she first saw Stanford through the keyhole in the door to her father's law office, there in the Smithtown House. It was 1880. He was twenty-seven and was already a successful architect. She was eighteen. Edward Simmons, a painter who was Stanford's contemporary and occasional collaborator, described him in a memoir as six feet two with "very long legs, broad shoulders, narrow hips, stiff tawny hair standing straight up, a great red moustache, beetling light eyebrows overhanging little bright grey-green eyes with almost white lashes," and added, "His hands were large and strong and hairy with long blunt fingers." The man Grandma saw through the keyhole was an artist, something that had not yet appeared in the mangrove swamp of Smith genealogy.

So there is Grandma, enclosed in her father's house—the crooked old lines, the cosmopolitan additions, the cage in the attic—which is itself enclosed in the universe of Smiths. There she is, peering into her father's inner sanctum, and there is Stanford, a man of volcanic creative energy, surrounded by her father's law books. Those same books were there when I was a child and are there still. They are bound in leather that is slowly flaking in the humid Long Island climate: Voorhys's "New York Code, 1855," Cranch's "Reports," Pomeroy's "Equity Jurisprudence." Grandma told my Aunt Claire that when she saw Stanford through the keyhole she had a desire to run her hand over the bristles of his hair. Soon Stanford began to court her and she took him for a ride in a pony cart, driving fast over a bump in a way that she knew would pop him right out of his seat.

Stanford and Grandma were married in 1884, and lived in New York, first in rented rooms on East Fifteenth Street and then in a rented brownstone on West Twentieth Street. In 1885, they had a son, Richard Mansfield White, who died at seven months. They first rented the farmhouse on Carman Hill for the summer in that sad year. Even while it was still a rental, Stanford began fooling with the grounds. A Reverend Timothy O'Slap complained in a local newspaper that while walking through the countryside he had passed Carman Hill and had found "a low and curious seat" situated there by "the husband of one of the daughters of Judge Smith." The seat was "surrounded by classic statues absolutely devoid of all clothing and standing out in shameless and conspicuous nudity among the green trees," he wrote, and he and his party had "fled in confusion."

Aunt Cornelia died in 1886, leaving to Grandma's mother, Sarah Clinch Smith, a quarter of a million dollars outright, plus a quarter of the residue of her estate, which the New York *Times* estimated to be worth five million dollars. A hundred thousand dollars, the equivalent of five million today, was left to Grandma. When Sarah died in 1890 (the Judge had died the year before), she left the equivalent of twenty-five million dollars to Grandma. Thereupon the Stanford Whites bought Carman Hill Farm, and Stanford went to work in earnest to transform it into the phantasmagorical world of Box Hill. First, one gable was added to the farmhouse. At this stage the house still looked rustic—bonnety with deep eaves and big-footed with porch. Two more gables went up, and the clapboard yielded to pebbledash—large pebbles flung into walls of wet cement. On this expanded scale the yokel proportions mysteriously became elegant. Box Hill is a sleight of hand.

*   *   *

After Stanford was murdered, in 1906, Grandma stayed on at Box Hill for almost three decades. There has never been an accounting of what happened to Grandma's fortune—under law, Stanford had control of it—but it was considerably reduced by the time of her widowhood. Still, my great-grandmother ran the house "like a Swiss watch," as my mother put it, with peonies in cut-glass vases, and a merry butler, in a striped cutaway, who liked children. Grandma ran Box Hill at full tilt as a monument to Stanford (or, as she referred to him usually, "Stanford White"). Although the contents of the Gramercy Park establishment were auctioned off, Grandma kept Stanford's eclectic collection in Box Hill more or less intact. She subsidized Box Hill with what little remained of Aunt Cornelia's money, and sometimes by selling off parts of her own collection of lace. My mother remembers Grandma setting out on expeditions to New York auction houses, getting into the back of her black Ford—Morton Treadwell, her black chauffeur, magnificent in his uniform in the front—with a packet of her lace which she would then put on her lap. On our walks, Grandma White used to show me Queen Anne's lace that grew in the fields, but only in adulthood did I learn from my mother that she had collected lace, and very expertly, though this was not celebrated in the family in any way. In the choreographic swirl of ornamental objects that make up the family universe of things, lace is incongruous: so feminine, not asking for attention; so retiring.

Morton Treadwell was part Native American, enormous, and very handsome, and he and Grandma were, in a certain way, close. They would go clamming in a beat-up scallop boat: he would row her out to the sandbars that appeared in the middle of the harbor at low tide, and they'd both dig there. Morton's Native American ancestors were local—were probably Setaukets—and my mother believes that Grandma's bond with him arose from a shared ancestral sense of place. It's a picture in which the Smith centuries merge with an even more extraordinary place-rootedness that went back untraceably into mists. Morton was also descended from local slaves, and in this too, my mother quixotically feels, he shared roots in the "old days" with Grandma which erased their differences in station. Grandma and Morton went on "Long Island vacations," as Grandma called their trips, during which they motored around to villages that were twenty, thirty, maybe fifty miles away from Box Hill and where Grandma would stay in a guesthouse, or a small hotel, and Morton would stay with one of his many relatives who were conveniently scattered all over the island.

In the neighborhood, Grandma was seen not as a person who went clamming in an old scallop boat—the way we saw her—but as a dowager queen, chauffeured around by Morton in his glorious uniform, she in a hat with a veil and wearing gloves and with calling cards to leave. In the neighborhood, she was perceived very definitely as a person with a story, including the story of Aunt Cornelia's fortune, and also including the Stanford story; in the neighborhood version of that story she rose above misfortune with the aid of character and good breeding. There is still a tendency in the neighborhood to feel hurt puzzlement that God should have allowed such an off-color disaster to happen to a daughter of Judge Smith. Old-timers in the neighborhood—though only just born at the time of the murder, or not yet alive—will still shut out inquiries into that disaster in a kind of inherited loyalty to Grandma. To neighbors and Smith relatives the idea is that Stanford had terrible manners—it's bad manners to get shot and have your sex life in the paper—whereas Grandma, coming from solid Smith stock, had solid good manners that carried the day. The element that is consistent inside the family and out is that, whether she was clamming or leaving calling cards, Bessie Smith White was just fine.

In the late thirties, Grandma began to turn Box Hill over to Papa and Mama and their large family of eight children—though she let go of it reluctantly. In early March of 1938, she went to a spa in Augusta, Georgia, where her sister Ella was escaping the cold, and wrote back to Mama, her daughter-in-law, at Box Hill:

Of course, *now* is the time, when I should turn over "Box Hill" to you and Larry—but no! I am naughty, unreasonable and very much ashamed of myself, and I just can't help it! Stanford seems to stand beside me, whenever I go there—he created and loved it so—and I can't even after all these years think of deeding it away, even to his son! I asked a lawyer if it would make any difference because of "Inheritance Tax" whether I gave it to you now, or in my Will, and he assured me, it would not—so you and Larry must try to forgive me, and let me go on leading this "dog in the manger" existence, and all I can do, now,—dear Laura—is to give you full power to do whatever you like with the place (only let me keep my room apart until I have time to really clear it out)—Please try to feel that it is "home", as much as Larry does. You have waited so long and so patiently for that "Home", and I have always realized how difficult it was for you to live in somebody else's home. It makes me so *so* happy to know that my darling Grandchildren will grow up there and learn to love it too, and I don't think, dear Laura, that anything you might say or do, could annoy me, or mar my love and great admiration for you! Sentiment does not count for much in this present troubled world, but I do not belong to this age—so remember that if a lump comes into my throat and I burst into tears while at "Box Hill"—it is certainly not from anything you and Larry have said or done—but just because I am a weak old thing, and am thinking of my gay and festive House as it was 50 years ago—there—it is easier to write these things than to say them—so—no more—but I know that you and I understand each other—and Larry can think me as unreasonable as he chooses, and has a perfect right to—finis. . . .

As to the Box bush, I think we can move it in April . . . but not to the north—it will die.

Soon thereafter, Grandma moved into the White Cottage.

Claire Nicolas White has recorded in a personal history of the

Smiths called "The Land of the Smiths" how in old age Grandma wore raggedy clothes more and more, and became preoccupied with old things having to do with her childhood. There was some old furniture in the attic of one of the barns on the Smithtown House property, for example, and she told Claire she could have any of it that she wanted. But when Claire chose a broken-down chair with a velvet seat, Grandma said she couldn't have *that,* because her father, the Judge, used to sit in it when he took off his boots in the evening. (The next day, though, she had the gardener deliver it to Claire.) In Claire's history, Grandma is described sitting on the porch at one of the many birthday parties of my cousins who lived in the Smithtown House. Oblivious of the small children milling around her, she was lost in reverie as she cracked nuts with a huge nutcracker that had belonged to her father.

In the nineteen-fifties, big Sunday and holiday lunches in the dining room at Box Hill would include whoever of my mother's generation was around and usually quite a few of my generation as well. A family story about Grandma White is that when in her mid eighties she became bedridden she always called Box Hill from the White Cottage at 1:10 P.M. on those days, just after everyone had started lunch, and when the call was announced Papa, sitting at the head of the table, would roll his eyes. The rest of the story is that on July 4, 1950, the call came that Grandma was dying, and Papa, at the head of the table, rolled his eyes. I don't remember this. What I remember is my uncle Peter striding into the dining room and announcing, in a loud, emphatic voice, "Grandma White is dead!" And then everybody at the table said "Aw!" in what sounded to me a falsely sad way (actually her death was merciful and had been expected) and then went on eating and talking. What seemed like a lid the size of the sky descended on me.

When the word "grief" is mentioned, or when I am sad for no apparent reason, that moment when Peter announced Grandma's death is what comes to mind. Peter said that Papa had been "with" Grandma at the moment of her death, and I always think of that as well: I remember looking at Papa's empty chair at the head of the table and thinking, He was "with" her. Did he hold her? Some days before her death, I had been brought to her room to say goodbye—though no one explained that this was the purpose—but the moment turned out to be not right. I glimpsed her through the open door, however: gray, in duress, but stoic in a groaning physicality. I wished for some spark of protest to fly from her to me, a spark that I could fan with my breath in cupped hands: for some essence of her being to flash out of the deep forest of her composure in defiance of what was happening—a demonstration of essence to affirm the defiant essence in me. But there was only numb acceptance. These pictures are still fresh, and I wonder now, What is it that keeps this old grief for a beloved great-grandmother, who died in the fullness of years, still unfinished?

The dining room at Box Hill had windows along one side and a wall of Dutch tiles along the other. The tiles were white, in different shades, with small figures of farms, animals, and people in a hot blue that flashed in the northern light from the windows. The tiled wall was bayed in the middle to make a fireplace: in daytime the flames were transparent with hot blue flashes all around. Near the windows, there were small gilded lions leaping upward from globes, and majolica plates running around the top of the room. On the end wall, behind Mama's place, there was a round mirror in a heavy, gilded frame. The mirror itself was convex, and reflected, in a miniaturized and distorted way, the entire room, including everyone at the table. The frame was elaborate and topped by an eagle with outstretched wings. It was the anchor in a room that whirled with joy.

With a transcendent eye, I see myself in the moment of the announcement of Grandma's death reflected in that mirror surrounded by family and history in that festive, ornamental room. And what I feel is rebellion against the fact that a person can go to the grave with so much buried within her. I feel fear to know that the forces of life do not necessarily rescue us, cannot be counted on to drive us out of our coverts into the open air.

BOX HILL

Besides going past Grandma's and up the Privet Path, you could get to Box Hill from the Red Cottage by taking a path through some scrappy woods to the Rhododendron Drive—the primary access to Box Hill—turning left on it, and following it straight up to the house. From way down the drive—from the depths of the woods—you could see all the way to the fountain that stood in full light in front of the house, its vigorously sprouting Ionic shape carrying over the distance, its old marble glowing softly against the clouds of leaves of two swamp maples on the lawn beyond. From a distance, the fountain seemed to hold the light like a sponge. In a scrapbook called ''The Box Hill Book'' Papa identifies the fountain as a cinquecento wellhead set on an ''Istrian stone ionic capital that

comes from some Roman temple, presumably on the Adriatic.''
Not that I knew such details when I was a child, but I knew the
fountain itself, first chin high, then chest high as I grew. The capital
alone was about three feet high. Over all the fountain was about
four feet high, and squarish, like the capital. Around the base there
were four bronze ducks, with backs that came off so that you could
hide things in them.

Deep down, Box Hill was plain. The original Carman Hill farmhouse was eventually swallowed in Stanford's expanding design—
but its proportions remained in the scale of the gables and the height
of the three stories. The stones in the pebbledash surface were from
the local beach, and the story was around when I was little that this
surface had been chosen to please Grandma White, because she took
such joy in the beachstones, and that she had flung the first handful
at the wet cement. It was, of course, Stanford who had chosen that
surface to please Grandma, but his part was somehow evaded in the
way the story was told. Still, he was there, however latently, in a
family anecdote, and—because Grandma's love for the little things
of the countryside, like beachstones, was an allusive language of
family love (as if in remembering that Grandma loved the landscape
we felt loved ourselves and safe)—this tale brought Stanford right
into the inner circle of family love. It is a love story in itself too, for
in it Stanford and Bessie are not only a couple but a happy one, with
a good future promised in that vigorous flinging of stones. The
pebbles were of many colors when you looked at them up close, but
in the sun they flashed white, so on the south side Box Hill was a
bright house.

Inside, it was festive. Its great rooms were party rooms in which
people became handsome and vibrant. The principal room was the
Parlor, or the Baroque Room, as it was later called—a room about
thirty by fifty feet at the western end of the house. Stanford knew
how to pick and place ornaments so that they would build to peaks
of ecstatic dance. In the Parlor among many other things were
Italian angels, a Madonna, a tapestry, a gilt Baroque altar, and two
life-size androgynous nudes—Venetian, also gilded, and holding lan-

terns—which stood by the Renaissance fireplace and came to be known as the Whoopsie Girls. The Parlor had windows on three sides, but its walls, like those of the front hall into which it opened, were covered in brown bamboo, creating a voluptuously dark background against which objects—and gilded objects especially—stood out as in an atmosphere more than as against a wall. Two exposed steel beams, painted gray, traversed the width of the room: they were needed to support the ceiling and there hadn't been sufficient height in the room to conceal them. They were decorated with cartouches, coats of arms, and similar objects, in gilt frames. From the middle of one of them a Portuguese votive ship in full sail was suspended, and from the middle of the other a Bavarian mermaid, crowned, elaborately clothed, holding a shield and a chalice, and with stag horns set in her tail. The horns swooped back and up, supporting sconces.

Box Hill was originally a summer house, designed to repel heat and retain coolness, and even after it was winterized the lightness remained. Gaiety was the keynote of the house—it was a total environment of gaiety, and in its gaiety, as in its lightness, it also repelled the slightest sad thought. Even after four generations had lived there, Box Hill seemed to know nothing of the struggles and tragedies of family life. The rooms were insouciant. It was a house of the fleeting moment of delight.

In adulthood I noticed that on the Place—and especially in and around Box Hill—half the spectrum of what I felt was blocked. I discovered the full spectrum of what I felt there in other places, as when, in my early twenties, I was taken to lunch for the first time at the Century Club in New York. The building at 7 West 43rd Street was designed in part by Stanford White (it was completed in 1891), who had much to do with the decoration and furnishing of the interior as well: in some details, but very much so in atmosphere, it was reminiscent of Box Hill. When I was thus unexpectedly exposed to the visual language of my childhood, a raw mixture of grief, fear, and a kind of obstreperous, anguished love rushed in. Underneath the insouciant, joyful atmosphere of the Place I felt awful disturbance, but my sense of that disturbance was latent, or blocked, as if with anesthesia, so that life there seemed to exist in a strangely bright band of experience, severed from other bands. In and around Box Hill, I was eerily happy and yet was also separated from myself, from that which was distraught and turbulent in me, and, perhaps, from that which might give me power, an edge in the world.

When I was an adult, before the world of the Place began to come apart for me, I dreamt of a huge country-and-Western festival at Box Hill, at which I was an anonymous guest. Everything in the environment had meaning for me that no one there understood. While a large band played outside, I wandered into the front hall into which a stairwell opens, three stories high. Ornamental objects from all over the house were falling, in silence, in a slow spiralling motion, down the stairwell. It was a peaceful scene, a beautiful picture: lions leaping off their globes were especially graceful in their falling, twirling gently, end over end. There was going to be a terrible crash, but I felt no dread. It was as if the crash had already happened. I woke up, in a state of calm in which I felt access to ordinarily unavailable depths in myself. I recognized in the scene an atmosphere of serene catastrophe that was profoundly familiar.

Because of the way Box Hill was built, with flanking gables, it was long across the front but was of only farmhouse depth. The south side of the house was a few strides from the north side; you walked in the front door, and in no time you were out the back. The thinness of Box Hill contributed to its lightness: the house, for all its appointments, never enclosed you the way full-fledged interiors do. On the north side, however, the house was in shade and from the outside looked stony-faced, as if it had interiors in the serious sense. A terraced lawn ran the length of the north side: it was called the North Terrace. A huge oak grew midway along the northern façade, so close to the house that it must have become rooted in the foundation. A piazza, or porch, ran around the southern, western, and northern sides of the house supported by white Doric columns. The piazza was about eight feet deep, then broadened at the northeast corner into a roomlike space enclosed by balustrades, inside of which were broad, built-in benches with fitted cushions. This part of the piazza had the feeling of a ship, for just beyond the western balustrade the land plunged down in a swinging way like the high seas. And above the woods to the north, the characteristic light was sunless and empyrean, a sea light. (Here the seas were calm.) For most of the day, the north side of the house was sunless too, but in the late afternoon a rich golden light, with inky shadows interspersed, would pour down the lawn. The shadows on the green lawn were, in contrast, grounding. When I became literary, the North Terrace in general but those shadows in particular sometimes gave me the reassuring impression of belonging to an established family in a novel.

Many years later I had a real family experience sitting beside my grandmother on the lawn near the oak. I was in my thirties, and Mama was in her eighties—she had long since turned over Box Hill to my uncle Peter and aunt Jehanne. I was sitting cross-legged on the grass next to her chair, busy with some needlework, as she was talking to Jehanne. Half-listening to the nuanced, deft, animated sound of Mama's voice, I became aware of her presence as something that I was *in,* a field that she generated around her which was beneath the surface—beneath the chat, beneath specific time, beneath her manners and practice of disciplined leisure—that was both calm and effervescent. I became aware of how the feeling of holes in my being disappeared when I was in that field, and, in the same moment, I registered that Mama would not always be there. I understood that she would die. And so, at that moment, I began to harvest her presence as if it were a field of flax, and I were gathering it into baskets, retting it, combing it, spinning it, and weaving it, until I felt I had something that I could hold, and take away with me, like the pillow that I was embroidering. There was safety for me within the atmosphere of serene crashing. I found grounding in that dizzying environment of orbiting things: it was safe, but it wasn't, but it was. But it was.

*   *   *

Sometimes on Lower Fifth Avenue I would be lying in bed and hear the lawnmower—an old-fashioned, sputtering lawnmower—cutting the grass in the yard of the black church across the street. Always for me that would be the sound of a lawnmower on the north side of Box Hill heard from a bedroom on the second floor when I was a little girl. Always it was crisp and sunny June. Just outside the window was the massive trunk of the oak that grew on the North Terrace. I knew that the mower was pushed by George, Grandma White's old gardener; I could visualize its oily, intricate engine which had no cover, and its three cylindrical sections of blades. The mower was improvised by George from a horse-drawn one: for my mother's generation, the evocative sound was of George geeing the horse and of the mower clicking and whirring. The sound of a motorized mower on a summer day is a common modern sound, but for me it might as well be the sound of a mower drawn by a horse: for me it's the sound of Victorian order, of a world in which the adults are in charge and the children are children. The sound reminds me of Mama's presence when she was the mistress of Box Hill and I was a child.

Mama's order had a lot to do with things—extra things, like butter plates and blanket covers, and silver coffee spoons I helped polish in the pantry—which all together created an atmosphere of confidence and supremacy, and yet there was something of chaos in Mama's order as well: the English cook and the Italian cook trying to upstage each other at Thanksgiving, the Italian cook bringing in garlicky turkey cut up in pieces, the English cook rushing in with sweet potatoes and marshmallows, when Mama probably couldn't afford any cook at all. My grandmother's orderliness was never static or repressive. A pile of letters on her desk would seem active, almost churning—not unlike the pile of unruly, dirt-encrusted iris bulbs that I once saw her disentangling from each other on the lawn.

When I look back on Mama's life, it can seem that her order was a kind of harness of restrictions—in her case, chosen restrictions, of

class and gender, without which she might have manifested herself
to the world in a large, adventurous way. For me, though, Mama's
order was heavenly. It had to do with thoroughness and ample
equipment and taking plenty of time. It had to do with taking plenty
of time with me. Properly. ''Properly'' was a word of Mama's,
sometimes rebuking—to my mother, for example. But not to me.
Properly was a bath, a big towel, and a bed with soft sheets, a
blanket, and a seersucker blanket cover that had two bands of lace
running like stripes down the sides. It was a kiss and ''Good night''
and a door closing with a clear, glass knob that would not turn again
till morning.

My grandfather was a big man, six feet two, and you could feel the
mass of him in his presence: two hundred pounds in his shoes—and
they were good shoes, with thick leather soles. And he had hundred-
dollar bills in his wallet, which he showed me when he paid me—a
dollar, perhaps—for weeding the drive. I felt insufficient in these
moments, for my efforts were so puny—the drive so long, the
weeds so many—and because of the enormousness of what would
have to be done to relieve the tension in Papa, to satisfy him, to
please him, to allow him to come to rest. Despite his shoes and his
wallet, and the sheer displacement power of his robust frame, there
was in Papa a quality of inexhaustible need continuously managed—
of controlled restlessness, like a hum.

As a young man Papa was dazzling, and even when I knew him he
was a very handsome man. But there was no vanity in him. Nor was
there in his restlessness any edge of violence, or in his energy any
sense that he might go out of control. He was not vain, but he was
indelibly elegant, and he had a swanky social life in New York,
where he was popular and conspicuous—as opposed to withdrawn
and restless, with a corona of irritation around him, as he was at
Box Hill. Papa was agitated in the family environment. He was not,
my uncle has observed, a family man. He bonded with institutions:
with Harvard, with the Navy, with McKim, Mead & White. Papa's

idea of how to be a good father, Bobby has said, was to buy his eight children sailor suits and take them yachting.

Papa was a dynamo: he had a surplus of mental energy, a kind of whirring of the mind, that helped make him restless too. Sometimes he ate a box of chocolates at a sitting, and he almost incessantly smoked Old Gold cigarettes—without inhaling. But his principal method of managing his energy was to keep phenomenally busy: reading detective books as if he were eating chocolates, reading cookbooks as if they were detective novels, and putting together volumes of genealogy as if they were cookbooks. Another pastime was translating "The Divine Comedy"—he started out of boredom on a transatlantic crossing, but his translation, when completed, was published by Pantheon Books to widespread critical acclaim. A story that Mama liked to tell about Papa was that one day he was looking intently at a book of art reproductions and listening to a complicated program on the radio while she was talking to him. She blew up, and said that he couldn't possibly be paying attention to the radio, the book, and what she was saying; and in response Papa told her exactly what she had said, and then, handing her the book, told her what the paintings were, in order, and what was written about them in the captions, and, finally, repeated to her what he had heard on the radio.

My grandparents had a Victorian marriage; they were partners in a social enterprise and had respect for each other as partners while not expecting intimacy. Within that framework, they were competitive, like siblings. Mama was always challenging Papa on some cultural or historical fact, and then they'd look it up, and Papa would always be right. It drove Mama crazy that he was always right, because she thought that through her mother she had a superior claim on European culture especially. Money was also an area of competition. Mama's was inherited and Papa's was largely earned, and neither would ever tell the other how much he or she had. Sometime in the early fifties, a piece of Smith property that everyone had forgotten about was noticed and was sold, and Papa got a nice chunk of cash and bought Mama a string of pearls. When he gave her the pearls, she asked him how much he had got for the land, but he wouldn't tell her, and she threw the pearls at him—though she accepted them eventually.

I remember Papa at extended-family lunches, with his children and grandchildren and Mama all talking up a storm. But Papa would be looking out the window, smoking an Old Gold cigarette, balancing the ash. Sometimes he would sit looking out the window that way until the cigarette had burned almost entirely down, but I never saw the ash accidentally topple. A story about Papa that is the opposite of Mama's radio story took place when my mother's generation was growing up. One day at Sunday lunch, as Papa was sitting at the head of the table, looking out the window, and balancing the ash of his cigarette, his eight sons and daughters, by prearrangement, quietly sank to the floor. Crawling on their hands and knees, they left the room. Papa didn't notice.

Papa had a closet he called the broken-china closet, in which he kept pieces of broken things that he intended to fix. Unlike most people, Papa got around to fixing many of them, though he never caught up with quite all. He spent many hours sitting on a large Oriental rug in the dining room at Box Hill touching up faded places in the rug with special inks, which he had gone to great lengths to acquire, and which he loved, because of the unobtrusive way they revived the old hues. On weekends one was apt to find him clipping the hedges in the Rhododendron Drive. The drive ran between the eastern and western ends of the property and was the axis of Stanford's design. One was especially likely to find him in the Rond Point (a French term of Beaux-Arts design), where the drive opened into a formal circle, also hedged with rhododendrons and graced by a Propylon, a soaring structure of six white wooden columns, placed along the Rond Point's shallow curve, supporting a frieze, the whole reaching a height of nearly twenty feet.

Then the Propylon blew down in a hurricane. Papa was horribly distressed. I could feel the depths of his distress as he fussed over how to make the Rond Point whole again. He couldn't afford to restore it to what it had been, and ultimately his solution was to truncate what was left of the columns and use them as high pedestals for large urns. Papa was always fussing, clipping, arranging: was good at both tending and creating spots—a column in a sun catch, a statue among pines on a hill. I associated him with his spots. I felt his warmth in the warmth and felicity of his spots far more than I ever felt it directly from him. "Locked up tight like a safe," as Mama put it. Papa had warmth, but I felt it apart from his actual presence, as if it were to one side, or in the place where he had just been.

Papa put together all kinds of scrapbooks and volumes of memoirs and letters, including reams of his own light verse. One of these is "The Box Hill Book." In it the growth of Box Hill, gable by gable, is recorded, as are the large grading and terracing projects that transformed the landscape around the house. Stone slabs for terracing came from the reservoir at Forty-second Street and Fifth Avenue in New York that was disassembled in 1899 to make way for the Public Library; white marble paving came from the recently demolished A. T. Stewart palace where Grandma White had spent her young womanhood with her aunt Cornelia. Six enormous wooden columns from an 1840 neoclassical church in Hartford, Connecticut, were floated across the Sound for inclusion in the southern façade, but because Grandma White found them pretentious (how different Box Hill would have been with them!) they were, according to Papa, "at McKim's suggestion set up as a propylon in the Rond Point of the new drive." Stanford himself is rarely mentioned in Papa's "Box Hill Book."

Papa's description of Box Hill is on the whole so piecemeal as to be a kind of dismemberment—in contrast to my experience of the Place as an enspelled environment in which I lost my edges. But along the way there is a picture of Papa as a boy, lying under a box bush, languid in the expanding world of his powerful father. Once or twice, the prose too becomes languid as Papa's irritable piecemeal inventory momentarily yields to a yearning dreaminess:

There were many huge cactus and a night blooming cereus, 18 ft. high. There were fancy conveyances, with fringes and kerosene lamps and jangling silver harness, driven by Michael Cuttle, an old Irish Coachman who was with us for 20 years, and who, I believed, was omniscient and altogether wonderful.

So there is Papa growing up in a world of Axis and Symmetry, Hierarchy and Procession, Proportion and Harmony—a unified world in which even small details are related to the whole, a world of both reason and joy. It's clear from the scrapbook that, while for me Box Hill was a preëxisting world in gradual decline, Papa saw it coming into being. The emergence took place throughout Papa's boyhood, from his birth, in 1887, to Stanford's death in 1906, and it's clear that had Stanford lived the emergence would have continued. Papa felt the decline of Box Hill keenly, but for him the rise and decline had been almost one motion.

No spot on the Place had more mystique than the knoll on which the statue of Diana stood—the family called the spot Diana or the Seat, because of a large, curved concrete seat, painted white, that was placed on the very crest of the hill, looking seaward. Called an "exedra seat," and constructed from a full-sized drawing of the original that Stanford had made in Greece on his honeymoon trip, the seat was extraordinarily comfortable. In front of it was a low wooden table, curved to match the exedra seat and set on two Ionic capitals that, according to "The Box Hill Book," came from the street-level arcade at Madison Square Garden when it was torn down. There were also "four cement casts from those on the proscenium arch at the theater" at Madison Square Garden which Papa had incorporated into the Orangerie, a shelter built into the hill behind the Seat, for equipment needed to tend the orange trees in tubs that lined the drive on the approach to the house in Stanford's time. Madison Square Garden was torn down in 1925. Papa would have been the one who did the scavenging and the incorporating of the bits into the spot we called Diana.

The statue was a half-sized cast of Saint-Gaudens's second Madison Square Garden Diana. It stood on a pedestal that was about four feet high, set just below and directly in front of the seat, aiming her arrow due north across Long Island Sound. From the perspective of Diana, the Sound was a field of blue bounded by the slate-colored hills of Connecticut on the far side, and on the near side by the sandy barrier that separated it from the harbor. The harbor, from the perspective of Diana, was often dark and still, like a woodland pond. This was the view from Carman Hill that had drawn Grandma when she was a girl.

In "The Box Hill Book" Papa notes with typical acerbity that Diana's arrow is on the wrong side of the bow, "a curious error." But he was happy at the Seat in a way that he was nowhere else in my observation. There his corona of irritation disappeared as he cooked at family picnics on a barbecue built of marble fragments, or read the Declaration of Independence on the Fourth of July. We were all happy there—we children pulling ourselves up by Diana's outstretched foot to stand on the pedestal with her. As a child I didn't know where all the bits and pieces at Diana had come from, but I did know that a statue like her had stood on top of Madison Square Garden; indeed I thought that ours was the very one. At Diana there was a strong feeling of an apex that was more than just the apex of our hill: there was the feeling of an apex of an edifice, an apex of family history, an apex of a great life—a convergence of Stanford's gift, productivity, publicness, and success, and also his huge and sudden death. At no other spot on the Place was Stanford so explicitly present. All the allusiveness of the unspeakable came to a point there. And at that point of convergence, where one would expect the disturbance beneath the surface of family life to press dangerously close, the family in fact became relaxed and without care.

Papa made one major addition to Box Hill—the library, in 1938, after thinking about it for thirty years. So he writes in "The Box Hill Book." He situated the library on the south side where there was an indentation between the front hall and a small dining room—called the little dining room—that was right off the kitchen and also faced south. By building in the indentation, he was freed from farmhouse proportions and could therefore set the library ceiling high. The room was very nearly, but not quite, a cube, and in this it was elegant in a more settled way than the rest of the house. In Papa's library, the walls were walls and the ceiling was a ceiling and they enclosed a space that was what it was and, in its fine limitations, imparted a feeling both of resting on a secure foundation and of coextensiveness with a social world.

When I was a girl, the library was the most used room in the house; in fact, aside from the little dining room it was the only common room that was built for private family life, as opposed to parties. Papa included a built-in glass-faced cabinet for small heirlooms—a christening cup, a tankard, and his paternal grandfather's watch—establishing a quiet mood of private history, different from the surf of anonymous plunder in the other rooms. The library was also the only room built to retain heat. Its southern exposure was not hooded by a porch, and in winter the sun poured in. Cocktails were had in the library, and tea, and the sherry and the cheese on Ritz crackers before Sunday lunch, and coffee after, with a box of chocolates with different fillings that you had to guess at. Papa chose his chocolate leaning forward with his tongue wagging out.

"The firm" was a term of the library, meaning McKim, Mead & White, Stanford's firm—though that detail wasn't clear to me as a child—which Papa had joined as a young man. To me "the firm" connoted Papa's functioning in the world—something reliable in the background of our family life. I loved the gifts from Papa's business connections which would be delivered to Box Hill at Christmas: crates of oranges from Florida and big baskets of candied fruits and wrapped cheeses set in fake grass.

Papa did not share his work life with us, however, nor did the family show curiosity about it or pride. After the Second World War Beaux-Arts architecture became virtually invisible, and the firm was relegated to functional buildings—"dormitories at Harvard, a lunatic asylum in Albany," as my mother put it. But there was, in some manner, on the outskirts of the library, the ghostly city of the

McKim, Mead & White of Stanford's day with its powerful roof-lines, its colonnades, pediments, and porticos, its halls and domes and palatial façades.

This ghostly city was paradoxically full of the roar of real destruction. Indeed, buildings in the ghostly city became specified in my mind usually when demolished. The most dramatic of these occasions was the destruction of McKim, Mead & White's Pennsylvania Station in the early sixties. I remember expressions of anger and a sense of almost unbearable helplessness in the library at Box Hill, with the sun pouring in. The helplessness and the anger had to do with not being able to stop the destruction: they had to do with the indifference that allowed the destruction to take place. There was a feeling of disaster and enormous loss that, weirdly, did not register in the world at all.

One morning nearly twenty years after Papa's death, when I was living on Lower Fifth Avenue, my mother called from the Red Cottage to tell me that she had discovered architectural fragments under a rhododendron in the Rond Point. She said that among the fragments were lions that had served as cornices and large ceramic medallions. Most of the fragments were made of concrete overlaid with a thick glaze—in some cases of enamel, in others of a substance that made them look like marble. My mother said that they were too heavy to move but that the enamelled colors had come up brilliantly when she rubbed them.

Mama was, at this time, living next door in the White Cottage. My mother had gone straight over to tell her about the fragments, and Mama had immediately guessed that they came from Stanford's Madison Square Presbyterian Church—that Papa had salvaged them from the demolition site with the idea of somehow using them to embellish the Rond Point. It was typical of Mama to guess the provenance of the fragments right off like that: to have facts about Stanford at her fingertips.

When my mother told me of this I only dimly recognized the

name of the Madison Square Presbyterian Church. For some reason, however—it was as if something unusual had been set in motion even before I saw the fragments—after the call I did a little research, a tiny amount but the first in my life of this kind. What I learned was that the Madison Square Presbyterian Church was completed in October of 1906, four months after Stanford's death; that it was regarded by many as his crowning achievement; and that, in the immemorial way of New York, it was torn down ten years later. I calculated that at the time Papa rescued the fragments he would have been twenty-eight. From this calculation, a picture formed in my mind of Papa as a young man, standing at the site of the destruction of his father's best work, salvaging bits.

The next time I visited my mother, she took me straight out to see the fragments. We went through a scrappy bit of woods beyond her house, and then turned right onto a winding footpath that threaded its way there between two rows of ancient rhododendrons—the remains of the Rhododendron Drive. My mother and I followed it in an easterly direction, toward the Rond Point, on a gently descending course. When family love is displaced onto land, every change that happens there has meaning: the calibre of the light and the texture of the clouds in a day, the big changes of the seasons, most of all the slow transformation of the infrastructure of the place itself as the decades pass. When the deflection of love is also a deflection of pain, the gradual decomposition of such a place can be excruciating, a kind of lifelong torture, and yet, at the same time, a hypnotic, unfolding story. As the place declines, layers of meaning are revealed. The Rhododendron Drive in its ruinous latter-day stages had become storied in this way in the extreme.

The Rond Point itself, however, was dreary. Its meaning seemed to be that it was without meaning. The once open circular space had become congested with saplings, briars, and honeysuckle. The columns had fallen down and rotted; the urns were gone; some statuary that as a child I had taken for marble, but which was white-painted plaster, had disintegrated; and the rhododendrons that formed the circle, by now gargantuan, were smothered by chinaberry vines, giving them the blinded, blunted look of a creature fumbling beneath a blanket. It was under one of the largest of these blanketed bushes that the fragments lay.

My mother showed me a way through the chinaberry cover to the interior of the rhododendron—a kind of cave, where an adult could stand in a colorless light—and there, sunk in the mulch and dulled by half a century of sediment, the fragments lay. There were eight of them: four lions, two medallions (one of these with a fishlike creature embossed in its center, the other with a flower), and two leafy marble formations in a scrolling motif. Although half buried, the fragments preserved in their skewed positions the heavy motion of having been thrown. Each also trailed chunks of the building from which it had earlier been torn, and the violence conveyed by these coarse ruptures—the concrete beneath the glaze exposed—similarly seemed fresh. I could understand why Papa had been unable to use them in a decorative scheme. Quite suddenly, I had a powerful impression of Papa's presence. It was a full, warm impression, and there was a masculine timbre to his presence: I was aware of him very much as a man. There was a heart there too. I felt that I was in the presence of a fully sexual man with an open heart from which flowed love but also raw, inundating grief.

Simultaneously with this impression of Papa came a scent of flowers so vivid that I momentarily assumed it was real, and looked around for its source. Even after I knew it was a phantasm of memory, the scent seemed strong in my nostrils, and even before I identified the memory the phrase "the scent of lies" came into my mind. Then I was back in the front hall of Box Hill as it had been during my childhood. There it all was: the dark polished red of the terra-cotta floor, the serpentine columns, the apple-green tiles of the staircase, and the deep golden-ochre of the split bamboo on the walls. It was a room in which I felt welcome. There at the bottom of the stairs were the wooden baroque lions—life-size, with long, backward-curling tails on which, to Papa's despair, I liked to climb. There at the eastern end of the hall was the Renaissance fireplace that you could walk into, with Atlas holding up the mantel. It was a

fanciful room. And there, flanking the fireplace, were the big portraits of Stanford and of Papa as a young man, in gold-leafed frames
that stood out in relief against the bamboo. The hall was banked
with white blooms that were softly brilliant against smooth dark-
green leaves. They were gardenias, I am almost sure, because that is
the scent that surrounded me under the rhododendrons all those
years later. I had just come into the hall from outdoors. I was
barefoot. The sunny wood of the piazza had been warm, but the
tiles in the hall were cool.

The white flowers were connected in a roundabout way to the
one occasion I remember when emotions were attributed to Papa.
The occasion was the release, in 1955, of "The Girl in the Red
Velvet Swing." From the family talk I gathered in a fractured way
that the title of the movie referred to a velvet-roped swing that hung
in a loft hideaway of Stanford White's and on which he pushed a
young woman named Evelyn Nesbit. I gathered that a sexual scandal
ensued, and that a man called Harry K. Thaw, who had become
Evelyn Nesbit's husband, shot Stanford. I was ten at the time the
movie was released, and this talk was the first I had heard of sexual
complications having to do with the murder—it may have been the
first I'd heard of the murder at all. Confusingly, the news of sex and
murder came packaged in the message that the movie was all lies
and that it was extremely upsetting for Papa.

The principal focus of the talk was that my beloved great-grandmother, who had died five years before, was, as Stanford's wife,
also portrayed in the movie—a movie that was all lies. It was said in
the family that the producers of the movie had waited for
Grandma's death to make it, so that she couldn't sue them about the
lies. Feelings of family loyalty were aroused in me that were deeper
than any I had imagined. I felt privileged in my outrage. The family
circled the wagons against whatever repercussions might provoke
further feelings in Papa. We circled them especially tightly during
the days "The Girl in the Red Velvet Swing" played at our local
theatre.

No one in the family went to *see* the movie of course: it would have been inconceivable to do so. But in the library at Box Hill I learned that it was a bad movie because it was a Hollywood movie, because its heroine was a person of low social station and questionable morals, because it was about sex, and above all because it told lies. The only specific lie that I remember hearing mentioned, however, was that Stanford White had drugged Evelyn Nesbit's champagne. The family talk implied that this was known to be a lie because Stanford White had paid Evelyn Nesbit's dental bills and also the dental bills of many other girls. The point was quite clear to me that doing this signified a good person, who would not drug a girl's champagne—and who was now, for his charity, condemned. The dental bills were often mentioned in this unusual period of discussion of Stanford White.

The danger in the life of my great-grandfather was implicit in what was conveyed, if not in the talk itself then in the calibre of distress that was present in the pregnant air. The essential ingredients of the story of Stanford and Evelyn were laid out in the library in this period. Perhaps because it was a story that reverberated right into conditions in my own life, thereafter, and well into adulthood, the mere mention of my great-grandfather—especially in public, unexpectedly—could jolt my system, disorienting me, blowing out my circuits with a horrible, smoking mixture of pride and shame.

Another confusing aspect of the talk in the library was the assumption that the primary injury the movie inflicted on the family was not that it misrepresented the story but that it raised the subject at all. It was publicity—more, and painful, publicity—and from this emphasis I got the idea that the bad thing that had happened in the family was not murder but publicity. The impression given was that the murder and the circumstances surrounding it had no significance for the family—as if the family were burdened only by the unfortunate obsessions of others. The publicity was the violent thing, and the movie was felt as a continuation of that original assault.

Most unforgivable of all, Cornelia Otis Skinner, an actress who then enjoyed considerable fame, had a role in the movie. Cornelia Otis Skinner lived down the road. She was a friend—particularly of

Papa's—a neighbor, and a ''lady,'' and one who had loved and admired Grandma White. It was unspeakable treachery that she had taken that role in that film. As soon as this treachery came to light, Mama wrote her a note disinviting her to my aunt Ann's wedding. It was clear that Cornelia Otis Skinner would never be spoken to again.

In 1956, one year after the appearance of ''The Girl in the Red Velvet Swing,'' Papa died of a heart attack. He was sixty-eight; I was by this time eleven. He was laid out in the Parlor at Box Hill, amidst the angels and ornaments, red velvet and gilt. That day, my mother had said what a wonderful thing it was that in death the eczema on Papa's hands had disappeared. I had never noticed the eczema, but now I did notice the warmth of him, in his brown tweed jacket. It seems to me in memory that this was the closest I ever got to my grandfather physically and the only time I felt his warmth coming directly from him.

Papa was my first corpse, and when I left the room I saw my mother coming down the stairs into the front hall with tears streaming down her face: she didn't use a handkerchief or wipe the tears away with her hand; she was just letting them stream, and her black hair was loose and streaming too. The emotion scared me. I needed to retreat from it into a kind of feigned innocence, to be a barefoot child outdoors. My cousin Benjy and I conspired in this pretense, spurting out of the front hall onto the wooden piazza; I can remember the springy feeling of running too, and the good feeling of the grass underfoot. We stayed out long enough to forget the scene in the house completely, and when we returned the hall was banked high with white flowers that shone against deep-green leaves and gave off a powerful scent. The scent was lovely, and the sight of the flowers was moving, arresting. Then I heard that they had been sent by Cornelia Otis Skinner.

In the normal course of events, having heard this I would have seen them as bad flowers, but for some reason I did not. They still seemed lovely to me, and I continued to see in them a loving gesture. Even now, my vision of them is one of depth and openness

of heart. How a mere impression could have withstood the imperative of family loyalty in the charged atmosphere surrounding Papa's
death I do not know. Perhaps it was the luminescence of the white
petals against the leaves, perhaps it was a readiness in me, perhaps it
was the momentarily freed vision that death occasions, perhaps it
was my mother's openness of feeling, perhaps it was incalculable,
inexplicable grace. But, whatever it was, my perception of the flowers disrupted the spell of the Place. Ever so minutely but with fatal
significance, the cosmos shifted, and in that moment I knew: it was
the family melodrama about lies and betrayal, and not the Hollywood one, that was untrue. There in my great-grandfather's warm,
charmed hall, the symmetries and harmonies that were the under-
pinnings of our sense of family blessedness slipped and became
skewed and thin, like a stage set gone awry.

In the cave under the rhododendrons I thought that I had, in that
moment in the front hall, seen straight to the bottom of family
truth. I had seen to the bottom of a well usually obscured by
brilliant reflections on the water. It was startling to me that I had
been able so completely to forget what I knew, had been able to
restore the concealing surface—halcyon, bright—so perfectly that it
was as if it had never been breached. But it is in the nature of this
kind of surface that, like reflections on water, it is automatically self-
sealing: the challenge is not so much to pierce the slick of reflections
as to maintain the break.

STANFORD

THOMAS,   717 6TH AVE. N. Y.

Stanford's father's name, "Richard Grant White," was affixed to the door of the Box Hill library, in black lettering on a round silver-colored plaque about four inches in diameter—an object Richard Grant White had probably acquired in one of his multiple careers. His was a name that floated in family memory with red hair, aggrievedness, versatility, and preposterousness attached, a vivid image that prompted affection, loyalty, and even identification: perhaps we in the contemporary family were a little odd too. The image was on the whole correct: he was indeed a misfit, though one who made splashes, a cranky bohemian who fancied himself an English gentleman yet was blackballed from the Century Club and was chronically broke and in debt, who had studied to be a doctor and also passed the bar but was, in practice, a music critic, a Shakespearean scholar, a linguist, a novelist, a lecturer, a cultural gadfly, a sonneteer, and an employee of the Custom House. He was all those things and yet was somehow, irredeemably, an outsider; was even, in a mild way, derided. An 1846 New York newspaper sketch describes him at Delmonico's "in an attitude of listless self-complacency—a tall, striking looking man, with a ruddy beard and moustache, setting off a voluptuous and decidedly handsome mouth—an epicure, an amateur, a dilettante, a gallant, a critic, almost a coxcomb," known for "prejudice, vanity, obstinacy," yet who "wields an intellectual battle-ax between his thumb and forefinger." A contemporary described him in a diary as "a decorated, and flamboyant gent . . . generally underrated and slighted." Richard Grant White has about him the aura of one born out of kilter, but his condition may have been exacerbated by disappointment in the area of inheritance. His father was a clipper-ship magnate who failed to switch to steam and went bankrupt, and died, in 1849, at the age of fifty-one, leaving his eldest son, twenty-seven years old and reared with expectations of wealth, penniless and—for the rest of his life—touchy where matters of social status or exclusion were concerned.

A matter that caused Richard Grant White great pain was that the English regarded Americans as inferior, rather than as blood brothers. That the English writer and art critic John Ruskin refused even to visit America—on the ground that it was a commercial place, with no culture—wounded him especially, although Richard Grant White himself was engaged in delivering a lifelong tirade to the same effect. "One had might as well live in a fulling mill or a boiler factory" as live in New York, he wrote, yet it had not always been so, and, in his opinion, this was what Ruskin had missed: that there were cultivated, unmaterialistic Americans like Richard Grant White, Americans who were essentially Englishmen. He loved being taken for an Englishman, and often was. In a letter to the editor of the *Spectator* he wrote, "What pleases me in being taken for an 'Englishman' is that it shows me I am free from many of these disagreeable peculiarities of which our British cousins make test points."

Richard Grant White didn't actually see England until 1876, when he was in his fifties, but he had studied that country for so long that, once there, he could find his way around the streets of London without difficulty. He wrote an account of this trip, "England Without and Within," published in 1881, that was serialized in its entirety in *The Atlantic Monthly* and was popular as a book as well. An entire chapter was devoted to English skies. Papa, his grandson, recorded in one of his scrapbooks that on this trip "he bought that magnificent travelling-case, the brass-bound mahogany box blazoned with his not very authentic heraldry and filled with an amazing array of silver mounted boxes and bottles: the whole contraption so heavy as to need a stalwart body-servant to carry it about." Papa adds, "Of course he had no such retainer."

Stanford's mother was Alexina—Nina—Black Mease, who came from Charleston, and who retained Black as a middle name when she married Richard so that she could be Alexina Black White. Indeed, she published a book of poems under that name. Not that this accomplishment was ever mentioned in the family circle as I knew it; though she lived for many years in Box Hill Nina was an unremarked presence in my time. Among the scrapbooks that Papa assembled were two "Ancestor Books," one for Mama's side of the family and one for his, and one of the exhibits in a section on Nina's ancestors was a certificate of bankruptcy issued to one of them in England, together with the flap of an old leather wallet, printed with his name—"John Mease of Houndsditch, 1776." Trouble with money converged on Stanford from two sides. Richard Grant White suffered from chronic insolvency, though it's something of a mystery why, since his literary output was prodigious and often commercially successful. In addition to "England Without and Within," a novel he wrote entitled "The Fate of Mansfield Humphrey," published in 1884, did very well too. (The novel was about a gentleman who goes to England and acts out the British caricature of an American, thus exposing the prejudice of his hosts.) In a more

academic vein, Richard Grant White's annotated Shakespeare was
the standard edition in America for many years. His "Words and
Their Uses, Past and Present: A Study of the English Language"
went through many editions and is still referred to from time to
time today. Richard Grant White was a champion of pure speech.

Except for a brief sojourn in Bay Ridge, Brooklyn, in 1850,
Richard and Nina lived in the neighborhood of Lower Fifth Avenue,
first on Thirteenth Street and then on Tenth Street, which is where
they raised their children—Richard was born in 1851 and Stanford
in 1853. Stanford was named for a friend of his father's who was a
piano dealer. Music was a great passion of Richard Grant White. In
addition to being a music critic and a Wagner scholar, he played the
piano, violin, and cello—and he owned a valuable collection of
musical instruments. From time to time, as debts pressed in, he had
to sell off parts of this collection. He also assembled a library so
distinguished that when he had to put up the best items for auction
the New York *Times* reported that such opportunities arose for bib-
liophiles only once or twice in a generation. (At his death, in 1885,
the remainder had to be sold to pay funeral expenses.)

Richard Grant White was also a worshipper of female beauty, and
he deplored any association with women who failed to please him
visually. "Twelve women at breakfast with me. All ugly, all ill
dressed, all with bad figures, all talked through their noses," he
wrote of an incident on a trip. He liked women to be young and
helpless and to require his guidance: he could be as acidic about
independence and self-sufficiency in a woman as about her failure to
be pretty. He had an extensive collection of erotica, and he made a
fool of himself by flirting publicly with very young women into his
sixties. It has been suggested that he took these tendencies a good
deal further. Aline Saarinen, one of Stanford's would-be biographers (there is a high rate of attrition among Stanford's biographers), who did her research in the fifties, wrote to her publisher
that "an ancient relative" had told her that Richard Grant White
had maintained a mistress, with children. Mama, who had lived for
some time with Nina in Box Hill when Papa went overseas in the

First World War, confirmed this rumor to Saarinen, and there is also an account by a contemporary of Richard's that he had a mistress, of whom he was very proud because she was English.

Yet Richard's letters to Nina are full of open, easy expressions of love. "Ah Darling, they make more of me here than I deserve," he wrote to her in 1857 from Cambridge, Massachusetts, where he was being somewhat lionized. In 1852 he wrote, "A few thousand dollars would do much toward making you and me happy, would it not, darling?" In the same letter, there is a confusing passage enjoining his wife to "kiss Richie the dear little monkey for his reputed father and tell him that I could not love him more if I really was his father." Richie—later known as Dick—grew up to be a big, red-headed man very much like Richard.

Confusion rises like thick smoke from the Richard Grant White family, but one thing is clear, and that is that Stanford was lovable. In one of Nina's poems, he appears as

> My boy Stannie, wee busy mannie!
> Aye, trottin' roun' the garden lot
> Wi' wheelbarrow, spade and waterin'-pot
> All bent and battered!

When Stanford's godfather, the piano dealer, gave his godson some shares of stock, Richard wrote to Nina, "Stannie, darling little soul, will have benefits showered upon him but my poor boy Richie will have few real friends." At two, Stannie gave his father a precocious drawing of a morning glory for his birthday. Both boys went to a public school on Thirteenth Street for six years; then the family moved to Bay Ridge for two years where one presumes the boys also attended public school, though it's possible that they were tutored; and then the family returned to Greenwich Village. Stanford covered up his public-school experience later in life, claiming that he had been educated by tutors. He fulfilled his father's dreams of success and yet inherited his father's touchiness about status.

You can see—almost feel—the artist in Stanford in photographs of him as a young man: standing with his legs apart in a studio, for example, his hair sticking straight up, he is charged throughout with a kind of straight-up energy that is full of the outwardness of doing and seeing and the inspiration of the world. He is dressed plainly, unself-conscious in a rough suit and sturdy shoes. This careless, engaged, passionate aspect never disappeared completely, even after he was hooked on buying excessive quantities of luxurious clothing that he couldn't afford—silk shirts in exotic colors, moosehide slippers. He would buy these things and then often forget to wear them. He could be a dandy, and he could also show up at a formal dinner with tails thrown over workaday trousers at the last moment—the artist who cannot be bothered with niceties of convention or dress. To the end there is this winning rough authenticity in Stanford.

He wanted to pursue a career as a painter, and so his father took him to the painter and stained-glass-window maker John La Farge for advice. La Farge looked at Stanford's work, and then told him that it was almost impossible to make a living as an artist—that he himself had had to struggle for years—but he saw that Stanford's subjects often included architecture and that they were sensitively rendered, so he suggested that Stanford become an architect. La Farge's advice—subsequently reinforced by the landscape architect Frederick Law Olmsted—was taken, though it has sometimes been said in the family that Stanford was really meant to be a painter, and that this was the tragedy of his life.

There is no record of any objection to this career course on Stanford's part, however. As his father could not afford to send him to the École des Beaux-Arts in Paris, the preferred architectural school of the day, in 1870 he entered the firm of Gambrill & Richardson as an apprentice, and apparently did so gladly. There he met the great H. H. Richardson in whom he found a surrogate father and a mentor. Richardson was an expansive epicure, given to excess, who hobnobbed with rich clients and enjoyed worldly success, ran up debts recklessly, and was very much a family man, who included his children in his work and his apprentices among his children. He had studied architecture at the École des Beaux-Arts and, though he did not design in a neoclassical style, he had absorbed into his work methods the hierarchical thinking and rational procedure from plan to final elevation which were taught at the École. These he taught his apprentices. Stanford worked on Richardson's masterpiece, Trinity Church in Boston, which was completed in 1877, and he is said to have been largely responsible for the design of the tower.

Augustus Saint-Gaudens, the sculptor, and Charles McKim, who were to become central figures in Stanford's life, were also working for Richardson on Trinity Church. Saint-Gaudens was boisterous and promiscuous, though no scandal was ever publicly associated with him: on the Place, in my time, he came to be a kind of substitute for Stanford, who could be invoked possessively and with love in an open, uncomplicated way that Stanford could not. Stanford had first met Gus in New York in 1875 when, climbing an empty stairwell in a building at Fourth Avenue and Fourteenth Street, he heard someone "bawling out" a theme from Beethoven's Seventh Symphony. Stanford "bawled" back, and in this way found Gus—like himself a big red-headed man—in his studio. Saint-Gaudens spent much time in Europe: in New York, he left the water running in his studio to remind him of the fountains of Rome. Like Richard Grant White, he later had a second family—with the model for Diana, Davida Clark; refusing to give up this double life even after his wife discovered it. This was in addition to habitual philandering.

Charles McKim, in contrast, was a high-minded young man, who came from a family of Quaker abolitionists; his sister was married to William Lloyd Garrison's son, and his family addressed one another as "Thee." Charley was a passionate devotee of Ruskin, whose philosophy of architecture was based on the principle that the purpose of architecture was the "pleasing of God." McKim was six years older than Stanford, five feet seven, and bald, though to the extent that he had hair it was red, including his drooping mustache. "Buoyant" is an adjective often used to describe him, but he was also fastidious, gentlemanly, reliable, controlled. He was, among other things, an athlete, in particular a great skater, and he had about him an athlete's grace. He was reserved and yet, of all the people around Stanford, he is the only one who, from this distance, seems to have registered—seems to have openly suffered from—the disaster of Stanford's life.

McKim was sentimental about love, but his marriage to Annie Bigelow, in 1874, was a debacle, ending in 1879, in divorce—a scandal always in that time. Annie sued on grounds of "gross misbehavior and wickedness repugnant to and in violation of the marriage contract," charges that are almost impossible to connect with Charley McKim. The divorce caused him deep pain, as did the ensuing separation from his daughter, Margaret—Annie would permit only supervised visitation. In "April Hopes," a novel by William Dean Howells published in 1887, which is purported to be about that marriage, the buoyant, kind, conscientious, and, to a degree, innocent protagonist marries a self-centered and erratic woman who has already, during their engagement, taken him for a brutalizing emotional ride. The implication of the novel is that the hero marries her anyway in order to re-create his relationship with his capricious mother. I can't guess why Charley married Annie Bigelow, and it should be added, furthermore, that—especially in this context, where things are often not what they seem—a modicum of doubt must be reserved in favor of Annie. However, the idea that Charley was attracted to trouble is certainly confirmed by the fact that, in addition to marrying Annie Bigelow, who was, at the very least, difficult, he hooked up with Stanford White, who was as erratic and troubling a life partner as one could find.

In the summer of 1877, after Charley, Gus, and Stanford had all finished work for Richardson on Trinity Church, Charley founded the architectural firm of McKim, Mead & Bigelow in New York, with William Bigelow, Annie's brother, and the architect William

Mead. That same summer Charley separated from his wife. In the summer of 1878 Charley and Stanford joined Gus, who was living in Paris with his new wife, Gussie, and the three men went on a trip through France.

Going to Europe for the first time was an overwhelming experience for Stanford. In letters to his mother he reported that the Elgin marbles made his "hair stand up and then lie down again," a Vermeer "squoze the tears out of my eyes," a Memling made his "nails grow." He exhorted Gus to fall on his knees before a Raphael and himself burst into tears before a Veronese, as he wrote to Nina, adding, "To think that so lovely a thing could be done and I could not do it!" Of Bruges, he wrote to her, "The architecture and the old town are enough to set you wild; but when you add to these the pictures, all there is to do is to gasp for breath and die quietly." He wrote regularly to Nina—large-spirited, open letters, in which he tells her of getting tight on wine with his friends and of his appreciation of pretty girls as well as of his aesthetic ecstasies. He shares with her his dislike of the wrong kind of women too— Gussie Saint-Gaudens, for example.

> I hug St. Gaudens like a bear every time I see him, and would his wife, if she was pretty—but she ain't—so I don't. She is very kind, however; asks me to dinner, mends my clothes, and does all manner of things. She is an animated clothes-rack, slightly deaf—a double-barrelled Yankee, and mean to that extent that no comparison will suffice.

Actually, Stanford failed to pay Gussie for his share of household expenses in the time that he stayed with them on this trip.

Stanford did like Gussie's sister, Eugenie Homer, even though she was a feminist and he got in "rows" with her. But she was pretty. (And she, too, mended his clothes.)

When Stanford returned from Europe in September of 1879, he moved back in with his parents, in the neighborhood of Lower Fifth Avenue, and joined McKim's firm. Bigelow had departed, and so the firm became McKim, Mead & White. Almost every reminiscence of Stanford in the office mentions a loud, reverberating voice; rushing feet, doors slamming; instantaneous aesthetic decisions; strewn, crumpled drafting paper; a gargantuan capacity for work; and a contagious obsession with beauty. The artist Edward Simmons wrote that Stanford had "a sensitivity so great that he could lose his personality." I associate Simmons's description with a softness in Stanford's nature—an immateriality, almost—much like the structureless, evanescent effect of his interiors, and like his latency on the Place and in our lives too. This recessive quality coexisted with the energy and the brashness. Henry Magonigle, a draftsman in the office in these early years, wrote:

> He had a "field," as an electrician would say, and his radiated energy was terrific. His habitual gait was something between a fast walk and a run; between the private rooms and the drafting room there was a double-swing half-door; it was White's habit to start on a dead run for that door, slide for the last few feet to check his momentum and bang the door open; his constant sliding back and forth through that door wore a trough through the wooden flooring that had to be repaired all the time.

Others found Stanford harsh in his criticism and offensive in his use of foul language. Still other reminiscences mention self-centeredness and a pattern of domineering, all of which were tolerated because of his charm—powerful when he turned it on—and his overflowing giftedness. He was the baby of the office, a big, inspired toddler, indulged, angelic, oblivious, tyrannical.

Magonigle also left some amusingly contrasting descriptions of Stanford and Charley. He wrote:

> [Charley] liked to sit down at a draftsman's table, usually in his hat and immaculate shirt sleeves, and design out loud; the room reverberated with architectural terms Cyma Recta;

Cyma Reversa; Fillet above; Fillet below; Dentils; Modillons. He was the most convinced authoritarian I have ever encountered.

Charley hardly ever drew; instead he would talk his way through a design, instructing a draftsman to draw a line and then, after much thought, telling him to erase it and draw it somewhere else. Often he would have a line redrawn many, many times. Stanford had a different style of working:

[He would] tear into your alcove, perhaps push you off your stool with his body while he reached for pencil and tracing paper and in five minutes make a dozen sketches, slam his hand down on one of them—or perhaps two or three of them if they were close together—say "Do that!" and tear off again. You had to guess what and which he meant. He almost never explained. A five minute visit from him left you limp with the reaction from the strain of trying to follow his thought as his fingers flew.

William Mead, the third partner, was deemed by contemporaries to be "the balance wheel" of the office. A medallion by Saint-Gaudens shows him struggling with two kites that represent Stanford and Charley. Mead was a taciturn Vermonter, very handsome with big, purple eyes and strikingly shapely eyebrows, who brought in little business, designed little, and spent a lot of time draped on a chaise longue in his office. However, it was he who brought a business sense to the partnership, and who took care of the practical aspects of the firm's work.

In 1876 Saint-Gaudens had been awarded a commission for a statue of Admiral David Farragut, to be placed in Madison Square Park. Stanford got involved in designing the pedestal, and so it became a joint project, though for much of the working time Saint-Gaudens was in Paris and Stanford was in New York. They corresponded but for the most part they fussed and toiled independently;

they were both great fussers. In May of 1881 the superbly original result of their collaboration was unveiled to the public. The convention for public statues then was an idealized figure on a foursquare pedestal. Saint-Gaudens's Farragut, in contrast, stands with his coat blown open and his legs apart. The central pier of the pedestal on which he stands is embellished with a shallow relief of waves—irregular downswinging lines, like the delicate lines of a pencil—pierced by a broad, downward-pointing sword, to enigmatic, mystical effect. The waves continue on either side of the pedestal through high-backed benches that flank it and are a continuation of it, the backs presenting themselves as walls that curve toward a spectator in a light embrace. The pedestal is feminine in feeling in a way that is surprising even today, especially for a monument honoring a military man. Two androgynous figures, Courage and Loyalty, sit in the waves on the flanking walls, and there are words here as well: biographical information about Farragut, prepared by Richard Grant White. Stanford's father was present at the unveiling, bursting with pride. The monument put both Gus and Stanford on the map.

With Charley, Stanford also designed a casino at Newport in this early period, a shingled complex of buildings which is cozy and elegant at the same time. A deep, arched entranceway, dark and medieval in feeling, leads into an interlocking series of spaces, full of green grass and light, where the textures of the enclosing shingled walls are varied, and a variety of towers and window styles adds to the picturesque effect. The casino, which was completed in 1880, had been commissioned by James Gordon Bennett, Jr., the publisher of the New York *Herald.* He had commissioned it in a fit of pique when a friend of his was blackballed from the existing casino for riding his horse into the reading room. Bennett became Stanford's lifelong friend: the young architect was moving into the circles of the overspending, bad-behaving nouveaux riches that his father deplored, while at the same time achieving the status in society for which his father hungered.

Stanford did a few houses in Newport that have the same grounded, comfortable quality. Richardson's style was strongly Ro-

manesque, and these buildings show that influence, with great, sloping roofs, deep eaves, and ample porches. An interior of this period
which has survived is that of Kingscote, a Victorian house in Newport which Stanford expanded in 1881. The dining room is notable
for a cork ceiling, and for sections of opalescent Tiffany-glass bricks
of subtly varied colors flanking a Sienna-marble fireplace, which
constitute the outer wall of the room. The cork, which is light-
absorbent, creates a dark, atmospheric glow; the bricks gleam, the
daylight shining through them. Magonigle wrote that for Stanford
light was the "most important element in design, and the way
surfaces can be handled to receive light, to be caressed by it."

Stanford's best work emerges from combinations of materials
rather than structural form, but he is also a master of the mysteries
of proportion, and particularly the proportions of interiors as well
as the feeling of a doorway as one passes through; the effect of the
size, placement, and setting of a window as one looks out. Here his
signature is a breezy warmth, a kind of grace, a feeling of goodness.
My mother was referring to this quality when she said that she had
experienced Stanford through "kindness in a measurement." The
virtues of Stanford's architecture are more like an emanation than
like any traditional architectural qualities: they are something ineffa-
ble, in which one also feels Stanford's presence in an uncanny way,
as if the emanation were of him.

Before Stanford was thirty, he was on his way to becoming the
most famous architect in America. The early eighties were big years
for him, and for McKim, Mead & White too: in those years the firm
designed many palazzi in and out of New York City for the bur-
geoning Gilded Age and became one of the most successful and
influential architectural firms in the country. The working style of
the firm was collaborative. No one project came from any one hand.
The pressure was tremendous, and Stanford in particular worked in
a whirlwind, but a lovely period sometimes opened up at the end of
the day, when the partners would sit down and, in a quiet mood,

discuss their work, comment on each other's efforts, and then leaf through volumes of classical architecture together.

With them would be Joseph Wells, an acerbic draftsman, who refused a partnership because he wouldn't put his name to "so much damned bad work." (Wells was in fact responsible for some of the most enduring masterpieces of McKim, Mead & White: the exterior of the Villard Houses in New York, for example.) Papa told a story—recorded on tape—that captures not just Wells and Stanford but Papa himself.

Wells was working at a drafting table, and my father came running into the room with a large photograph of the façade of the Cathedral of Poitiers, which was a very rich, juicy Romanesque church. He plunked it down on Wells's drafting board and said, with great formality: "Mr. Wells"—they were great friends, but people were not called by their first name in the office at that time—"Mr. Wells, damn it, that building there is as good in its way as the Parthenon." Wells took the pipe out of his mouth and looked up at my father and said, "Stanford"—which was a terrible breach of etiquette—"Stanford, fried eggs, in their way, are as good as the Parthenon," and then went on drawing.

Wells lived in the Benedict, a building on Washington Square that had been designed by McKim, Mead & Bigelow. It was a building for bachelors, which Wells was all his life—and a cranky, misogynistic one to boot. In the eighteen-eighties Mead also lived there, and McKim had rooms in another building on the Square. Stanford continued to live with his parents nearby, but it was Wells's rooms at the Benedict that became the focus of social occasions. The painter Thomas Dewing was a member of the group that gathered there, and Saint-Gaudens, of course, was often there too.

The members were initially bonded by an interest in the arts, a passion for beauty. They had concerts: in 1882, Saint-Gaudens brought in a chamber group to play, but Wells, characteristically, judged it to be inferior and replaced it in 1883. Stanford had inherited a sensitivity to music: a friend observed that the only time he saw Stanford sitting still was when he was listening at these concerts—and then he was absolutely still. The occasions were informally known as "smoking concerts," and women were usually excluded, but somewhere along the way activities were taken up from which women were not excluded, for eventually the concert group became the core of a sex club. In Stanford's mind, certainly, very beautiful, very young women were on the same continuum as the beauty he adored in art.

In Stanford's late twenties—the period of the smoking concerts—something in him turned. He had at first been a hero to Cass Gilbert, who came to the firm as a draftsman in 1880 and later became one of the era's greatest architects. In 1880 Gilbert saw Stanford "as a man of extraordinary ability and of the most attractive and engaging personality." But in 1882, when Stanford was only twenty-eight, Gilbert wrote in a letter to a friend that he was "getting a little sick of his arrogance, and his claiming all the credit for everything done in his office" and that he had "heard things and observed things . . . that make me respect him none the more." Even Wells thought that Stanford was "fast losing those qualities and traits of character which made him one of the best of friends"; that he had come to care only for being a social figure; and that he was washed up aesthetically as a result. Although we must remember that it was the aesthetically fastidious Wells who made this judgment about Stanford's work, it is true that the kind of forthright originality that was evident in the Newport Casino and the Farragut monument disappeared from Stanford's later work. After that, the excellence in his work became harder to pinpoint—became an emanation.

In the late seventies, Charley McKim's good friend Prescott Hall Butler, a well-connected aspirant to the bar, was getting his legal education by clerking for Judge John Lawrence Smith, on Long

Island. As an honorary member of the Smith family, Prescott invited Charley out to visit at the Smithtown House, and Charley quickly contracted that sentimental ecstasy of place which was a peculiarity of the Smiths: "the Holy Smith Empire" was his name for Smithtown. Charley's attraction to the Smith family reflected all that was pure and idealistic in him—that which longed to believe that people were essentially good and honorable and that life was wholesome. He also became a special friend of the Judge's youngest daughter, Bessie, then in her late teens. Charley was fifteen years older.

Prescott Butler married Cornelia Smith, the Judge's oldest daughter—known as Nellie—and asked Charley to design a house for them on one of the hills above the harbor in St. James, right next to Carman Hill. This brought Charley out to St. James often to oversee the work. On these visits Charley began to extol Stanford to Bessie, and perhaps on returning to New York extolled Bessie to Stanford, though that's not recorded. By now an honorary member of the Smith family himself, he saw to it that Stanford was invited out to the Smithtown House in the summer of 1880. Because of Charley's carefully laid preparations, when Bessie spied Stanford through the keyhole in her father's office—Charley was in the office too—she knew that they were being matched. So there was Stanford on the other side of the keyhole, soft and powerful, kind and rageful, hugely warm and—in the sexual compulsion that was already setting in—icy cold. He was already a very successful architect, and was also on the course that would eventually lead to his death.

Charley hovered over the courtship, and when, at last, the two became engaged he wrote to Bessie:

But how can I say it, It—that which I want to say—that I wish for you both all that is good and best and happiest—and to you that you are very welcome among us whose office is now yours.

We will pull in one boat and we will pull all together. And

when you bring him (Stan) to dine with me, very soon I hope, he shall carve and you shall pour out the tea after dinner just as if I were the guest.

Stanford and Bessie were married at the Church of the Heavenly Rest in New York, on February 7, 1884. Gus Saint-Gaudens's wedding present to them was a relief in white marble of Grandma as a bride, head and shoulders, in profile, altogether about two feet high and one foot wide. Stanford designed a handsome frame for it: the piece was a fixture of Box Hill when I was a girl. It hung just inside the front door, softly white and very striking against the brown bamboo. Marmoreal Grandma. Saint-Gaudens liked Bessie. Later he held her up as an example to his wife for the silent stoicism with which she bore Stanford's infidelities.

The bride and groom took a six-month honeymoon in Europe and the Middle East. In Constantinople Stanford bought a carpet out from under two men who were sitting on it carding wool—it's not known what became of that carpet—and a mosqueful of tiles which he sent home: they sank in a shipwreck during the Atlantic crossing. In Greece he bought some illuminated manuscripts that he then lost, and carefully measured the dimensions of an exedra seat. In the Tyrol he and Bessie ran into some Smith cousins. Bessie's letters home express amazement and delight; there is one from Rome in which she describes Stanford's approach, slamming doors and whistling—sounds she identifies as her "cowbell," telling her of his movements. She also recounts that when she admired from a hotel window a pot that a woman was carrying on her head in the street below, Stanford went right down and bought it for her. The pot was around the stables for a long time when I was little. Later on in the honeymoon, Bessie became weary of the constant social activities, and longed for a swim and a sail on the Long Island Sound.

THE BOYS

BEYOND THE GARDENS of Box Hill, the Place was a quilt, every bit of territory patterned in its own way and fitted to the next. There was a cluster of outbuildings that we called the barns: a carriage house, its shingles black to brown, with a roofline that was bowed in front giving it the look of an open brow; the inward-looking stables attached to it; a very old barn that we called the cow barn; a stone garage for Grandma's black Ford; a water tower; the chicken coops; and an enormous and progressively collapsing gray-shingled structure that had been built to house orange trees in winter and which we called the elephant barn. A three-story farmhouse standing right up like an ostrich among the barns was the home of my uncle Bobby and aunt Claire.

For most of my childhood, the stables were dead and empty, the sleighs in the carriage house gathering dust and barn swallow droppings and the saddles hardening on their racks in the tack room, except for Mama's big taffy-colored sidesaddle which stayed soft. This sidesaddle had its own freestanding wooden horse and I liked to sit on it because the leather crunched deliciously. When I was very little, though, Angelina, Say When, and Steinway blew and munched and shifted their weight in the stalls. The stables were shadowy and the air was warm with the horsy smell and the smell of hay and manure, and the water in the concrete water trough was dark. Steinway was enormous and gentle, and later Mama loved to tell how, at age two, I rode him in the Smithtown Horse Show. I don't remember the horse show, but I remember Steinway's black mane and chestnut withers from the perspective of the saddle, on a scale that reflects a toddler's relative size. I remember his shouldering gait beneath me and the look of the ground passing by beneath his big neck. I remember feeling just fine up there; it didn't occur to me to worry; after all, I was on Steinway. At some point, I must have been in the stables at night, because when I wonder about the connection between people—about what it is that we are to each other truly—I think not of language and faces but of the shifting of warm masses in the dark, creatures in each other's presence, *there:* the stables at night.

Right next to the stables was the water tower. It was octagonal and dark-shingled and rose from the barn cluster organically, three stories tall, thick and tapering to a flatly conical roof.

There was a spring on the shore of the harbor from which water was pumped up to the tower and stored, and from there carried through a system of pipes that carried it to the houses on the Place. My mother was touched by how this water manifested the blessedness of our locality, and even Mama, who was otherwise indifferent to the charms of Long Island, said years later, when the system was dead—and said it in a tone that came from depths beneath her usual personality—that in the bathtubs the water had been blue. When I was about six the pump failed altogether, and the tower was drained and the Place was switched to town water. After the switch, my mother would drive down the hill to the spring about once a week to fill bottles, usually empty gallon jugs that had originally contained Dad's purple wine. Fresh from the spring, the water frosted the glass.

The water tower made the cluster of the barns charismatic. But the key to the cluster was the oldest building on the Place: the cow barn, swaybacked, with a weathervane on its witch-peaked roof. Most of the outbuildings—the carriage house, water tower, garage, and elephant barn—had been designed by Stanford and laid out by him in a knowing, chosen way. But the cow barn, belonging to the older, improvised countryside, was set stubbornly into a hill and had accumulated there the irrational authority of ancient location. With that authority it quietly undid Stanford's balanced layout. Even though the carriage house seemed by far the most important structure there, and even though the tower had the most charisma, it was the cow barn, with its quirky placement, that gave the area its character: the organic character of the utilitarian rural landscape— Grandma's landscape of Carman Hill Farm, to which the cow barn had originally belonged.

It was in the cow barn that Papa had had a studio built for Mama, which she had turned over to her son Bobby as soon as he was grown. This studio was at the back of the cow barn, at the end of a passage that, because the structure was set into a hill, was pitch-black. When you opened the studio door, however, you stepped into a high room painted white and full of light from windows set near the top of the north wall. There was grass up there, growing against the windows, and above the grass a blue sky. (In my memory that sky is always blue.) There was wet clay in Bobby's studio, and plaster and armatures, and wet clay on armatures wrapped in plastic, with the clay messing the plastic. The statues were mostly male heads or torsos down to the penis, and the clay on the torsos was laid on in a coarse, thumb-swatch texture. There was at least one horse once, and one woman, and I also remember a time when many, many drawings of horses were pinned up all around in an impromptu way.

Bobby had chestnut-brown hair parted on one side and brushed over, just like Grandma White's, so that his brow was open. Compared with his brothers, Peter and Johnny, he was short—he was about five feet nine. Whenever it was possible he was bare-chested and barefoot. His feet were small and broad, his insteps were high and tightly arched, and his gait was springy with impacted sexuality. When he sculpted he would slowly move his perfect body around the statue as if wrapping it in a sculptural dance. Bobby loved to talk, especially at meals. He might talk about wonders of nature— something he had read about fossils, perhaps, or something to do with the sea. He would talk as if to a great audience. He had warmth, but he was also far away, in his own dreams.

Bobby and Claire's house was a plain farmhouse with high ceilings and tall windows on the south. Inside, each object was discrete and tranquil as if in a still life. There were paintings on the walls but there was also the skull of a cow, and a sword too, and they, and the furniture, and even humdrum things like a pipe or a plate, shone in those rooms like objects in a Vermeer. In Bobby's environment objects acquired a singularity that cast a spell, that spun a dream.

Everybody was in love with Bobby, and so was I, from earliest days, I am sure, but in my case an even stronger feeling was the wish to *be* Bobby. He had a bow, and so, by the time I was seven, I had a bow. He wore a hunting knife on his belt; by the time I was nine, I did too. Bobby kept his bow over the double doors to the living room in his house. It was a fibreglass hunting bow, dark green and laminated, and bent back on itself in a double curve when strung. At night when guests were there, he would take it down and string it and talk about its seventy-pound pull. In the daytime I'd see him go with the bow to the Box Hill fields and shoot one arrow straight up. Just one. I'd do the same, though I never could stop at just one.

Bobby built an arbor in the garden around his house—just like an Italian arbor, with a little statue in it. Bobby's arbor was built on four posts as if it were a room, and inside he placed a big wooden table with two benches and some chairs. At meals in his arbor, Bobby would talk. My aunt Claire was the poet, but it was Bobby who sailed the seas of spoken language, and it was always the high seas, and the wind was always fair, and the words plumed gorgeously under his prow and unrolled behind him in a sparkling wake of aristocratic English. I remember Bobby talking about proportions in his arbor: about Italy, where entire hillsides were covered with roomlike arbors that you could walk through, one after another, and they would all be nice, and then you would come to one in which the proportions were perfect. Bobby was at a loss for words to describe the effect of that mystical rightness of proportion—and when Bobby was at a loss for words it was dramatic. He would express the experience by showing awe in his face, and you would see him standing in that perfect arbor in Italy looking up and around, experiencing the awesome effect of the proportions as if it were a vision of God.

My mother's brother Johnny was also around. He was in his twenties then, as were Bobby and my father, I realize now: so very young. They were boys, really, but to me they were men. Well over six feet, with a lock of black hair that fell across his forehead, Johnny was handsome without vanity, virile without salaciousness, and a vitality that seemed like rage surged in him always. He was always deeply tanned and always wore a green work shirt with the sleeves rolled up. I remember him on the lawn outside the stable by the water tower leaning back on one foot, drawing on his cigarette from the bottom of his lungs, his face tilted to the sky—a characteristic posture. His voice was resonant, his English clear, rich—Shakespearean, almost—and rounded with an inflected energy in it exactly like Papa's.

Johnny had a kind of tragic yet heroic stature in the family, based on his good looks, his madness, and his horsemanship, which had a wild streak. When I was very small, and there were still horses in the stable, he would thunder around the countryside in the wee hours of the morning on Say When, with Steinway and Angelina running loose alongside, and startle the neighbors in their beds.

He'd hitch up a horse to a trap and then gallop full speed down steep hills. He would ride onto the railroad tracks and then hold Say When there as a locomotive approached, allowing him to bolt only at the last moment. Bobby and my mother saw Johnny as romantic, but Johnny himself was absolutely unromantic in his outlook on himself or on the world.

My mother, Mary, had seven brothers and sisters, but she and Bobby and Johnny formed a subgroup in the middle of the family, bonded by experiences they had shared when they were growing up. One of those experiences was a sojourn in a school in Bavaria when my mother was between ages nine and eleven. During the Depression my grandfather's architectural business dwindled to nearly nothing and my grandmother's solution to the shortage of cash was not to cut back but to move with the children to the Schloss Neubeuern, an eighteenth-century Bavarian castle set on an abrupt outcropping of rock in a long valley of orchards and flowering pastures that wended its way into the Alps. This was in 1932. Papa stayed behind, minding the mostly moribund office, translating "The Divine Comedy," and going through the McKim, Mead & White files, drawing out and destroying masses of material having to do with the private life of his father.

The Schloss was the ancestral seat of the Baroness Wendelstadt, whose sister-in-law, the Countess Degenfeld, had been her partner in running a school for highborn boys ever since their fortunes were ruined in the aftermath of the First World War. Mama had heard about the school from her sister Hester, who had had an introduction to the Baroness and had visited her the summer before. The setup there was convenient for Mama, because the school-age children could be in the boarding school and the little ones with a nanny, while she herself could be a paying guest of the Baroness— yet a friend, sharing her social life.

The school had two divisions, one for older boys, which occupied one half of the Schloss itself, and one for younger children, situated in the next village, Altenbeuern, in a charming house called Hinterhör, which had previously served as a summer house for the residents of the Schloss. This is where my mother and Johnny, who was eight, were put; Bobby, at age eleven, was with the older boys in the Schloss. Aside from two girls at Hinterhör, who were day students, my mother was the only girl in the entire school.

The Countess lived at Hinterhör, and was theoretically in charge of the children who lived and went to school there, but my mother's perception of her was that she didn't give a damn. Compared with the regal Baroness, the Countess was not an aristocrat born but, rather, was more like a sexy adventuress—"the type who says 'Oh, lovely, lovely, haw, haw, haw,' " as my mother described her to me. "She was charming and courtly, good-looking, with tremendous vitality, but cold and untrustworthy, too. She paid no attention to the school—none, zero." As it happens, the Countess was the model for the character of the Marschallin in "Der Rosenkavalier" ("Marschallin" means "wife of a general"). The character falls in love with a younger man and is in despair when he leaves her, but then she gets over it easily enough.

The actual running of the lower school was in the hands of Fräulein Buss, a woman of Prussian extraction who was about six feet tall, had eyes like a Tartar's, muscles like a man's, and straight black hair that fell to her waist when loosed but was usually coiled around her head in an enormous braid. Fräulein Buss was in charge of the children night and day—in charge of teaching them all subjects and in charge of supervising their meals, the orderliness of their rooms, and their recreation. Whenever a student made a mistake, Fräulein Buss would hit him or her on the head, hard, with a stick. My mother found her studies very difficult. She was, for instance, trying to learn Latin from the perspective of German, a language she didn't yet understand. She was therefore hit often. This was shocking to her as well as painful. She had experienced some abusive and erratic caretakers, but, she told me, "we had never been hit in our home."

From the start, my mother was scared all the time at Hinterhör.

Every morning before class she would throw up, and on her way to throw up she would run past the door of the suite where her three little sisters, Cynthia, Sarah, and Ann, were being cared for by their English nanny: in a scene of Victorian orderliness. Sometimes on holidays, the Hinterhör children ate at the Schloss, and on the way to the dining room they filed past the door to Mama's suite. My mother would dart in and just sit there near her mother for a moment. Usually, Mama was scrutinizing newspapers from Paris and London, trying to figure out what the political situation in Germany was, and my mother did not feel particularly welcome. At other times, when she had Mama's attention, she told Mama that they were being hit, but Mama didn't respond—and this, in a way, my mother says now, was the scariest thing.

Johnny, being a year younger than my mother, was having even more trouble with his lessons than she, and so was hit even more. He was hit all the time. All the children suffered under Fräulein Buss, but none so much as Johnny.

Photographs of Johnny at the time of the sojourn in Germany show a sensitive-looking and very beautiful little boy. When Mama came for charming lunches with the Countess at Hinterhör, Fräulein Buss would put her arm around her and flatter her and tell her how beautiful her children were.

Everywhere one looked from the Schloss or Hinterhör, there were spectacular views of the Alps, rising singly and abruptly from the valley floor. The mountains had names—my mother speaks of them almost as if they had personalities, almost as if they had a capacity to love as well as to be loved: to the west was the Wendelstein, to the south the Toten Kirche, or Church of Death, so named because so many climbers had died there, and, to the east, most tenderly invoked by my mother, the Heuberg, or Hay Mountain. In the spring and autumn, the children would take bicycle trips in the valleys and hike in the mountains and in the winter they would be taken on ski trips. These expeditions usually lasted several days: they would stay in peasants' houses, or in huts in the mountains. In winter, they would tie skins on their skis, so as not to slide backward, and would climb all day until they reached the top of their mountain, usually in late afternoon. A sublime image of our Red Cottage life was my mother's descriptions of skiing down through virgin snow at sundown, around hemlocks—starting in sunlight and descending into night.

One day, Fräulein Buss was showing around the wife of a general—a Marschallin—who had a son in the school. As they entered the dormitory where the children, including my mother and Johnny, stood waiting, Fräulein Buss was flattering and fawning over the Marschallin. Eager to show off how tidy the children were, Fräulein Buss pulled back a curtain in front of some shelves where the children's belongings were kept. The belongings were in order except for some of Johnny's handkerchiefs, which were not lined up evenly in their pile. Fräulein Buss turned and hit Johnny on the head as hard as she could.

It seemed to my mother that the Fräulein's motivation was not so much to punish Johnny as to show off to the general's wife how strict she was. Watching—but, of course, unable to do anything— she thought in that clinically lucid way that children can think, That blow destroyed Johnny. At the time, my mother tried to tell Mama about that incident in particular, but Mama was unresponsive. Throughout her adult life, my mother occasionally tried to tell Mama what had happened to them at Hinterhör, but especially to Johnny, and each time Mama would just let her run her course as if she were complaining, as if she were a pest. It's true that my mother was difficult to listen to when she talked about Germany. She became pent up and seemed to be trying urgently to communicate something that would not come out—as if what she was saying weren't strong enough.

Echt was a word that entered the family vocabulary during the sojourn in Germany: it means authentic, or real, as opposed to ersatz, and my mother applied it particularly to a peasant way of life in which, as in the Alps, she found connection and comfort. Hinterhör itself was echt, in that it had originally been a rich peasant's house and there was still a big pig-farming operation there, and a plum orchard, from which quantities of plum jam were made in a waist-high cylindrical stone vat cut out of a single boulder. There were also pear trees, and from the pears a mildly alcoholic pear wine, called *Most*, was made in a big stone trough. My mother loved the plum jam—"We lived on plum jam," she said—and the *Most*: she even came to like the cold pickled herring that was served with a boiled potato on Fridays. She liked Regina and Emma, young local women who worked in the kitchen at Hinterhör and waited on table; they were kind to her. She liked the clothes that the Bavarians wore—the dirndls and lederhosen, the knickers and loden capes. She liked the sculptures of butter that peasants would bring to weddings and other events at the Schloss—"The Baroness was something high and mighty: peasants came all the way from Switzerland to honor her," she said—although the children were left to run unsupervised at these events and after nightfall the peasant men would drink beer and become raucous and frightening.

She liked the peasant houses where the children sometimes slept on trips—houses warmed in winter by cattle kept on the ground floor. She liked the bone closet in the graveyard in Altenbeuern, where old bones were put helter-skelter on shelves to make room for new bodies. She liked the way the men smoked and talked on the balcony in the church during Mass. She liked a narrow passage between the church and a big barn—she liked the smell of manure there and thinks that she may have gotten high on it—even though sometimes there was slaughtering going on in the barn when she passed by.

In 1933, the second year of the family's stay, my mother walked through the manure-smelling passage every morning, because she had graduated to classes in the Schloss, though she continued to live at Hinterhör. Every day, she walked the mile from Altenbeuern, leaving Johnny behind at Hinterhör with Fräulein Buss. Life at the Schloss was somewhat more tolerable, in that, although there were beatings, the rules were clear, and beatings took place only when rules were broken. But that year a different kind of danger arose. The Nazis came to power, and peasants all around turned out to have been in the Nazi underground. Abruptly, they appeared in brown uniforms, each with a red armband imprinted with the *Hakenkreuz,* or hooked cross—the swastika—black, in a white circle inset in the red. Overnight, the peasants stopped saying *"Grüss' Gott"*—"Great God"—when they met you, and instead, without exception, said *"Heil Hitler."* You might be walking down a track beside a field, my mother said, and along would come a peasant on a bike, and everything about it would be normal except that he would be wearing a brown shirt and a red *Hakenkreuz* armband and would say *"Heil Hitler"* as he passed.

Textbooks were suddenly changed. History that had already seemed odd to my mother because of its German perspective was now distorted beyond recognition. It turned out that a number of the students had been in the Hitler Youth, and they too were not only suddenly wearing uniforms with the *Hakenkreuz* but giving orders to their teachers. Favorable mention of the French was impermissible, for example, and the ban was enforced by students in brown uniforms. One of them—"a princely boy," according to my mother—appeared to be a kind of officer. He wore an officer's cap with his uniform and always stood with the headmaster and the Baroness at school reviews. He also appeared to have the power to give orders to both of them. A teacher was found to have a cache of guns under his bed—he was probably in the anti-Nazi underground—and it appeared to be the princely boy who gave the order that he be fired.

The fact is that the Baroness and her entourage, while appearing to conform, opposed the Nazis; indeed, the private half of the Schloss was a scene of intrigue, with royals passing through incognito on missions of good in a "Der Rosenkavalier"ish way. Once, the butler/head valet guessed the identity of a Russian count by the crown on his underwear and silently acknowledged him by decorating the table with autumn leaves of the count's colors. There was an air of excitement. High-level gossip swirled. Mama, my mother has said, was having the time of her life. For the children in the school, though, life was simply difficult in additional ways. Gym became a martial drill. You had to stand very straight, and at first my mother stood so straight that she stuck her stomach out, and then she was punched hard in the stomach by the instructor. She learned to throw hand grenades. Instead of games like hare and hounds, the children now played war games. Bobby developed heart trouble from being made to run up mountainsides with a heavy pack on his back.

That same year the mountains became infested with machine-gun nests, and the sound of machine-gun practice ricocheted around the Schloss. Military gliders coasted off the mountainsides. The gliders were a way of evading a provision of the Treaty of Versailles that forbade Germany to train military pilots in airplanes. "We were in the middle of an enormous war machine," my mother told me. There was a bad incident concerning Jews in Munich, which she heard about. Papa came over for Christmas that year, and on the way to Kitzbühel, in Austria, for New Year's, the family passed through the town of Kufstein, near the Austrian border, where they saw a pool of blood in the square that somehow had to do with Jews. My mother also heard stories of people getting smuggled out of Germany in coffins. "A child can sense political terror like a smell and it was rising around us," my mother told me. "It was an atmosphere of terror in which we had to turn to our abusers—who were themselves vulnerable and endangered—for protection."

When I was growing up, terror might be provoked in my mother at any time—by a strange dog on a familiar path, by an unexpected noise. World-flooding terror. She never seemed to protest being in a condition of terror: indeed she almost seemed to expect it, as if terror were a part of her; as if it lay in her like an aquifer. As an adult, I came to understand the extent to which that aquifer paralyzed her; came to see that Hinterhör held her hostage and her failure to protect me arose from that. As a child, however, I understood only that things had happened in Germany that were very bad. Yet most of my mother's references to Germany in the Red Cottage were made in a tender tone—were to the butter sculpture, or to skiing into the valley in the evening. My mother sang German in a particularly language-loving way, turning its masculine fierceness into sounds that conveyed a depth of heart, as if the language were a membrane against which unspeakable love and sorrow pressed. There were some old wooden ski poles with leather webbing in the Red Cottage when I was growing up, and a pair of lederhosen that I wore for a while, and several rough brown loden capes. All these objects were luminous with a benevolent significance. The combination of the terror and the tender sense of benevolence was confusing, though a kind of confusion that was familiar to me, and that I accepted. Only as an adult would I come to understand that the depth, the luminousness, and the benevolence reflected the desperation of a child inventing warmth and safety out of things.

At Christmas in the Red Cottage we would have real candles on our Christmas tree (as they did in Bavaria). Our Christmas tree was usually in the dining room, and the tiny flames would cut into the atmosphere of the room in an unearthly way as rays from a midafternoon winter sunset shot through the oaks to the west like spears that landed in the room. Then the atmosphere would become dusky and waterlike, the kind of half-light in which electric bulbs have no power (but tiny flames stand out). Dad would stand by with a bucket of water as we'd sing—our mother's voice in the lead—''Lo! how a Rose e'er blooming'' in the gloaming in our tinderbox house.

Johnny was part of the threesome with my mother and Bobby, but Johnny was not a part of the life of art and talk because he was not an artist. He was not an intellectual. He was not an enthusiast either. He was just Johnny. In the war, he had served in the Navy in the Pacific on at least two ships that had gone down, though he could not recall those experiences. Another anecdote about him that had somehow gotten back to the family was that he had stayed at his post as a gunner on the bow of a ship under direct air attack by the

Japanese when everyone else had run for cover—he stayed because he had not been ordered to leave. Even on the Place this was not regarded as romantic or heroic. After the war he was accepted by a college in Annapolis that specialized in the classics, one of the toughest colleges in the country. A few months after matriculating, he called from what turned out to be the railroad station in Philadelphia and said that he didn't know where he was. After that he gave up trying to get into life. One day on Grandma White's lawn there was an incident in which Johnny got into a high-spirited argument with a man who was doing some kind of work for Grandma. Johnny was carrying a shotgun, and when my mother came along and tried to intervene in the argument he put the shotgun to her temple, and they walked to the Red Cottage that way. Later, when my mother said, "Johnny threatened me with a gun," nobody paid any attention, as if the words were somehow weak, unable to cut the air. Even decades later, if my mother, trying to get at the truth of Johnny, said, "Once he threatened me with a gun," the words still didn't cut the air.

Johnny's room on the top floor of Box Hill was manly and sane, with a sleigh bed, a Navajo rug, a jackknife on his bureau, and his gun leaning in the corner. Johnny looked good with a gun—a shotgun was in just the right proportion to his body, and the brown stock and the black metal barrel would rest naturally in his excellent brown arm. No one thought to take the gun away from him after the incident with my mother.

It was like that with Johnny: the frightening aspect of him didn't register as alarming. Sometimes at Box Hill, when I was four and five, he would swing me around by the arms far too hard and fast, and after it was over it would be as if the experience hadn't happened. The world would return to itself unaltered except for a little fissure, a little crack from top to bottom in my actual vision. In that crack, the texture of the world swarmed, the way it does in a heat mirage on the road in summer: sometimes a day would pass before the swarming fissure went away.

* * *

My father and Johnny went riding together often, and Dad developed some fairly wild habits on horseback this way. Dad was a "natural," my mother always said, meaning that he could take up tennis or riding with no previous experience and would almost immediately be right up there with the best of them. One day Johnny and Daddy took Aldo Bruzzichelli, a Florentine man in his forties who lived nearby, out riding. Aldo had had no previous experience on horseback, and I guess he wasn't a natural. There was a straightaway by the railroad tracks where the horses were used to galloping, and then a sudden right-angled turn which the horses also knew and took without breaking stride. Aldo was unprepared for the turn, however, and he flew off and broke his back. Though Aldo fully recovered, my father was so deeply remorseful that he never rode again. Mama, in contrast, conveyed the opinion that anyone who couldn't stay on a horse on Long Island probably deserved what they got.

My father realized that he couldn't have a regular friendship with Johnny after a day in the Red Cottage garden when I was three and Johnny held me with the small of my back resting on the top of his head and said he was going to bend me from both ends till my back broke. My father says he locked eyes with Johnny and held him there, talking to him, until Johnny threw me into the bushes and ran away. I do not remember this, but it's consistent with my sense of him then. And even so, I did not register that Johnny was crazy. The attitude I learned was that if he rode crazily that showed what a good horseman he was, so comfortable on horseback that he once fell asleep at a gallop.

One day when I was still very little, Mama said casually at Sunday lunch that maybe it was too costly to continue to keep horses, and after lunch Johnny went out and shot Say When in the head right there in the stable. Shortly afterward, there was a fire in Smithtown, and Johnny followed the sirens on his bicycle, carrying a machete, and when he got to the burning house he climbed up to the second story and tried to save the clothes in the bureau drawers. The police came and arrested him, though it's not remembered for what crime, and he was released only on condition that he be institutionalized for insanity. Johnny then went to a series of places, including the Hartford Institute where he was treated by the eminent psychologist Abraham Maslow, but there was no improvement. This treatment was very expensive and eventually Mama and Papa felt that they could not continue to pay for it, so he ended up in a Veterans Administration hospital. There he was given seventy-five sugar treatments which caused his weight to go up to two hundred and fifty pounds, and a hundred and fifty electroshock treatments. He came out, and went back in, and then the word "lobotomy" became a part of the family vocabulary, and in particular "frontal lobotomy": "full frontal lobotomy." He was back on the Place, and then up in Vermont or back in the hospital after that, though he would come for long visits: to me he was the same old Johnny. One of the things that I learned about a full frontal lobotomy was that it was supposed to turn you into a vegetable, and it showed what fine stuff Johnny was made of that he could come through a full frontal lobotomy and not be a vegetable at all.

FAME

FAME KEPT STANFORD latent in the family right into my
time, simultaneously separating him from us and holding us hostage.
Like a kind of golden weather that had flipped into a black storm,
Stanford's fame had turned and headed at the family at the moment
of his death, while at that very moment he himself slipped over the
horizon to a place where he was beyond accounting. In this transi-
tion Stanford became, from the family point of view, merged with
his fame and also effaced by it. The fame made him nonhuman and
dangerous. After Stanford was murdered the family retreated into a
sanctuary of silence and privacy, but it was a sanctuary encircled by
a storm with golden edges. The Place became the calm eye of the
storm, and so it remained. Some of us born into that sanctuary

could not easily find our way into the open, moving river of continuous time outside the family, into the world.

Even my father had a sense of being held hostage by the Place; he was in a struggle with its vortical pull. The most explicit way that he would express this would be by railing about Stanford (using his name openly where others didn't), dismissing Stanford's work as imitative, and identifying what he did not like in the family, which was a self-absorption and a sense of specialness that both excluded him and drew him, as the "Stanford White thing." He used to tell about how when he got back from the war he'd wanted to take my mother and me to live in New York—the picture was always of an apartment on Mulberry Street, in Little Italy, because we could live there cheaply—but this prospect seemed unsafe to my mother; she wanted to move into the Red Cottage. The story was that one day in this period of indecision my father was on the second-floor landing in Box Hill looking out at the fountain, the sarcophagi, and the Tapis Vert below and he thought, I'll flip a coin. And then he thought, No, I should be a good boy and do the right thing—which, in his mind, was to go along with my mother's wishes. And so at the end of his odyssey from California to Paris—a journey toward his own fame, it must have seemed—he found himself instead, year after year, walking along a path that ran just inside the line of shipmast-locust trees along the road, on the way to his studio in the cow barn.

In the early fifties, my sister Beatrice and I were taken by our parents to a concert at the Circle in the Square in New York. Half the program was my father's music and half was the music of Morton Feldman, a composer who was experimenting with the element of chance in music. The concert was attended by a lively audience of Expressionist painters of the Tenth Street school and their entourage—an electric, palpably intelligent audience. Dad's part of the program consisted of three settings of poems by Robert Herrick, sung with exquisite sensitivity by my mother, and a cello sonata. Feldman's music was written in squares that indicated units of silence or loosely defined sound—there was a range within which the performer could choose notes, but there were not many notes. I was only ten. I didn't know what was going on: the music was interesting, though baffling; it was exciting to be there—but it became clear in the discussion period after the concert that something had gone wrong. My father, in rage and scorn, would barely answer questions put to him by the moderator. In adulthood I learned that the audience was there to celebrate Feldman's experimentalism and had no interest in my father's neoclassical music. Perhaps rightly, my father felt that he had been set up as a reactionary foil. He had been blindsided by a development of which he had been unaware—that respect in the cultural world for the kind of highly evolved music he wrote had been replaced by a frantic desire for what seemed to him mere novelty.

We drove home from the city that night, my mother and father in the front seat in turbulent silence, both of them bewildered and violated, my mother's own terrible disappointment—for she had worked hard—effaced by my father's continuing rage. We little girls sat in the back in our dresses, riding home through the night to the empyrean world of St. James.

Not that I imagine that my father, had we moved to Mulberry Street as he'd wanted, would have written music based on chance, nor do I mean to suggest in any way that he ought to have. My father's obliviousness of fashion was magnificent to me then, as now. His passionate relationship with music put him beyond the reach of the blandishments of the world: for him, not money, or fame, or glamour, or even prestige among peers, could begin to compete with the rewards of composing purely. Nothing on earth could match that which he sought when he jumped up in the middle of the night and rushed out to his studio to compose. Four years before the Feldman concert, he was to conduct a piece of his own at another concert in New York, and rather than buy a baton he cut a lilac switch and painted it with black enamel. Why should he spend money on a baton? His purity could border on arrogance. A year after the lilac-switch concert Leonard Bernstein conducted a piece by my father, also in New York, and swayed and wiggled during the performance in a way that my father regarded as lewd and drawing attention away from his piece. When the concert was over he did not go backstage to thank Bernstein—that he was a young unknown composer notwithstanding. He simply walked out. This unworldliness made my father a "natural" for the Place where fame seemed to be a matter of entitlement, something that it would be degrading to work for precisely because it was a kind of birthright. My father might have derided the "Stanford White thing," might even have felt excluded, but he brought to the Place attitudes that fit right in.

It seemed a given of my childhood world that my father and Bobby would naturally be famous some day, a feeling that arose in part from the golden glow of Stanford's latent fame. It was as if—because of Stanford—we on the Place were natives of fame. The feeling of entitlement had a centripetal effect, however. Paradoxically Stanford's fame—or worldliness—reinforced the unworldliness of the Place, deepening our separation from ongoing time.

Furthermore, Stanford's fame was preserved intact on the Place independent of his changing stature in the world. Unspoken of, Stanford's fame remained fresh and vast, despite the fact that with the exception of the moment of "The Girl in the Red Velvet Swing" his celebrity had long since faded. (The novel *Ragtime* by E. L. Doctorow, in which Stanford was a character, and the movie based on the novel, came out much later.) As for his standing as an architect, the whole neoclassical period was from the thirties until the seventies in a kind of hole of anti-fame. Indeed, by the fifties the modern aesthetic was so dominant that Beaux-Arts buildings were seen as worthless imitations—just garbage, best swept away. As a result, for much of my life the inexplicable pain and silence conjured up by Stanford's fame was all the more isolating because—in actual fact—Stanford was hardly famous at all.

Today, the Beaux-Arts style is valued again, especially its extraordinary contribution to our cityscapes. Consequently, Stanford once more has real standing in the world. But in the family Stanford's fame was consistently felt as huge.

*   *   *

The hugeness of Stanford's unspoken-of fame on the Place reflected unresolved family pain, but it also reflected in preserved form the actual scale of his fame in the time that he lived. In an article that appeared in *Vanity Fair* six years after Stanford's death John Jay Chapman wrote:

> He was a personality of enormous power, a man of phenomenal force. He affected everyone he met. I always think of him as the embodiment of a particular period in American life—a period of effervescence, and of the sudden combining of elements that had long lain in solution and came together with a certain emotional violence.
>
> He had the vitality of a giant. He had the same divine frenzy for making himself known that great politicians are born with. He was pervasive. Not a day passed without one's hearing something new about him. . . .
>
> He swam on a wave of prestige that lifted him into view like a Triton that typified the epoch.

Stanford rode a surging national sense of imperial greatness, a mood of power and dominance in the world. His career was merged with a fantasy of the United States triumphant. Indeed, architects, because they could give expression to the dream of imperial grandeur through public monuments and buildings, had a kind of heroic stature in the public eye in those days that is hard to imagine today. It was widely believed that the identity of the nation could be formed by architecture, and consequently there was passionate controversy over which style was best suited to its emergent power. The neoclassical style—championed by McKim, Mead & White—prevailed, as the architectural character of the official areas of Washington, D.C., attests. The neoclassical style was the worldly style—as opposed to the Gothic style, its principal competitor, which was of the spirit. Nineteenth-century neoclassicism is a style that cele-

brates exclusive and total power, a style that not only erects buildings but controls the environment around them too. Because every
inch works to reinforce the authority of the whole there is no
acknowledgment implicit in the neoclassical style of realities beyond
those that it celebrates. The authoritative rationality of the style
excludes mystery, puzzlement, wildness, weakness, suffering, and
love. With its unself-questioning assertiveness, the neoclassical style
aggrandizes society, political power, and the works of man. It became the style that would reflect the nation back to its citizens,
teaching them how to think and feel about their country.

The influence of McKim, Mead & White in this period was wide
and deep. The firm had an impact not only through the buildings it
actually designed but as the premier training ground of future architects. A stint as a draftsman there was a highly coveted position for
aspiring architects, and those top men who got the job subsequently
fanned out across the country, founding firms that did work patterned on the architecture of McKim, Mead & White. (In the peak
years, from 1890 to approximately 1909, the firm employed as
many as a hundred and eighty draftsmen at a time.) The alternative
for a talented would-be architect who did not get his training at
McKim, Mead & White was the School of Architecture at Columbia
University, where Charles McKim, who had designed the university
campus, had also taken the study of architecture beyond engineering
into the realm of aesthetics. He did this by including the history of
architecture in the curriculum, emphasizing the classical masterpieces that also inspired the work of the firm.

McKim, Mead & White was not associated with the neoclassical
style from the beginning, however. Indeed the firm fell into it rather
casually. In 1881—still early days in Stanford's career—the firm
was approached by Henry Villard, a railroad magnate, who wanted
an edifice designed for him that would contain six domiciles for
himself and his children, with their families, on a lot at Madison
Avenue and Fifty-first Street. Stanford drew up plans for a French
château, but then he had to go out of town and handed the project
over to Joseph Wells, who took it only on condition that he have a

free hand. While Stanford was gone, Wells scrapped the château and replaced it with plans for a cinquecento palazzo. When Stanford returned, he fell in with Wells's plan without protest and the result was one of New York's great landmarks, the Villard Houses, in my time owned for many decades by Random House, and by the Archdiocese of New York. (Today it is a part of the Helmsley Palace Hotel.) The exterior remained Wells's, but Stanford took on the interior, taking up this new style with a natural fluency: the Villard interiors are perhaps the greatest of his interiors extant today, and they represent his first crack at the Renaissance mode.

As the years passed, Stanford became fanatical about the neoclassical style as the only appropriate one for public buildings, maintaining, for example, that all the Gothic buildings at West Point— West Point is almost entirely Gothic—ought to be torn down and replaced by classical structures. When his advice was not followed, he called it "a public calamity, a body blow to all those who are striving to raise architecture out of the heterogeneous mush." The issue of Gothic versus classic also arose in connection with the neoclassical design of Stanford's Madison Square Presbyterian Church. The design was attacked by critics as pagan and secular; there was a prevailing opinion that Gothic was the most suitable style for a religious building. Stanford retaliated by saying that Gothic reflected a Catholic and medieval mentality: that classicism was closer to the spirit of the early Christians and was therefore the appropriate style for a Protestant nation.

This ideological ardor was uncharacteristic of Stanford, who was not otherwise inclined toward intellectual constructs. Books, for him, were wallcovering. In general, his approach to architectural style was purely aesthetic and playfully eclectic: he could be as lighthearted in his choice of a style, and even in the mixing of styles, as he might be about choosing a costume for a ball. Yet concerning this matter of the appropriate public style he came to fight with quasi-moralistic fervor for the style of secular power against the style that was spiritual, individualistic, irregular, and full of darkness and mystery. It was not only the Gothic that drew his opprobrium, however. In his later years, he even turned on his mentor Richardson, asserting that Richardson, who had continued until his death to work in a style heavily influenced by the Romanesque tradition, had left America the worst architectural legacy possible. What is striking about Stanford's zeal in this matter is that while, in general, his charmingly harmonious aesthetic belies an emotional state that was voracious and out of control, in espousing a style of imperial connotations, the style of voracious appetite for power, his art and the inner forces of compulsion that drove him were, for once, congruent.

Stanford subscribed wholly to the idea that the new robber barons—the Whitneys, Goulds, and Villards who were McKim, Mead & White's clients—were the American descendants of the great Renaissance merchant princes, a new upper class that would be the backbone of the imperial nation. Architects, in his view, fulfilled an additional patriotic mission by building appropriate housing for members of the new class, so that they could better fill their princely roles. The sense of heroic architectural mission was unaffected by such facts as that Villard went bankrupt in the spring of 1884, three months after moving into his mansion, or that, conversely, Ogden Mills (heir to a mining fortune) occupied the sixty-five-room mansion that Stanford had expanded and redesigned for him at Staatsburg, New York—it was completed in 1897—for only a few weeks a year in the autumn. (His sister, Elisabeth Reid, had bought the Villard Houses in 1886 and hired Stanford for further work on the interior.) It's hard for us to see a moral mission in such improvident extravagance, but Stanford, though he was touchy about matters of status, or perhaps because he was touchy about them, was not a clear thinker where issues of class—and particularly excess—were concerned. In 1896, he went to Madison Square Garden to hear William Jennings Bryan, the leader of a pro-labor movement, pitted against Eastern conservative mercantilism. Stanford was swept away and became Bryan's champion until he realized that Bryan was attacking the clientele of McKim, Mead & White. Abruptly he took a position against Bryan as a demagogue.

In addition to properly housing our new Medicis, the architects of the time, and perhaps Stanford more than any other, took on the task of teaching them good taste. This mission included helping them buy suitable furnishings and adornments for their palaces; indeed, Stanford relied for a good portion of his income on dealings in art to fill the houses that he designed. The statue attributed to Michelangelo recently discovered in the French Embassy in New York, formerly the Whitney mansion—designed and decorated by Stanford—exemplifies the service he provided his clients in this respect. He had an eye. But with this went a shamelessness about looting Europe of its treasures. He stripped palazzi not only of objects but of their ceilings, their mosaics, their very doorjambs and window frames, paying their impoverished owners the lowest price that he could. Once, when he saw a fountain in an Italian village square which he wanted for a client, he simply went to the police and made a deal for them to look the other way while he had the fountain wrenched out and carried off. He was of the opinion that it was the prerogative of an ascendant nation to appropriate the treasures of civilization.

Stanford's declarations to the customs officials of the ascendant nation were not always accurate, his rationale being that the value of an antique is a relative matter. He himself was partially responsible for this relativity: the volume of his European purchases was said to have raised the price of antiques all over the Continent. (He sent shiploads back.) He was not always honest with his clients either, not above designing a room so that a tapestry he had already bought would fit on a wall exactly. He designed his friend Henry Poor's dining room to receive a baroque ceiling that he had bought at a low price and stored in a warehouse, then pretended to have miraculously found "just the right thing" in Italy, though at a high price, of course. This sideline was supporting his own accelerating spending habits, including the acquisition of art for himself. Stanford stuffed his large house on Gramercy Park with paintings, tapestries, statuary—including a cast of the MacMonnies "Bacchante," and *two* copies of Diana—a sculptured gilded coffin and nine harps ("a flight of harps,'' as they came to be called), two imported baroque ceilings, two Renaissance mantels, twisted columns, nudes, Madonnas, a fountain with trout in it, palm trees and orange trees, and much red Genoese velvet. The Gramercy Park house was crammed, and slightly mad in a way that the interiors that Stanford produced for clients, and even the interior of Box Hill, were not. To a modern eye, the home that Papa grew up in looked a little like an out-of-control emporium.

Stanford was a voracious acquirer, but he was also extraordinarily generous. He would give money away, especially to artists in need, even when he himself was in financial trouble. He also often waived his fee for work on public buildings or worthy institutions: he designed parts of Grand Army Plaza and the entrance to Prospect Park in Brooklyn for nothing, for example, and he charged neither the University of Virginia nor New York University for his considerable contributions to their campuses. Not only did he work gratis for the Columbian Quadricentennial Celebration in New York City but he also stayed up five days and nights running just before it started in order to make sure that absolutely everything would come out right. As a result, he ended up in ''howling pain'' with a bleeding ulcer that kept him in bed for five weeks, much of that time on morphine.

Stanford in his middle years, from 1890 on, often became obsessively involved in public extravaganzas, and also frequently fell ill, from grippe, infections, and other ailments, although he was still a young man. He worked compulsively and fell into the habit of turning up at the office in the wee hours and designing all night: he had a capacity for going without sleep which raises the possibility that he was using drugs. Whether he was or not, he indulged in alcohol heavily and regularly. His course was self-consuming, cometlike.

When Stanford's golden fame turned into infamy, it became amalgamated, in a way, with the destructiveness in the underside of his life. As infamy, the fame became a force that blindly savaged the family, just as Stanford's compulsions had savaged him and others as his life went on. That dangerous fame was implicit in the Place, and yet the style of the Place was joyous, harmonious, and charming. Had the style been the kind of neoclassicism that forthrightly glorified power and domination, it would have been more congruent with the blind brutality of the fame. Instead, the joyous charm of Box Hill overlaid its violent subtext, and so created perversity, much as it did in Stanford himself. This contradictory overlay made the Place a confusing environment to grow up in. Further adding to the confusion, because there was not much money left in the family the familial sense of stature was drawn from a heritage of taste. It was sensibility that put us a cut above the rest of the world: we were artists in a mode that somehow also made us socially superior. In this way the domineering aspect of class superiority was avoided. Yet the physical embodiments of that sensibility—the long drive, the Tapis Vert, the box garden, the house itself—though joyous and light nevertheless conveyed something more than sensibility. They conveyed dynasty, wealth, and power.

What was finally most confusing to me as a young girl was that, while this message told me I belonged to a dominant family and in so belonging was, surely, supremely safe, I was in fact unprotected there, for unaccountable, destructive forces continued to exist unacknowledged within the family sanctuary. And while the covert, unaccountable power all around was dangerous to me, especially as a little girl, it was really dangerous to all members of the family since it was, as a force, almost by definition blind. Johnny certainly, while terrifying, was as much a victim as a perpetrator of this unwitting violence, for his mother's failure to protect him in Germany was a passive form of violence. Indeed, from this perspective violence was an independent force that savaged the family, making of an individual a victim or perpetrator according to its whim. Our sense of Stanford's terrifying fame, however silent, was the only manifestation of this condition in our lives, the only form in which the blind force that roved in our family life was acknowledged at all.

*   *   *

A part of the heroic scenario of the new merchant class in the Gilded Age was a great deal of extremely silly social life; innumerable costume extravaganzas and improbable theme parties, such as one held inside at Sherry's on horseback. It was a world in which crushing volumes of wealth were normal. Although even with Bessie's money behind him Stanford was only modestly endowed in this arena, he was its impresario. He was a maniac for parties, always available to advise, to decorate, to manage the festivities, as a part of his calling to teach the new rich how to be rich in style. John Jay Chapman wrote:

> If you were walking down Fifth Avenue and caught sight of a turkey red curtain at the upper window of a new Renaissance apartment you knew who it was that had hung his flag there. If you went to a Charity Ball, and saw on the stage a set of gilt twisted wooden columns eighteen feet high and festooned with laurel, you looked about till you found Stanford on top of a ladder draping a tapestry.

There is gaiety in this picture, but there was heaviness and pretension in these festivities as well. A photograph of the period shows Stanford and Bessie as portly and aging (though he was in his midthirties and she was in her late twenties), decked out in the attire of a knight and a Byzantine princess to a point of near-immobility, literally: Stanford was in chain mail. (Mrs. Stuyvesant Fish, for whom Stanford built a New York house modelled on the Doges' Palace in Venice, instructed Stanford to design a ballroom in which a person who was not well bred would feel uncomfortable.) And yet mixed in with this kind of stuffiness was behavior that was so bad that one feels embarrassment merely to repeat it. James Bennett, for whose New York *Herald* Stanford designed a superb building, also in a Venetian style, generated many tales of bad manners. One is that he urinated in the fireplace at his engagement party. His most memorable moment, however, was in a Greek monastery where, on being shown a lighted lamp and told that it had not been extinguished for a thousand years, he snuffed it out and said, "Well, now it has."

In another photograph, Stanford sits with others—all in immobilizing costumes—behind one of two long tables, one above the other on a tiered dais in front of which is a lion skin with a roaring head. The roaring lion's head, being a lot closer to the camera than to the table, is disproportionately large: it looks like the vanguard of a voracious double wave, the two tiers of costumed worthies cresting behind. How confident that wave was of its passage into a great future, when in fact it was rolling right into oblivion.

Stanford, both in his personality and in the causes he served, became merged with the onsweeping imperial mood of the Gilded Age, and yet the most salient characteristic of much of his work is seductiveness. Stanford was always seducing, and through his architecture most powerfully and enduringly of all. The Henry Poors, whom he bamboozled in the matter of the baroque ceiling, were seduced. Though the cost of their home far exceeded the estimate (they went bankrupt a few years later), the Poors were "enraptured" by their new dwelling, seeing it as a reflection of Stanford's personality and charm. Rosecliff at Newport, Rhode Island, which Stanford designed for the heiress Tessie Oelrichs—it was completed in 1902—is literally a valentine. The white exterior is a lacy variation of the Grand Trianon at Versailles, and the first thing one sees on entering is a double staircase that forms the outline of a heart.

Rosecliff included such appurtenances as a trompe-l'oeil ceiling of painted clouds and a chandelier equipped to release twenty-five thousand dollars' worth of French perfume at a time. In keeping with this standard, Tessie hired Barnum & Bailey to entertain at her son's tenth birthday and, in 1904, gave a Bal Blanc for which she attempted to induce the United States Navy to anchor the Great White Fleet offshore for scenery. When the Navy refused she had full-scale facsimiles of the ships constructed. She was a girl after Stanford's heart in her extravagance and love of show, but she was not hoodwinked by him in the matter of a space he left on a prominent wall surface in the reception salon that fitted perfectly the measurements of an expensive tapestry he had acquired on a recent trip to Europe. (Stanford was left holding the bag on that one.)

Tessie ended up living alone at Rosecliff, talking to imaginary guests; she died in 1926. The house then passed through a number of different hands. One of the owners, an actress, returned to New York in the fall of 1942 without closing the house for the winter properly. The pipes froze and burst, flooding the second floor and caving in the trompe-l'oeil ceiling. The perfume chandelier came down with it, and water cascading down the heart-shaped stairs froze in place. Almost always there is a disaster somewhere behind even the most sublime of Stanford's seductions.

But in the architecture itself, especially in the interiors, there is a stillness that arises out of the combinations of textures, often unusual and often in rich dark colors that are altogether expressive, amounting to a form of personal presence that is outside time; it is this stillness that is seductive. Sometimes the stillness borders on eeriness because of the unstill context—the onrushing wave, the destructiveness of the age—of which it is a part. But the architecture survives its historical context, because the stillness in it is the stillness of fantasy and, in that, is apart from history and the world. The true context of Stanford's work is not high society or the imperial nation but a celestial dream, a dream arising out of his own immersion—his drowning—in aesthetic delight. In his interiors the onlooker drowns a little and becomes lost to the world too.

Stanford consumed beauty and it consumed him. In a memoir, his friend Royal Cortissoz wrote:

Sometimes whistling would fail him and as though in despair of all he felt he would burst into song. Beauty did possess him. That is why those of us who loved him are proud to stand up and be counted in devotion to his name.

It is Stanford's obsession with beauty that amounts to a presence in his interiors, especially that texturing of walls and ceilings that seems to dissolve edges, making one feel that one is standing in a mirage rather than in a room. What is frightening about Stanford is that this obsession with beauty existed on an uninterrupted continuum with his destructive qualities, driving him to rip apart palazzi and plunder vulnerable young girls. He and others deemed this kind of behavior acceptable precisely because the palazzi and the girls *were* beautiful, and, of course, because the nation was ascendant and the clients were rich and—in the case of the girls—Stanford was not just successful and rich, but so hugely likable. Underneath the entrancing Stanford White surface is predation. Behind the aesthetic sophistication of a Stanford White interior is the blindly voracious, irresponsible force, both personal and that of a whole class, a whole nation out of control.

The trance of beauty with violence and chaos underneath is an ambiance in which I feel at home. I feel safe in that strange serenity, as I do at Box Hill. Yet when I encounter it outside of Box Hill I also feel danger. For me, to stand fully aware in a Stanford White interior is an experience of extremes: of fear and safety, of yearning and an impulse to flight, of disturbance and peace.

Through happenstance, I have found myself living—almost unwittingly—in Stanford White environments. I spent two years at Manhattanville College in Purchase, New York, where the administration building, the central building on the campus, had formerly been Ophir Hall, a Norman-style castle redone by Stanford in 1890 to serve as the country retreat of Mr. and Mrs. Whitelaw Reid. Later I worked as a secretary at Random House in what had formerly been the Villard Houses. Though any Stanford environment was richly associative for me, I tended to experience those associations on a subliminal level. Even when I recognized the provenance of a given location, I avoided thinking about Stanford's connection to it, as a way of not knowing, a way of keeping clear of a whole universe of my history. This tension of knowing and not knowing is intimately familiar to me and brings with it another kind of stillness, a stillness of my adulthood, an immobility of my own interior, the stillness of a Ping-Pong ball that has ceased to bounce. New York City itself—where I have lived most of my adult life—continues to be, despite the ongoing destruction of architecture of all kinds, a Stanford White environment. Although Stanford achieves his most seductive effects in his interiors, even his exteriors can ensnare. And his snares are all over town.

The American Academy of Dramatic Arts is just up from Madison Square at Madison Avenue and Thirtieth Street. Completed in 1907, the building was originally the old Colony Club, a women's club founded over the protests of the husbands of its members. Stanford supported them, however, and when they needed an architect he took on the job. The façade of the Colony Club is brick with white limestone trim, in a delicate Federal-revival style with domestic proportions. (No need for imperial language in a women's club.) The grayish-pink bricks of the façade are set with the headers—the ends of the bricks—facing out, and the squarish shape of the headers is arresting, both because it defies convention and because headers have a rough surface. The over-all effect is to make one *aware* of texture: the building is quietly but powerfully sensual and, with its grayish-pink color, latently glows.

At a glance, the Robb House, at Park Avenue and Thirty-fifth Street—completed in 1891—looks sombre, even stuffy, because the surface has become blackened with soot. But when one looks closely at the façade one sees textured bricks and terra-cotta tiles of different colors, including pale yellow, while the base of the building was of a light-colored stone. Even in their darkened state, these differences in color and texture have their effect. The interplay among the brick, tile, stone, and among the black iron grilles, the darker shadows of the inflected façade, and the delicacy of carved florets and other ornamental pieces that punctuate the design, creates an experience of delicate sensibility and breezy warmth. The façade seduces.

Just to the west, on Thirty-fifth Street between Madison and Park, is the unreservedly lighthearted little house that Stanford designed for his friend the collector Thomas Clarke, completed in 1902. The style is Grecian with a Fragonard touch. A luxurious two-story window very nearly overwhelms the small brick façade: here grace, elegance, and charm are all just tossed off, to flirtatious effect. Then around the corner, on Fifth Avenue and Thirty-sixth Street, is the Gorham Building, completed in 1906. The Gorham is a commercial structure eight stories high with an overhanging copper cornice, the underside polychromed and gilded. The windows are unframed which makes the façade seem a smooth plane, with one ironwork balcony placed perfectly in the middle. The stillness of the Gorham Building is in the perfection of the scale of cornice to façade, and of the placement of the balcony.

In contrast, across Fifth Avenue at Thirty-seventh Street is the ruined grandeur of the original Tiffany Building—also completed in 1906—noisy with decay and complaining. Built in the style of a Venetian palazzo, the Tiffany Building is a pitiable derelict in every detail. Its white marble facing is now irregularly soot-stained and caked with pigeon droppings. Its Italianate balconies are crumbling. Its cornices in this context of decay are sad in their very elaborateness, and the light gestures, such as Corinthian capitals and expanses of glass, now appear trapped, the whole floundering in humiliation and further degraded by gimcrack signs and storefronts on the first floor. The Tiffany Building reminds me of a terrible studio photograph of Stanford taken toward the end of his life: fat, pleading-looking; all dressed up in a rich man's pin-striped suit, though at the time he was on the verge of bankruptcy, he is almost unrecognizable.

Up Fifth Avenue, at Sixtieth Street, is the Metropolitan Club, Stanford's magnificent monument to the egos of parvenu businessmen. This club was started by J. P. Morgan in a pique, because some of his newly made millionaire cronies were refused admission by the exclusive Union Club. Morgan told Stanford he wanted a "gentlemen's club" and "damn the expense," and Stanford obliged, though he nearly killed himself trying to get the job done on time; in the last weeks Morgan had made a bet he couldn't do it. He worked around the clock. Tripped up by strikes, he hired scabs on the day before the club opened to bring in mantels made by nonunion workers and other scabs to install them, with charwomen standing by to clean up the mess. Stanford was there himself, overseeing it all. And he was there in the morning too. On February 27, 1894, having had no sleep, Stanford was standing in the reception line next to Morgan to greet the members.

The result of Stanford's obsessive work is a miracle. Despite the pretensions implicit in its scale and style, the Metropolitan Club is joyous and light. The courtyard is elliptical. The façade is white marble. The two-story entrance hall is faced in gray-veined marble, and a double staircase that ascends one vast wall is graced with scrolling leafy ironwork bannisters to lacy effect. The stairs themselves are still carpeted in burgundy, as they were by Stanford. In some of its details the club verges dangerously toward a silliness of excess. For example, in a painted relief on the ceiling of the ballroom bare and amply bosomed angels look down from an elaborate garden. But instead of creating a feeling of glut the relief has the air of architecture dressed up for make-believe. Large windows with deep insets yield a more serious architectonic pleasure. They look across Fifth Avenue to a statue of General Sherman by Augustus Saint-Gaudens. There is General Sherman riding high on his horse, sword outthrust, led by victory, the trees of Central Park providing a soft texture behind.

The library windows, on the other hand, face into the elliptical courtyard. The wings of the Metropolitan Club that enclose the courtyard also half enclose the view and where that enclosure leaves off, Stanford's Harmonie Club directly across Sixtieth Street encloses the rest. The Harmonie, completed one year after Stanford's death, was a comparatively small club, for Jewish businessmen. Its façade is also of white marble, densely articulate with classical language. The surface is complex, shallowly inflected with delicate

Corinthian pilasters, a frieze of scrolling foliage, elliptical windows, and fine Ionic columns. This backdrop of fluency and right proportion is framed by a corner of the Metropolitan Club: by its great overhanging cornice with copper verdigris and lions, white marble scrolls and leaves and rosettes underneath. What you see from the window of the Metropolitan Club library is a world entirely created by Stanford White, a kind of outdoor enclosure, and there is, as so often in Stanford's architecture, something that radiates, something that—despite the harmonious, light-filled, rational nature of his style—even pulses faintly, in the animistic mode of a garden at night.

The club in which Stanford himself was most comfortable, however, was The Players down on Gramercy Park, a club for people in the theatrical profession, people who at that time were not considered quite acceptable in society. Stanford had a hand in The Players too, but only insofar as he made changes to the preëxisting brownstone in 1888. The Players is characterized by the old-fashioned intimacy of its domestic brownstone scale, and its eccentric array of portraits. In other men's clubs there are portraits too, but usually of male worthies dressed in suits. In The Players the portraits are of great actors and actresses (despite the fact that women were excluded from membership) in costume, at the high points of their greatest roles. One sees Ellen Terry as Lady Macbeth and Edwin Booth as Richard III at full emotional throttle with appropriately high-contrast lighting. Taken together so much drama creates a hilarious effect.

The artist Edward Simmons, who belonged to The Players and often collaborated with Stanford on his interiors, wrote about him in a way that captures his humanity more vividly than any other account. In a memoir he described Stanford as

always in a hurry, dashing about here and there and with his body always slightly bent forward—he took very short steps—trotting along the sidewalk like a busy little girl.

Simmons also wrote that Stanford was "as strong as a prizefighter" and that his proper clothing would have been a wolf-skin and a battle-axe, that he should have worn his hair long, that he made Simmons think of "Vercingetorix in his cave with all his spoils piled up around him." A Simmons image that stands out among all the recollections of Stanford for the vulnerability it conveys is of Stanford swimming nude in a pool: the whiteness of his body reminded Simmons of tallow. "I got to know this very simple person," Simmons wrote, "who was a child and an artist and never became an adult."

One day in February, 1896, Simmons found Stanford sitting in The Players Club all by himself in a puzzled, confused state. When Simmons asked him what was wrong, Stanford "started and came out of his mood" and then told him that he was just back from the University of Virginia. In October, Thomas Jefferson's masterpiece had been devastated by fire and Stanford had been hired to restore it, and to expand the campus as well. On this trip he had had a chance to look at Jefferson's blueprints, and what he had seen had brought him to a halt. "They're wonderful, and I am scared to death. I only hope I can do it right," he said to Simmons. This is the only moment that I have found in which Stanford seems to question himself, the only time when he senses limitations and responsibility too. The only time he comes to a stop. There is Stanford alone in The Players Club amidst characters at peaks of theatrical intensity, for one moment truly present, for once in his life encountering himself.

The encounter was insufficient: His contributions to the University of Virginia are today known on campus as "the mutilations of 1896." Both Jefferson and Stanford were attracted to the classical vocabulary but for opposed reasons: Jefferson for the democratic associations of that vocabulary (there is an implicit modesty in his work) and Stanford for the imperial ones. In Jefferson's design, the campus consisted of two rows of pavilions, combination classroom-dormitories that face each other across a green called the Lawn. At one end of the Lawn was the Rotunda, which served as a library, from which the Lawn descended between the embracing pavilions, creating a prospect that was open at the far end to a magnificent view of the Blue Ridge Mountains. The campus was organized around that view and took its deepest meaning from it. It was the relation of the architecture to that view made this cluster of buildings both passionate and contemplative. But right in the middle of the opening to the mountains Stanford erected a big neoclassical building flanked by two others that are connected to the first by walls cutting off the view altogether. This was not something Stanford did without struggle—the University needed new buildings and he had to put them somewhere—but nevertheless he did it. The consensus of time is that he made a very big mistake, but it was perhaps an inevitable mistake in that it reflected the difference between imperial and democratic neoclassicism. In the imperial vision there is no preëxisting landscape, no outside power, no mystical cosmos. There is no encompassing mystery and there is consequently no humility either. There is magnificence in the imperial vision, but it is the magnificence of man alone. The neoclassical architecture of imperialism is about power without love and without prayer.

The tragedy of Stanford White is that combined with his softness and sensitivity there was something in him that was hard and unfeeling, something blind and crushing—incapable of the responsiveness that humility brings. One can see how hard he tried with the University of Virginia buildings, and also how doomed his efforts were. He knew to restrain himself; his buildings are delicate and sophisticated, and reflect in many ways the very best that he had to give. Yet in the context of the open tenderness and authenticity of Jefferson's architecture, the very sophistication of Stanford's buildings exposes a kind of emptiness—as if the buildings were a performance, a kind of dressing-up; a charade. In Jefferson's architecture, in contrast, there is thoughtfulness, humility, love, and, above all, conviction.

*   *   *

The Players Club is a few doors away from the Gramercy Park house that was Stanford and Bessie's home for most of their life together. Their house was rented: Stanford never owned a house in New York. The Whites gave parties frequently, but Bessie in some ways felt out of her depth in the role of society hostess. In the early days, for example, she was intimidated by a French chef whom Stanford hired. She told my mother that mercifully the chef was a kind man, and had guided her in shaping menus. There are indications that Stanford tried to change Bessie. He made her smoke against her will, for example, and disapproved when she put on weight. According to my grandmother, once when Bessie went out to St. James for a spell, Stanford, who was no sylph himself by this time, sent her roses every day with the telegram "Fat is fatal." Mama always said this phrase in a musing way, as if turning it over in her mind: the side of Stanford that was not so nice.

Bessie nonetheless was responsible for the domestic sphere of the Gramercy Park house and especially for raising Larry. According to family lore, Stanford told Bessie she could "have" Larry until he was eighteen and then she could hand him over. And, indeed, other than enrolling Larry in St. Marks—a boarding school in Southborough, Massachusetts: a bastion of the upper class—when he was six years old, Stanford was not much involved with his growing son. An exception was a time when he heard that Larry was thought a sissy by the other boys in the neighborhood because he was too dressed up when he went to the park. Stanford went home and fired the nurse, but it was Bessie who was responsible: she had Larry in dresses when he was as old as five. When he was older she made him wear white gloves and, one year, a peculiar tam-o'-shanter that other boys mocked; he recalled being chased by a bunch of boys because of his hat and escaping only by hiding in a manhole.

From time to time, Stanford retreated to a salmon-fishing club in Canada to recuperate from the effects of high living. Occasionally Bessie would accompany him. When she did not, however, a companion observed that Stanford wouldn't bother opening his wife's letters, because, he said, he did not want to read about how Larry had gone swimming or how Larry had not gone swimming. Stanford, who kept a little black book with the birthdays of many women written in it, asked Larry in a letter to remind him when his birthday came around. This was when Larry was at St. Marks. Not long afterward, Larry came down with a life-endangering case of pneumonia and Bessie, in New York, nearly went mad with anxiety: Stanford did come through that time, going with her to the school and arranging for an express train to make a local stop to pick up their sick son.

The liveliest connection between Stanford and Larry, visible from this distance, cropped up in Larry's teen years around the subject of automobiles, for which both father and son had a passion. "HOW ABOUT THE AUTOMOBILE?" Larry writes in one letter from school, and, in another:

Thank you for your letter. I am "orfle" glad you got the Renault. What kind of a body are you going to have on it and will you paint it blue. I still want an automobile very much, if you are not *too* bust. Even if I did have one I would still ride horseback a great deal and would use the auto principally for going over to Fire Island.

Your loving son

Larry

(His signature is accompanied by a drawing of an automobile.) Stanford told Larry that if he could take apart an engine and put it back together he could have an automobile. Larry did this, and he got one.

There was a tension between Larry and Stanford that had to do with privileges that Larry enjoyed and with a suavity that these advantages bred in him. Stanford was never smooth, and he came to feel that Larry was spoiled. On Larry's side, tension may have been generated by Stanford's infidelities to Bessie, and in this there would have been a repetition of history: Stanford was always extremely solicitous of *his* mother, Nina, who had endured a philandering husband, and indeed may have endured a husband who was supporting an entire second family. Nina lived with Stanford and Bessie, and then just Bessie, from Richard's death in 1885 until her own in 1921. She was there throughout Larry's childhood and well into his adulthood.

Even given the tension between Stanford and Larry, however, it is a jarring fact that Stanford did not include Larry in his will. Daisy Chanler, Larry's mother-in-law, who had been a friend of Stanford's, said on several occasions that she was sure Stanford took this harsh action because he thought Larry was spoiled and needed to struggle. The irony is that by the time of his death Stanford had only debts to leave his son, in addition to the job of protecting Bessie from scandal. Stanford, of course, could not have foreseen the circumstances under which Larry would discover that his father had cut him out, but surely under any circumstances it would have been a hurtful message. Larry, in turn, left his daughter Sarah out of his will, because she had become a nun—not an altogether unreasonable action, as she would have been required to turn the money over to her order. Nevertheless, I remember when the will was read, the day after Papa's death, in Mama's bedroom on the second floor of Box Hill. Sarah, in her Dominican habit, looked as if she had taken a blow to the solar plexus which she then absorbed with nunly discipline.

There is a photograph of Stanford walking with McKim and Mead on the North Terrace at Box Hill, probably taken around 1900. Papa, running after the partners, is about eleven or twelve. He is somewhat gawky and inhabits his body in a spontaneous way that conveys a vulnerability and humanity that one did not see in him as an adult. He is running toward his father, reaching toward his father who, leaden, bloated with dissipation, is absorbed with Mead and McKim, and oblivious of his son.

*   *   *

The emergence of Box Hill was recorded in sketches and drawings that I found in Avery Library at Columbia University. In the earlier drawings the old roads show up, and I was fascinated to see how these delineated the unlandscaped terrain. Even as an adult, it was startling to me that Stanford's layout was superimposed and in some ways at odds with the lay of the land. As the Place begins to come into being, there are some full-scale renderings by draftsmen, along with other lightning-speed renderings by Stanford in which he is trying out many radically different ideas of Box Hill.

In the Avery collection one can be right there with him, fidgeting with the Rond Point, coaxing the box garden into the light of day, envisioning things that never came to be—a swimming pool behind the barns, for example, with statuary and elaborate plantings to embellish it—and planning the barns themselves. Those were perhaps the most touching drawings to me: seeing the trial and error, watching as at last the familiar outline playfully appeared—the bowed roofline of the carriage house carrying through the stables to the charismatic tower with its pointed roof like a Chinese hat. Stanford played and played. And then up comes the Place as a whole, up comes what I as a child just assumed was the format of Providence. Up came the outlines of our blessed location where the whorl of a fiddlehead fern was the whorl in an Ionic capital and both of these were the whorl of a storm that could be seen in its entirety from Diana as it travelled across the Sound. Up came the world in the bright band that drew its intensities, its stillness, from a silence within Stanford's encircling fame.

Bessie's sisters all inherited money from Aunt Cornelia, and three out of four of them built fancy houses for themselves in St. James. Stanford, though neglectful of his wife and son in many ways, was generous to the point of compulsion with his in-laws. He loved big families with many needs that he could fill, and the Judge John Lawrence Smith family had plenty of those. Bessie's sister Kate wanted a house in the shape of a Maltese cross, and he tried to persuade her to change her mind but in the end obliged, with a four-story shingled and gabled structure that stood at the top of a very steep hill and, because of its unusual shape, had many triangular rooms. He expanded Ella's Sherrewogue, an old Smith homestead, and Nellie's Bytharbor. He also took on the care of the houses he had designed, constantly seeing to tedious details like malfunctioning plumbing, and to decoration and redecoration, but also getting involved in aspects of family affairs, in New York as well as in the country. For example, when Kate's daughter Isabella was six he drove her to school often and she loved him madly because he let her drive the car herself. He would also take care of theatre tickets, or make arrangements for trips abroad. After the Judge died, Stanford and Nellie's husband, Prescott Hall Butler, became the paternal figures in the Judge Smith family, with Prescott taking care of legal matters and Stanford tending to other concerns. (Kate's husband, James Wetherill, was an unworldly clergyman, and Ella's, Devereux Emmet, was an aristocratic sportsman.)

There were spats too. Stanford could not run the Rhododendron Drive in a straight line to the road, because the line ran straight into Kate's property. Kate could have solved Stanford's problem by selling him a small triangle of land, but she refused because, she said, Smiths never sell their land, even to Smiths. (A rich Smith history could be written entirely in terms of land sold and bought and sold again by Smiths to each other, not to mention real-estate transactions with outsiders.) There were tensions in the wider Smith clan as well, having to do with Aunt Cornelia's money, which, Smith aloofness notwithstanding, was hard on cousins who had grown up swimming and clamming with Judge Smith's daughters, but who had no comparable inheritance. "Lord Protect me from Envy," Ella's cousin Dorothy Smith wrote in her diary after attending a dinner for a hundred on gold-plated service given by Ella at Sherrewogue. But Stanford was Cousin Stanny to these unrich cousins too.

The Judge Smith daughters gave parties in their lovely houses, and Stanford had a hand in them, also. He especially liked costume parties. In particular, he liked classical costumes, and a number of photographs show Stanford and the Smith sisters, with houseguests, dressed up in togas with wreaths of laurel on their heads, posing near Diana or, most improbably, cavorting with seagulls and horseshoe crabs on the un-Aegean shores of Long Island.

Judge Smith's daughters were unlike other wealthy members of New York society in that, as Smiths, they regarded their country places rather than their city residences as their primary homes. Gold-plate dinners aside, they maintained habits of enjoying the simple pleasures of place. Picnics were a favorite: picnics on the water, picnics on horseback, moonlit picnics. One day, there was a rowing race in the harbor. Isabella, who was twelve by this time, won, but fell over backward as she crossed the finish line, her legs wheeling up into the air, her skirt over her head. The next day, she received several pairs of bright-colored silk stockings from Uncle Stanny.

He was there, there on the harbor, on the Nissequogue River, on the Sound beach. I overemphasize this perhaps, because he was so absent, so excised, when I was growing up, so pulsingly invisible above all. It's startling to hear about him, for example, from his grandniece, Isabella's daughter Kate, as—sitting on the porch of her own house on the harbor—she tells me about her mother and the stockings. Even more, there is a jolt from coming across him in an ordinary snapshot, all bundled up on the steps of Sherrewogue with Grandma and Aunt Ella, just standing there hunched and shivering: the wind off the harbor in winter is damp and sharp.

MUSIC

WHEN THE TELEPHONE rang in the Red Cottage in the daytime, it was sometimes for my father, and my mother would go to the back door quickly and halloo "Frank-OH," the "OH" on a high soprano note. That would be after he moved from the studio in the cow barn into one in the woods on the edge of the Red Cottage garden, though in fact my mother's halloo could carry past the White Cottage and up the length of the Privet Path—could carry as far as the barns, to summon us children home. But what I remember is my father in summer charging like a linebacker out of the studio in the Red Cottage woods and across the deep-green, half-grown long grass under pulsating trees. As a young man and later too, Dad was slender, but for a few years in his thirties he put on weight and had his hair cropped short so there was a feeling about him of mass—on these occasions of mass forcefully propelled through space from the studio to the house. It made me angry, the way my mother hallooed to him automatically, without even asking who it was, or if the person could call back at lunchtime: the way she just interrupted my father's work, although his running to the phone betrayed no reluctance. The sight of him running contradicted the idea that Dad's work was sacred and that one day he would just naturally be famous. My mother's rushing to halloo and my father's running—head down, torso nearly flat out, legs churning under him—said that we were just a family in a green place with a father who had hopes but no guarantees. In other words, we were what we were right then, and not some other family that would become retroactively golden when our father was famous.

The phone number in the Red Cottage was 6613. The Bobby Whites' was 6616. Box Hill was 6642. Phones rang less often everywhere then than they do now, but especially seldom in the Red Cottage where the texture of life was disrupted by sudden noises. Long-distance phone calls were downright rare, and in our house making one was surrounded by stress that had to do with cost. Thus it was momentous when, once in a blue moon, we made a family call to Grandpa in California, during which each of us in turn would "say hello" and have a two- or three-sentence, time-tense conversation. It was Dad who generated the suspense, his eyes showing dollars and cents like a cash register, as my mother would say.

Yet sometimes, late at night when he was drinking whiskey and roving around like a bull in the house, he would call California and talk for a long time. From upstairs I'd hear the singsong drone of his voice, and I'd drift off, and wake again, and the drone would be singsonging on. I know that he called California, because once I crept partway down the stairs to listen and I heard him say "Dad." I listened eagerly, hoping to discover something deep and intimate about him, something that could come to the surface only when he was by himself in the depths of the night. But what he was talking about was us girls, one by one, in a kind of litany, saying what grades we were in and that kind of thing. I was astonished that he was talking about us at all, and especially that he was recounting such banalities in a heavily sentimental way. I thought that after getting drunk and wild to the point of making a long-distance phone call he should have had something more profound to get off his chest.

The Red Cottage was near the public road, separated from it only by a cedar hedge. But there were few cars on the road then: it was like a broad, calm stream that moved silently by. We would hear the mailman's car come and stop; we would hear him open the mailbox and shut it. Twice a year, for each of us, at Christmas and on our birthdays, there was a card from our Grandpa in Palo Alto enclosing five dollars, and in between there were letters to each of us written in blue ink in Grandpa's flowing cursive script. Grandpa's writing was as regular and as readable as the printed script on his cards, and he always closed with "X"'s for hugs and circles with a dot in them for kisses. A fresh, loving feeling arose from his writing like a scent. We all took these cards and letters and gifts of money for granted, and were not made to write thank-you notes, or letters in return.

Once, however, my sister Beatrice wrote to our father's aunt Kate, who was a school principal in Eureka, California, for information to fulfill a grade-school assignment in family history, but this educator wrote back that the family history was best forgotten. What a rebuff that letter was! Later, I understood that Aunt Kate was ashamed—that behind the bedtime stories that Dad told us was a history that was felt to be one of poverty and disgrace. On my mother's side the names of Chanlers long dead and only remotely related were incandescent with significance and powerful with the emotions they evoked. On my father's side—beyond the juvenile realm of bedtime stories—nothing was significant, and there was no feeling: that was the principal message. On my mother's side, even though substantial aspects of the family past were sunk in silence, the presence of mighty narratives in the background was always felt. On the Rousseau side, there was, in comparison, a void. The blankness of landscape and family history around them made the Rousseaus seem small and exposed against darkness. Even the public history that surrounded them—the frontier, the Depression—seemed to have come out of the night and then shot by, leaving them stranded.

There was, however, something—largely fragments of bedtime stories that could be pieced together into a history of a kind. I knew, for example, that our great-grandfather François Rousseau was, when a young man, forced to flee Quebec because of involvement in a brawl between the English and the French; that he had an apprenticeship as a carpenter in New York and then was hired as ship's carpenter on a vessel headed around the horn; that he jumped ship in San Francisco, taking with him only his tools. This was in 1848. He went north to Eureka, to look for employment, but his temper was so bad that he could do only solitary work. He ran mule trains in to the miners in the Sierras once the Gold Rush started, for example, and later rode for a local version of the Pony Express.

At a rest stop where he ate and changed ponies he met our great-grandmother, who was the cook. She was seventeen. (He was nearly forty.) At age twelve, she had been sent to America from Gothenburg, Sweden, alone by her parents, because they could raise only one fare. My father thought her first name was Evangeline, and didn't know her last—a lapse that would be unthinkable in my mother's family. As an adult I learned from some family documents that my California aunts had kept that in fact her name was Christeen Johnsen. In the same cache I found a picture of her dressed in a heavy wool jacket—a mannish-looking jacket—with a high white collar, but she is petite and pretty, in a birdlike way, with very bright eyes and a sharp, smiling look. She looks to be a brightly self-contained person, merrily accepting the conditions of her life. Her appearance prompts one to see human life as a fleeting thing, like the life of a bird, but everything about her also conveys something lastingly good in a situation where little else is encouraging.

François and Christeen married and lived in Eureka, and had three children who lived to adulthood: Kate, Jess, and Francis, our grandfather, born in 1883. Christeen adored her tough old bird of a husband. A bedtime story about him was that when he had to have one leg amputated and there was no anesthetic, he just drank a lot of whiskey. Another story was that at one point he owned half of what is now downtown San Francisco with a partner, and they sold it. But then the partner ran off with the money, and our great-grandfather took off after him to kill him. He never found the partner, but he was gone for years. It was not the first time that he abandoned his family. In those periods when he was gone, Christeen took in washing to support herself and the children.

There was this story, too. One day when Francis was a boy, he saw his father laying out strings on the ground, and when he asked his father what he was doing his father said, gruffly, "I'm building a *house!*" That emphatic "house!" stayed with me. In my mind it was a house erected against the great dark void of historylessness but which, for this very reason, I could not take further than the abstraction outlined by the strings on the ground.

But in the same cache in which I discovered the photograph of Christeen, I found a photograph of The House on Fourth Street, as the house Grandpa Rousseau built was identified. It was, clearly, a real house, with a real street number: I decided to go to Eureka to find it.

The houses in the neighborhood of Fourth Street were two-story clapboard structures with steep peaks, often with two windows close together centered under the peak—but sometimes placed to one side—and on the first floor a plain, small front door, almost always on one side, and a single window balancing it. The windows seemed small in the expanse of clapboard, though not small enough to be a stylistic statement. On the sides of the houses there were hardly any windows, and those few miscellaneously shaped. The only aesthetic statements were small, diamond-shaped windows right under the eaves on the side. You would have to say that, taken part by part, these houses had almost no style. Even if you looked at them whole you might say that their character arose out of a kind of absence of style. But when you saw them all together under a gray, drizzling, February sky, with the Humboldt Mountains—stubbornly plain—behind them and the unresponsive Pacific horizon in front, they made a clear statement of the stark smallness and insignificance of human life in a universe that is large and indifferent.

Grandpa Rousseau's house was exactly as it appeared in the photograph except for a tiny little porch, now rotting, built over the front door. The shades were drawn, a window was patched with cardboard, and rain-soaked possessions—a hat, a doll—seemed abandoned on the decrepit porch. It was occupied, I discovered, by Laotians who were illegal immigrants—hence the drawn shades—when they invited me in I saw that they lived so lightly in the house that it seemed empty and unfurnished. It was plain white, with high ceilings, with plain daylight coming in the side windows, from the plain gray day. There were two big downstairs rooms, a kitchen in back, stairs that were substantial, with a heavy bannister, and, upstairs, four plain rooms with banked ceilings. The message of the house was as flat as a flat brain-wave, flat as the white light flowing in the windows from the gray day leaving no shadows on the white wall.

After old François's leg was sawed off, he couldn't work, so they sold the house to William Ayres, a quixotically idealistic newspaperman who was a neighbor, and moved to San Jose, where Christeen went to work in a cannery. Not long after the move, François died. Kate and Jess, who were older, continued with their schooling, but Francis, my grandfather, who was only fourteen, went to work with his mother, evidently because he was a boy. When he was eighteen or so, Kate, who was ten years older than he, and bossy and ambitious, insisted that he go to "business college" where he could learn to be a clerk: it was at business college that Grandpa picked up his Hallmark-card script. But the life of a clerk did not appeal to him. Instead, he became a machinist and went to work for Bethlehem Steel, and married William Ayres's daughter Jenny—as he had known he would from early childhood, when they had played house together. In photographs of them Francis is almost always looking at

Jenny in an all-consuming way, handsome and sturdy, while Jenny looks straight at the camera with large, calm brown eyes. Grandpa had a great capacity for love.

As an adult, I learned that Jenny was a schoolteacher in Eureka before she married: in fact, she was a star teacher who worked in the wild mountains above town and had been named Teacher of the Year by the state. Jenny's four brothers had wondered if Francis was good enough for their sister, and William Ayres wondered if the Christian Science tradition in which Jenny had been raised and the Rousseau Catholicism would mix well. But in spite of these objections Francis and Jenny became engaged in 1905. From photographs in which Grandpa is looking at Jenny, one would conclude that there was no stopping him. After they got engaged, however, he had to wait for a decade because that is how long it took them to save enough money to build a house.

The site of their house was in a partly developed area called the Amazon Track on the outskirts of San Francisco. Jenny and Grandpa designed their house together, and when building started Grandpa, who worked at Bethlehem Steel in the San Francisco area, was able to supervise the work. It was a solid house, not large but ample—a testament to their cautious delay. In 1915 they married and moved in. Jenny liked things to be a certain way. She had a linen tablecloth and napkins and Haviland china, and she made beautiful clothes for her three children as they came along: a little white coat lined with ermine and a matching cap for Eileen, who was born in 1917; knickers and a cap for Frank, my father, who was born in 1920. Jeanne, the youngest, was born in 1922. All the Ayreses were musical; Jenny, in particular, had a fine singing voice. She took Eileen, her eldest, to piano lessons with an old Italian and when, in ear training, Eileen couldn't hit the note, Frank, playing on the floor, sang out the note in perfect pitch. The teacher said "Let me teach *him.*"

One can see in photographs that as time passed, Jenny began to look stressed and careworn: a young mother used up by three young children, perhaps. Grandpa, compared with his father, was a para-

gon of virtue—a dedicated family man who held a steady job. But
he had an untamed side too, which was stubbornly outside society.
My mother said of him that he was the only man she had ever met
who seemed to have no feminine component whatsoever. He
swigged coal oil as a "physic," and cured colds by taking a hot bath,
sweating under blankets, and then jumping into water that was ice-
cold—probably an Indian remedy he learned from his father in
Eureka. He never used antiseptic, even though he had once got
lockjaw when he sliced off a bit of his heel with a weed cutter and
then, according to a cousin, plastered it with mud full of chicken
shit.

In 1924, when they had been married for nine years, and Jeanne
was two, Jenny got breast cancer. Some of the six months before
she died was spent at home. Once, her dressing fell off and my
father could see the cancer, and he could also see that his mother
was scared. She died in the house in August of 1925, when my
father was five. Afterward, Eileen became terrified that she would
forget what their mother had looked like, and asked if they could
keep her body in the back of the closet so that she could pop in to
refresh her memory from time to time.

On my mother's side, we lived in a swirl of objects, some of
totemic significance, many of a less personal kind of importance—
museums might be interested in buying them, for example—that
reflected our own importance, or so it seemed to me as a child. To
me it was a given that this world of mythologized objects was what
gave meaning to our life. It struck me, therefore, that on my father's side, the objects that had family meaning were, in comparison, few. They were, furthermore, ordinary, and had meanings as
keepsakes rather than in themselves. In this there was an authenticity
of feeling to which I was unaccustomed, combined with an evanes-
cence that scared me. I heard in the bedtime stories, for example,
that all Grandpa inherited from his father was his set of tools. Dad
told us that when he was a little boy he took the tools and, in a kind
of trance, dropped them down deep cracks in the ground, one by
one—"down to China" was how he put it when his father asked

him where the tools were. Dad said that this was the only time his father thrashed him.

Dad had one possession from Jenny, his mother—a pair of gold cuff links—and he gave them to me when I was ten or so. He communicated to me little sense of value or meaning having to do with the cuff links, or perhaps this gesture of recognition and connection was such a reversal that I was unable to absorb it.

I lost Dad's mother's gold cuff links somewhere out in the field between the Red Cottage and the woods, where occasionally a silver cup or a spoon or a porringer from a christening turned up, battered by the tractor. My father said nothing when I confessed that they were gone. My mother, however, conveyed to me by tone and body movements that the death of Daddy's mother when he was so young had been a tragedy for him. After my mother made this clear, I had no outlet for my remorse other than to search in the rough grass. But the cuff links were small, and the grass had just been mowed.

After Jenny died, Grandpa's mother, Christeen, came to take care of the children. She was, by all accounts, a nurturing presence. Grandpa's sister Jess, who had been living with Christeen, came too. Jess had married a ne'er-do-well in Eureka, who had subsequently died under a train. After his death, however, she had got a job as a stenographer in the San Francisco area—a job that she loved and considered very modern. She continued working as a stenographer for several years after she moved in with her brother's family, but then Christeen became too old to handle the children and the household and Jess was drafted to take over. She did not want to give up her independent life to take care of her brother's children, but evidently she had no choice.

Five years after Jenny's death, the family—Christeen and Jess included—moved to Palo Alto. (Grandpa also sold a shack in the countryside thirty miles south of San Francisco, where they had vacationed together when Jenny was alive.) They moved not to Palo

Alto proper but to Donohoe Street in East Palo Alto, a part of the town that was still half rural—there were fields all around the house and some of the roads were unpaved. It was an area in which people struggled to get by, supplementing their incomes with what they grew. The East Palo Alto house stood on one acre on which Grandpa did some farming as a hobby, to the delight of his city-bred children. Later, when he was laid off in the Depression, they depended on it.

When Dad told us about his childhood, the setting had always sounded remote, lonely, and rural, and the picture I got—to the extent that I got a picture at all—was that that was all there was. That was California in that time. I didn't understand that right next door was Palo Alto proper, the Stanford University town and a hub of cultural activity that was strongly connected to San Francisco, a cosmopolitan city by then. The lonely farawayness that I picked up from Dad was that of a poor place that was in fact surrounded by prosperous, busy places—a kind of isolation that is entirely different from the kind that comes about because of actual remoteness.

Francis lived in a dream of his marriage to Jenny, and that dream, rather than real memories—the children were too young to remember much—was what lived on in the household. The grip that the past had on Francis was made vivid to me by a story that David Ayres, the son of one of Jenny's brothers, Milton Ayres, told me as an adult. Three years or so after Jenny died, David told me, the two families went for a picnic on some high dunes near San Francisco. At the picnic, Milt tried to convey to Grandpa that he and his brothers all knew how much he had loved their sister Jenny, but that they felt it was important for both him and the children that he get on with his life. Milt said that he and his brothers would not in any way see it as a betrayal of Jenny if Francis married again. In fact, he said, they would see it as a good thing, as the children needed a mother. Francis was stunned by this statement and took a long time to reply. Finally he said, very slowly, that the children would be all right. Jess would raise them, he said. As for himself he would never, ever, look at a woman again.

Francis's manner was so serious, almost pompous, that Milt was embarrassed. To break the embarrassment he grabbed Francis and started them both running down the dune, but he got them going too fast so that they fell head over heels most of the way. At the bottom Milt got up and was brushing himself off, laughing and apologizing for what he had done, but then he looked at Francis and his words died in the air. Francis seemed not even to know that he had rolled down the dune, much less to be hearing Milt's apology. He was staring into space, still lost in the mood of eternal fidelity to Jenny.

As it turned out, the children were not all right with Jess at all. Jess was an angry person and abusive to the children. Christeen was able to control Jess somewhat, but then, in 1932, Christeen got sick and started to die. There was a story about this period that Dad told us at bedtime in the Red Cottage: one day when Christeen was in her last illness and was bedridden, and Dad, then eleven, was in the room, she suddenly ordered him in a brusque way to leave. Shocked and hurt, for she had never before spoken harshly to him, he obeyed. When he had gone, she died. The hurt stayed with him until, when he was grown, he realized that she had been concerned that in her dying she might not be sufficiently in command of herself to prevent something from happening that could upset a boy. Our father would be visibly moved when he told this story and indeed how Christeen's act of love and awareness rings out like a bell in the tale of this struggling little family.

After Christeen died, Jess was no longer restrained. She yelled at the children a lot, and scolded unceasingly at meals: they usually ate with their stomachs in knots. And the food itself was often an ordeal. Aunt Jess was a health nut, and in the morning she made each of the children swallow a raw egg whole, followed by a quart of water and a soup bowl of mush, all taken fast so that they could catch the bus. (Eileen invariably threw up.) In addition, she some-times hit the children. These punishments were meted out arbitrarily: Jess could be pleased one day by something the children did and hit them for it the next.

The children didn't tell their father about this, because they were afraid of his temper, afraid of what he might do to Aunt Jess. Francis never laid a hand on his children, my aunts said (the thrashing that my father got for losing François's tools must have been an exception), but he had a temper. He would take out his anger on the dog sometimes, making them cry, and he would grab hold of Aunt Jess in a way that scared them. Jess was not intimidated, however. When Grandpa or another adult crossed Jess, she would choke until she began vomiting; once, she brought up something that Eileen thought was her liver. On those occasions, Eileen was sure that Jess was going to die, but Grandpa paid no attention.

Grandpa worked many hours overtime and he turned his entire paycheck over to his sister. Once he discovered that she had given a large proportion of the money to the Catholic Church and that was one of the times when his anger impressed the children. Sometimes when Jess began to scold at dinner, Grandpa would just leave without eating and go sit out back with the squabs and the chickens, and, later, Jess would feel guilty, and send Eileen out with an eggnog for him; he would drink it, but only because he suspected that Eileen would get in trouble if he didn't. Thus the children lived with a sentimental, idealized fantasy of their parents' marriage while the reality in their house—the relationship between the adult man and the adult woman, and the way the children were treated—was full of conflict.

After Dad's mother died, there was nothing much in the way of musical training for him until, at seven, he was encouraged to take up an instrument at school. He chose the trumpet and, in a few days, hit high C. This is an achievement even for an adult. The music teacher, Mr. Snow, was very proud of Dad, and had him show off to people how he could hit high C. Mr. Snow was connected to the Stanford University band, and my father became the mascot of the football team. He would march out on the field in front of the band wearing a tiny uniform and playing his trumpet. Grandpa drove him faithfully to the games. Everyone in the family was proud.

When my father was eleven, he sought to play his trumpet in a little orchestra that had been organized in Palo Alto by a young Russian woman named Elise Belenky, a pianist, who had studied at the École Normale in Paris. She was the first person to properly evaluate his gift, which neither he himself nor his father had understood as being very much out of the ordinary. "He was good, that's all there was to it," Mrs. Belenky said to me. "He was better than anyone in the orchestra he wanted to join." First, she told him, he needed a more challenging instrument. She encouraged him to take up the piano, which he did.

Mrs. Belenky recalls that Grandpa was in no way awed by his son's gift—that he just wanted to do the right thing. He brought Dad to his lessons and orchestral sessions punctually. Both father and son were very quiet; when the lesson or the performance was over, they always left right away. Mr. Rousseau, Mrs. Belenky said, was clearly an uncultivated person, a person who worked with his hands. He was barrel-chested and short, and his arms were long. My father, in contrast, not only grew to a willowy six feet but had a sensitivity that was refined and extreme and very vulnerable—a sensitivity that would be extraordinary anywhere but was almost freakish in the obscure precincts of East Palo Alto.

Grandpa was a man's man and he had trouble with Dad's sensitivity. Once, for example, Dad was being bullied at school and Grandpa taught him how to fistfight; he knocked an opponent down right off, and then was nauseated. Dad couldn't stand heights, and Grandpa didn't like that either. When some work needed to be done on the roof of the house, he made Dad go up there to do it, shaming him for his fear.

After encountering Mrs. Belenky, Dad began practicing every waking hour he was not at school, on an upright that stood in the living room at 310 Donohoe Street. This was Jenny's piano, which had come with them from the house in San Francisco. There had been times when the children had gathered around to play and sing from Jenny's songbook, with Eileen on the piano and Dad on the trumpet and Grandpa on the guitar, singing out of key. These had been happy times with a light feeling, according to my aunt Jeanne. The music my father began playing after studying with Mrs. Belenky, however, brought in a different mood—one not altogether friendly to the others in the house. Aunt Jeanne said that, though she was proud of her brother's talent, listening to him practice for six hours at a stretch in their small house could be hard. He would fly off the handle if there was any noise when he was practicing. A folding door to the living room made a little sound when it was opened and if anyone went in to get something he would become enraged. Once when he was practicing, Jess came in and said, "It's time to go to bed," and he said he would go to bed when he was done practicing, and Francis backed him up. Jess started choking, but Francis ignored her and Dad went to bed when he wanted.

When Francis was laid off in 1934, and at that point they became downright poor, living off what they could sell of the fruit that grew out back, and eggs. Eileen remembers a charity coming by that Christmas with a turkey complete with trimmings. Francis angrily turned the turkey away, saying that he would accept no charity. They were better off than some, however: on the telephone pole by the house was a little marker that hoboes had set up to indicate that this was a house where they might get something to eat.

When I was twelve our family went to California for the summer. Almost everything about California was unfamiliar—the absence of change in the weather, the garden like a garden in a magazine around Aunt Jeanne's pool. But 310 Donohoe Street, where Grandpa still lived, had such depth and associative resonance that it was as if I had known it always. And in a way I had, for 310 Donohoe Street was a subtext of the Red Cottage. Though it has long since been torn down, it is still vivid to me, and a part of this vividness is that in my memory it's chopped up and incomplete: there are incomplete doorjambs, a bit of old sink seen from another room, linoleum, cracked and rotting at the edges. There is a couch with unruly springs that is difficult to sit on—chopped in my mind's eye like a Braque. There is an upright piano, two bedrooms that for some reason I don't want to enter. The neglect in Grandpa's house was stubborn, angry, but stale. It was a house like an old loose bandage on a wound that for ages and ages had refused absolutely to heal. It was a house with no context: there were houses around, but they were strangely unseeable, perhaps because Grandpa's house was left way back in time.

In front of Grandpa's house when I visited there was a sign that said "Beware: One Man Dog." (There was no dog.) Out back where the pear and apricot trees grew and the raspberries and boysenberries that had supported the family in the Depression— now untended and run amok—there were feral cats that might attack you and, of course, the squabs in their old stinking cages. Grandpa would say, "Let's have dinner," would grab a squab by the wings, chop off its head, throw it in a barrel where it would flutter around with blood spurting, and then throw it into boiling water for plucking.

I gather that as Grandpa grew older, long after his children were grown, he became something of a drinker. He'd watch TV all day, going to the refrigerator for sips of the beer that he kept there. This was in a house where, in the basement, there were "mystery fruits" in Mason jars, preserved by Jess—long dead by then—when Dad was a child. In later years three ten Donohoe Street had the bleakness of stasis and neglect, of an absence of future.

How Grandpa's love stayed so fresh in the stasis of his deteriorating house I do not know. But it did. It was there in his letters, like a flower, and it was there in person. His "grandkids" he called us. We "tickled him," he said. When we were both grown up, Jeanne's son Rick told me that Grandpa picked him and his brother Roy up at school every day and baby-sat for them whenever he was wanted. Often too, Roy and Rick would stay over at Grandpa's. Grandpa impressed Rick with his cursing. He slept on a bed that was a mattress lying on open springs, and when he snored Rick could hear the springs resonate. The house was filthy. But for Rick it was a place where he was loved. He described a scene that always brought back to him exactly what it was like to be there with Grandpa at 310 Donohoe Street. It's a picture of himself sitting on the dilapidated couch on a hot summer day looking out the door, watching and hearing the cars on the freeway that had been built at an angle across the neighborhood and hearing also the sound of the TV, "The Honeymooners" or Groucho Marx, and the creak of the springs in the couch. Looking at the cars on the freeway through the open door and hearing the creak of the couch.

After he started studying with Mrs. Belenky, Dad was taken up by two rich ladies in Palo Alto proper, Mrs. Slater and Mrs. Sessheimer, who were connected to San Francisco and to the international world of music. (Mrs. Sessheimer had launched Yehudi Menuhin.) They would have parties to which Dad, even when he was only eleven or twelve, would be invited and at which he would sometimes play. Mrs. Slater had a huge record collection, and an extraordinarily beautiful garden in which my father liked to sit. More and more Dad stayed at Mrs. Slater's and Mrs. Sessheimer's houses, and sometimes he stayed with Mrs. Belenky. He began performing publicly—first locally, in W.P.A. orchestras that had been formed for out-of-work musicians, and then all over the state. When he was home, he practiced non-stop.

After a while Mrs. Belenky saw that there was a further dimension of my father's gift which needed to be developed. She told him to walk in the fields around his house and see if any "musical thoughts" came to him. He objected that he didn't know how to do that but she insisted that he try, and told him that if he did have a "musical thought" he was to put it out of his mind until the next day, when he could go for another walk, recall his musical thought, and see if anything came to him to add to it. She forbade him to write his musical thoughts down or to try them out on the piano: he was to wait until he had a completed idea, and then he was to come to her and perform it. Only after that could he write it down. In this way, my father discovered a perfect, empyrean realm. As he put it later, he discovered how music could touch upon the mystery and beauty of creation. "That possibility has kept me fascinated all my life," he said. "Nothing else has ever come close. I could get out of myself with this thing that is in touch with that mystery and beauty. It's the only thing that interests me in another person too—how he reacts to that."

As time went by, Mrs. Belenky saw that Dad needed instruction in composition more expert than she could give, so she asked her friend Henry Cowell, a well-known composer, if he would do this. Cowell agreed, but on condition that the lessons take place with her present, in her house. They lasted only two months, however, because Henry Cowell was then arrested and sent to San Quentin for molesting young boys. Later, he was pardoned. In any event, though this is a striking incident in the context of subsequent history, both my father and Mrs. Belenky say that Henry Cowell did not molest my father in any way—that the lessons took place in a room with the door open; and indeed Mr. Cowell had insisted on this arrangement to make sure that nothing could go wrong.

By the time Henry Cowell was sent to San Quentin, my father had injured a nerve in his right arm by practicing too much. This closed off his future as a performer. With Cowell gone, Mrs. Belenky saw no recourse but to send her prodigy away from the fields of East Palo Alto, to study composition with the great teacher Nadia Boulanger in Paris. Grandpa sold a vacation shack the family had in the Santa Cruz Mountains for five hundred dollars. Then, when Igor Stravinsky visited San Francisco, Mrs. Belenky approached him on my father's behalf: with his support, she was able to raise the rest of the money my father needed. Off Dad went across the continent by train and then on, by sea, to Paris. He was sixteen.

*　　　*　　　*

In 1934, when Mama and the children returned to America from Germany, my mother was eleven. First she went to Turkey Lane, an impromptu school that Archie Roosevelt—Teddy's son—and his wife, Grace, had set up in Oyster Bay. At Turkey Lane nine girls of varying ages were instructed by an English tutor. Classes took place in a freezing room above a garage where the students sat on lion skins under stuffed moose heads and cobras that looked down from the walls. After Germany, English history from an English point of view made no sense to my mother at all. Two years later the tutor eloped with one of the students. My mother was thirteen by this time, however, and was sent to Noroton, a very small convent boarding school situated in a Queen Anne mansion on the coast of Connecticut and run by the Religious of the Sacred Heart, an order of nuns that had been founded to educate the daughters of aristo-crats in France. In this school she learned a deep court curtsy, useful for presentation to Louis Quatorze.

Papa was obsessed by my mother's beauty and talked at family lunches about whether she would marry an earl or a raja. A young man from St. James, who was some years her senior and was en-gaged to marry someone else, fell in love with her, causing a scandal both in St. James and at Noroton. Grandma White said, "You are a bad woman." My mother was devastated: the remark, she says, was "like an axe to my root." There was much that was good at Noroton, but by this time my mother was unable to absorb it. The school had broad ledges running under the windows on the third floor, and one night in a storm my mother climbed out of a third-floor bedroom window and crawled along the ledge to the window of the next room. The girls inside the room screamed on seeing her—her black hair long and streaming, and her white face looking in.

After Noroton, my mother wanted to study dance, but Mama abhorred ballet—she thought it ridiculous—so my mother studied drawing in New York instead, going to art school in the morning and sketching dancers at a ballet school in the afternoon. After a year she complained of eyestrain, and Mama said, "Oh well, then you might as well switch to music," and sent her to her brother Teddy. This was in 1942.

Theodore Chanler was a lovable man, a funny man, and a brilliant composer who was regarded by many, including Nadia Boulanger, Aaron Copland, and Virgil Thomson, as a future bright light of American music. He was also a tortured man who could not accept his homosexuality, and an alcoholic. His wife, Maria, had lesbian tendencies: their household was a teetering mixture of art, religion, drink, and confusing sexual vibrations. My mother says that she and Teddy had a lot of fun. "When we were alone doing music together it was like being up in the tree house, though there was something sexual, too—a lot of giggling." When they were together Maria was apt to start bouncing a ball around the piano, getting the dog to run after it, or else she might send Teddy out on a two-hour errand. Maria spent a great deal of time in bed. When she had sent Teddy out, she would invite my mother into her bedroom where she lay in state, dressed in a black negligee and drinking whiskey-on-the-rocks. She would talk to my mother till Teddy came back, gesticulating with the drink in her hand, rattling the ice, raising off-color topics.

One summer morning in that same year, my mother was out at Box Hill for a visit and decided to go to seven-thirty Mass. She got into the family station wagon and headed down the Rhododendron Drive, where she "mixed up the brake and the accelerator. I thought I was pushing on the brake," she explained, "but the car kept going faster and faster. I couldn't understand anything. So I gave up and the car smashed into a tree."

Three days later, while she was lying in a darkened room, recovering from a concussion, Teddy called and told Mama that Nadia Boulanger was teaching at a summer school in Dubuque, Iowa, and my mother *had* to go. He would pay for it, he said. Mama said, "She can't go, she's had a concussion," but Teddy said it didn't matter, she had to go and he would pay for it. And so my mother took the train to Dubuque. For weeks Nadia Boulanger was inaccessible, but as soon as my mother got there she met my father, who had travelled from Paris with Nadia. "He was my daily companion," my mother said. "We talked and talked and talked. I remember sitting on some children's swings talking. We fell in love. We were lost people. I remember vividly having the picture in my mind of us gravitating toward each other like lost people floating in the ocean."

ROKEBY

WHEN I WAS a little girl, my grandmother was in her vigorous sixties. Zipping around in her black-and-white Thunderbird with her long shins and narrow feet, she was my model for engagement with the world. When I went places with Mama, I felt as if we were really going places: it's only now that I see that we were flying around in her cage. I felt safe with Mama, flying around in her cage.

She got her cars at Glamore's Ford, in Smithtown, trading in the old one for a new one every two years. Mama believed in Glamore's and the Ford Motor Company and wore an ''I Like Ike'' button, while her children drove beat-up foreign cars and voted for Adlai Stevenson. Mama couldn't resist Ike, because he was a general. She liked war. She remembered how as a girl she had relished postcards of Havana Harbor with a little fuse in back that you could light to blow up the *Maine*. In 1917, when she was twenty-nine, she had rushed down to Washington, with her sister Hester, to hear the Senate declare war. When she was in her eighties and the world was in the grip of the nuclear predicament, she would puzzle over her young self's warlike propensities as she lay in bed in the morning. But I don't believe she had really changed. In that same period, she had a South Vietnamese general weeding her garden, and when he didn't recognize her Western herbs and pulled them up she said that he couldn't have been a very good general and fired him. Mama liked victory.

Mama believed in supper for children at six, with a menu such as peas, mashed potatoes, roast chicken, a glass of milk, and pudding with a cookie. In the Red Cottage we had bohemian food, like pasta, or lentils, or herring. Once, when Mama came over to the Red Cottage on a summer evening and saw no signs of a supper of any kind being prepared, she asked us children lolling in the long grass what was going on, and my sister Madeleine said, "We're just drifting in boats." Mama told the drifting-in-boats story again and again, gasping with surprise. How could she have been surprised? Once, all the clocks in the Red Cottage had broken and my mother said she liked it that way and wasn't going to get them fixed or get a new clock, and Mama said, "If you will not accept a clock from me I shall blow up your house."

For Mama, there were people who were important and people who weren't. She referred to the friends of one of her daughters as "odd job lots of people," for example. Chanlers—her family on her father's side—were important, certainly. Above all Mama's mother, Daisy, and her father, Winthrop Chanler, were important; in comparison with them Mama was shadowy as was her whole life. When John Lindsay was elected mayor of New York Mama said, "It's nice to have a white man in politics." (Lindsay's predecessors were Vincent Impelliteri and Robert Wagner.) When Mama was old she grew roses, and once she drove by an old man tending a beautiful rose garden in the working-class part of the village, and she almost stopped, but she didn't, and then thought about it for weeks afterward. She thought about driving over and knocking on his door and talking about roses, but she couldn't do it. In a way, Mama's racism and snobbery were a highly restricting form of shyness. I'm not sure why, but Mama thought that I was important. Grandma White too had thought that I was important—but as a little girl, the way the apples from her old apple tree were important as apples. Mama would remark on my red hair (a latent reference to Stanford), or on how I had a naturally good seat on a horse. With her, there were expectations of outstanding performance connected to being important.

The important Chanlers were Mama's eight aunts and uncles, her father Winthrop's brothers and sisters, who had been famous for eccentricity and escapades. Mama's aunts and uncles were connected to the idea of money in the family, but the real Chanler legacy was stories. Some Chanler stories were short; Uncle Willie's way of communicating with an inattentive waiter at Delmonico's: he took off his wooden leg and threw it at him, catching him squarely between the shoulder blades. Some Chanler stories were long but could be reduced to an image or a phrase; "French leave," which ordinarily is a term for the covert departure a lover makes on hearing the tread of his paramour's spouse on the stairs, in the family was a reference to the manner in which Uncle Archie escaped from the lunatic asylum. Another story was that when Uncle Bob Chanler married the famous opera singer Lina Cavalieri, in Paris, and signed over his fortune to her, Uncle Archie cabled him, "Who's loony now?" This phrase entered the language overnight. Comedians, columnists, and preachers snapped it up, and it inspired a comic strip of that name. Even today "Who's loony now?" surfaces from time to time, in a headline or in jocular repartee, its origins long forgotten. Archie's quip is the most famous of the Chanler achievements.

The Chanlers, not Stanford, were our myth. We were Chanlers, so it was always surprising when people identified us as "the Stanford White family," thereby showing that they had no idea who we were. The Chanler stories were light and, above all, funny, yet there was an urgency in the way the crazy things the Chanlers had done were recounted. It was as if somewhere inside these stories—which were for the most part little more than snatches, vignettes, and splinters—there was the flash of a grail-like truth. Something about our family that we needed to know.

Though Mama herself was not throwing wooden legs or taking leave of asylums, it was through her that we were Chanlers. This was a confusing thing about Mama. Her good wool suits and her pearls and the way she had her hair done regularly—in contrast to the bohemian style of the other women on the Place—somehow coexisted with the Chanleresque attitude that the purpose of life was to generate outrageous stories. None of us ever got used to it. When one of my sisters grew up and was arrested for shoplifting in Italy and had to escape through the Alps on a flatcar—with no coat and only a small basket of possessions—she cringed to think of her respectable grandmother's reaction. But when Mama found out she said, "You're the only one around here who's having any fun," and wrote her a big check. Mama's handbag was tidy, and the money in her wallet seemed a natural extension of the tidiness there, but mostly she wrote checks. Her handwriting was freewheeling but steady, like clouds being blown fast while keeping their banked formation.

Only two of the original Chanlers were alive in my time, Aunt Alida and Aunt Margaret. Aunt Alida, whose married name was Emmet, lived in a big house on Stony Brook Harbor that we visited often. (Alida Chanler and Ella Smith married brothers, Temple and Devereux Emmet, which is how Aunt Alida ended up on Stony Brook Harbor.) She had a great Empress's head with a Roman nose, strong high cheekbones, one regally direct eye, and another that was crossed, so that her gaze clashed like swords. She was domineering yet absent-minded. "Psyche Sleeps" was the title she gave to a book of sonnets she wrote. She wore enormous rings on her fingers, and full-length gowns in which she served high tea. Aunt Alida's teas were splendid. They included several kinds of cake, and tiny scones split and drenched in melted butter, and, of course, there was Aunt Alida herself, breathing hard, her massive visage with its clashing gaze concentrated to frowning behind the looming silver service.

With my cousins Ben and Sam—Uncle Peter's sons—I often played cards with Aunt Alida, old-fashioned games, like euchre and casino. She would teach us these games, and then—once again, concentrated to a frown and breathing hard—cheat, and consequently always win. After she became partly bedridden the card table would be set up in her bedroom, and we learned to maneuver her into the chair with its back to a mirror so that we could see her cards and beat her at her own game.

Aunt Alida was a Catholic convert. Enormous wooden rosary beads hung on the wall at the head of her canopied bed and she had a penchant for dousing people and objects with holy water which she kept in plentiful supply. One story had it that Uncle Archie once visited her in a bright-red car, with an enormous black manservant and chauffeur. As Archie had been reported in the newspapers to have had conversations with a Confederate officer in Hell who had described Satan favorably, Aunt Alida therefore concluded from the color of Archie's car that his manservant was the Devil and drenched him as well as the car in holy water, hoping that he would flee. The manservant was unperturbed, however. Aunt Alida knew that her brother was superstitious; her next strategy was to frighten him. She had two enormous gilt-framed portraits that hung in her front hall rigged so that they crashed down, spontaneously, it seemed. Archie, with car and manservant, left instantly.

At tea, a few of Aunt Alida's eight aging children were usually around: Willie Emmet, six feet eight and skinny as a beanpole, peering at us through a crack in the door; his sister Marga, broad-shouldered and big bosomed, with silver-white hair swept back, declaiming in a breathy passionate way, but deaf, and so unable to participate in an exchange; Jane, with a rag-doll figure but bolt upright in her chair, silent and staring outward under iron-gray bangs. The Emmets were abstracted and quixotic, with theatrical voices that could suddenly develop a melodramatic quaver or go into a theatrical crescendo in an archaic upper-class accent mixed with a German "r" that they had acquired from a series of Fräuleins that Aunt Alida had hired as governesses. One afternoon, in the Red Cottage garden, Willie Emmet was having tea with my mother under the apple tree. He was sitting on a kitchen chair and he was talking non-stop. As he talked he began to lean over to one side, lowering his head, lower and lower, always talking, with my mother listening, until his head rested upside down on the ground: he continued talking even then.

The Chanler stories surged around in family life like a flock of birds, creating an atmosphere of whimsicality within which what was disturbing about certain incidents in the family—Johnny with a gun, for instance—was lost. Also lost was the fact that the Chanlers were orphans and this despite the fact that they were famous for being orphans—they were known to the world as the Astor Orphans. This was because they were the great-great-grandchildren of John Jacob Astor, but of both the Astor connection and the orphaning I heard not a whisper in the library at Box Hill.

What I did hear of was Rokeby—the house in the Hudson River Valley in which the Chanlers had grown up. The way Mama said "Rokeby" was full of longing, almost brokenhearted, and projected a cradling kind of place deep in the world. The word Rokeby conveyed a promise of deep connectedness and peace: of coming to rest in family love. No other word in the family vocabulary conveyed such a feeling of homing.

Rokeby was serious, but Aunt Alida's sister Margaret, who presided at Rokeby in my time, was, like all Chanlers, funny. Many of the stories about Aunt Margaret had to do with her intolerance. She was intolerant of divorce, which she called "plural marriage," and of trousers on women, which she called "the divided pedestal," and of alcohol, which was banned at Rokeby in her time. Divorced people were not allowed in Rokeby either, even though that category came to include several of her brothers; nor were Catholics, and that meant her sister Alida. Mama's mother (Daisy Terry Chanler) had, like Aunt Alida, converted to Catholicism, and we, her Catholic descendants, were banned from Rokeby too. Mama was born at Rokeby when it still belonged collectively to the then youthful Chanlers. Aunt Margaret, who was sixteen at the time, spent hours adoring Mama in her crib. But when at two or three weeks of age Mama was baptized Catholic, Aunt Margaret declared that it would have been better if she had been murdered.

When Aunt Margaret became the proprietress of Rokeby, however, she allowed Mama, and only Mama of our clan, to visit, on the ground that Mama had been born there. This is typical of Aunt Margaret's reasoning, in which Rokeby itself becomes a kind of power overruling some of the rules that she herself has made. When I was seven Mama decided to take me to Rokeby: I, who was not born in the house, would be swept through the gates on the swoosh of Mama's exemption.

Mama drove from Long Island to Rokeby as if she were riding a steed through an exotic countryside, soaring over hedges and streams. Once we were on the mainland, she pointed out rock faces rising beside the highway and said, "Look at that. You'll never see anything like that on Long Island." There was another component of her mood, something I recognized later as an adult when she talked about Rokeby—a sense of shyness lifting, of going to the place where she could be herself. We zoomed up a drive to a house that was big and white and hard to read architecturally. It rode the crest of a hill like an unwieldy ferry. Then we got out of the car and everything was very still. Aunt Margaret came out. She was small and wore a long dress, and had a nut-brown look about her. She was not effusive at all, but she was welcoming and kind. She told me about the big cacti that stood in front of the house in pots. They were called century plants, she said, because they bloomed only once in a century. They had bloomed only a few years ago, and so we figured out that I would be a very old lady or quite possibly dead when they bloomed again.

*   *   *

There were originally eleven Chanlers, from Archie to Egerton, but a daughter died in infancy, leaving ten. Their parents were John Winthrop Chanler and Margaret Astor Ward, a great-grandchild of John Jacob Astor. Margaret inherited Rokeby from her grandfather, William Waldorf Astor, John Jacob's son. But she never lived in it, for she died within the year. The children, in turn, inherited it from her, and moved in with their father immediately after her death. Within the year, their father too had died, leaving the ten children—Archie, Wintie, Elizabeth, Willie, Marion, Lewis, Margaret, Bob, Alida, and Egerton—ages thirteen to one. A board of trustees, mostly elderly Astor relatives, discharged their duties to the children from afar, largely by surveying the household accounts.

The Chanlers, from start to finish, lent themselves to storytelling, but somehow the heart of their story—the catastrophic nature of these successive deaths—was lost in the fanfare of minor myths and tales that arose around them. Even Lately Thomas, an established biographer who took the Chanlers on as a subject in his book *A Pride of Lions,* does not seem to register the catastrophe. His book is dedicated to ''Fantasy,'' a strange choice for a biographer under any circumstances, and it is typical of his approach that the chapter that ends with the death of the children's mother is followed by one that opens with a list of the social luminaries who attended her funeral. As for the Chanlers themselves, it would seem that in the face of these disasters they resorted to stoicism. The only expression of grief that I have found is an indirect one in Aunt Margaret's memoir in a section that has to do with animals at Rokeby:

Unlike horses, oxen are not credited with affection for humans. Nevertheless, one of them fancied my father. He would move to the farmyard gate on a Sunday as soon as we were in sight. The night before Winthrop Chanler died this ox managed to get out of the barn, moved up to the mansion, stood under my father's window and lowed pitifully. I saw and heard him, for my window was next to my father's.

Rokeby was a children's republic. Bob's goats were in and out of the house unsupervised, and a herd of dogs accompanied the children everywhere. "Chanlers always sat up with a sick dog," Aunt Margaret wrote many years later in a memoir. Mary Marshall, an impoverished relative from the South who was not a strong authority, was the only non-paid, parental presence. A tutor, Bostwick, was sunk in deep silence much of the time (Bob was discovered at nine trying to read a book upside down); sometimes there were additional instructors, a piano teacher, a French teacher. And there were a number of servants, most of whom came directly from feudal Ireland and regarded the children with deference, inculcating in them a sense of their own importance that was wildly out of scale with the society in which they were to live their adult lives. On Sundays, the servants' day off, nothing was done for the children in the normal way, although the boys did spend time outside the servants' wing conducting dogfights, which the servants considered a blood sport suitable for young gentlemen, and therefore encouraged over the objections of Mary Marshall. She could not intervene, because her authority did not extend to that wing.

Dogfights were not always intentional. Bob ended a particularly vicious one between two of the dogs, Spot and Jody, in the drawing room, by biting Jody's tail. Fights were not always between dogs either. Aunt Margaret later wrote in her memoir:

> Challenges were flung to you, awake or asleep. Words poured out of you in defense. Very early the rule was established that there was to be no striking during quarrels. "Take it out in words" hurt nobody. I have seen a frenzied boy whirling around his head the long green baize contraption filled with shot, used to keep draughts off the floor. The rule was "no striking."

The children devised games "gentle and violent," according to Aunt Margaret—one "a gruesome witch game." Another that she recalled took place in the dim hall, and was called "still pond; no moving!" Second sight abounded at Rokeby. Old Jane, a black nurse of whom it was later said that she was the only one who could handle the Chanler boys, had second sight, and after she died she became a ghost that could be heard sweeping the floor in the tower room where she had expired. Another nurse, Mrs. Meroney, was regularly in communication with her dead brother.

Irish wakes were held in the house frequently: in addition to the Rokeby servants there were several tenant-farming families on the Chanlers' four hundred acres, and then there were the men who ran the Rokeby farm proper. In her memoir Aunt Margaret wrote of the wake of a boy who had been murdered in one of the tenant farmers' cottages. It was winter and there was deep snow on the ground; she remembered watching from the window as the boy's coffin was carried away on a sleigh over the hills. Two Chanler children died as well in the Rokeby period: Egerton, the youngest, of a brain tumor when he was three, and Marion of pneumonia when he was four-teen. Lewis was the closest in age to Marion and after Marion's death he nearly died himself of peritonitis. Similarly Alida, who was closest to Egerton, nearly died after his death, but in this instance no cause was recorded. "Were we all to die?" Margaret wrote. Before most of the children were grown, Mary Marshall, at fifty, was dead too.

And so the enduring parental figure in the children's lives was the house itself. In her memoir Aunt Margaret wrote of Rokeby, "The place from the beginning has been beloved by those who owned it— by those who might have owned it—and by many who have been only occasional guests. [It inspires] immoderate affection. I myself am capable of praying that he who comes to hold the place without love may be unhappy in his life and death."

*   *   *

On reaching their majority, each of the Chanler children came into two hundred and fifty thousand dollars (equivalent to roughly ten million dollars today). Archie, as the oldest, was expected to become the master of Rokeby and was left an extra hundred thousand for the upkeep of the house and land. The girls were left an extra fifty thousand each in case they didn't marry. Archie was also appointed executor of the will upon reaching twenty-one, and guardian of the children. He declined these roles, however, deeply disappointing his brothers and sisters, who saw in his abdication a violation of their father's sacred wish.

When the Chanler girls emerged from Rokeby to enter society, the Astor aunts found them in need of remedial polishing. As for the boys, Bostwick, their tutor, later said that hog farming was the only occupation he was equipped for after coping with them. (Indeed, he became a hog farmer.) And yet the Chanlers also had an extreme polish overlaid on the barbarity that Rokeby life engendered. Possibly they had acquired a backward-looking tendency as they yearned for their parents; others have speculated that the feudal values of the caretaker-servants influenced them in this way. In any event they all had qualities of formality and courtliness, of eighteenth-century grace and quixotic high-mindedness, qualities that made them seem old-fashioned in their own time and not quite of this world.

Sometime in the late eighties, Archie, then in his mid-twenties and moving in New York society, met Stanford White. They became good friends, with Archie looking up to Stanford, who was ten years older. Stanford was invited to Rokeby and was soon friendly with all the young Chanlers. These lovable, wounded socialites with big personalities and a tendency to do as they pleased were perfect for him. He took them all under his wing.

Much was needed at Rokeby, but one of the most obvious needs was for someone to do something about the house itself. There was no central heating. In winter, water in glasses at bedsides would be frozen in the morning. The plumbing consisted of a privy just east of the house, albeit a large privy, with a mansard roof and two sections—one trimmed with pine for the servants, and one trimmed with walnut for the quality folk. Stanford had a basement blasted out underneath the dining room, and put in a furnace, and upstairs he put in bathrooms. He rectified mistakes in taste that the Astors had made, such as replacing wooden mantels of a simple, classical design with fancy Italianate ones of marble (Judge Smith made the same mistake). He tried to make Rokeby efficient by creating a curious confluence of two interfacing second-floor landings—one in the servants' wing and one in the main house—which he connected by a door, so that servants would be able to have access to the family bedrooms without using the main staircase. He put in a number of other doors where they were needed, and changed many of the first-floor windows to French doors. He also combined two of four drawing rooms into one large one, and covered the walls with a silvery-green patterned silk and the floor with a green carpet to bring the lawn through the French doors and into the room, he said.

All eight of the surviving Chanlers came to accept Stanford as a fixture in their lives. Each of them was in frequent correspondence with him and was involved with him in one way or another, enjoying his willingness to arrange trips and theatre tickets and parties for them, to acquire desired objects and dispense advice and information and even, when necessary, advance cash and not complain when the reimbursement was slow. When the three girls decided that they would like a house in New York, it was Stanford who found them one they could afford. He went on to renovate and decorate it, taking into account the needs of each. He also continued to keep an eye on Rokeby, of which the three girls had become the sole proprietors through an arrangement made by their brothers. The Chanler boys assumed that their sisters, because of various defects (Alida's crossed eye, a hip disease of Elizabeth's, and Margaret's supposed plainness), would never marry.

To the Chanlers it was a matter of the utmost seriousness that they distinguish themselves, to honor their parents and to solidify their identity as a family, though how exactly this was to be done was unclear. Archie went to Columbia Law School, graduated, and was admitted to the New York bar in 1885. Instead of practicing law, however, he decided to become an opera singer. Margaret later developed this ambition as well, but Archie, who had by then abandoned singing to stalk the Apache chief Geronimo out West, discouraged her from pursuing it for reasons that are not recorded. In the summer of 1884 Archie and Wintie, the brother nearest him in age (later to become Mama's father), decided to make a grand tour of Europe, a way of life that as a gentleman of leisure Wintie would adopt permanently. In Rome Archie fell in love with Daisy Terry, who was a first cousin once removed: Daisy's parents were expatriates and she had been born and raised there. But it was Wintie who got Daisy; they married in December of 1886. Archie seems not to have been put out by this, for the summer after he had met Daisy in Rome he met, at Newport, Amelie Rives.

Amelie Rives was an exquisitely beautiful, highborn novelist from Virginia: one of her later novels was called "Virginia of Virginia." She had purple eyes, wrote dramatic, perfumed letters in an extravagant script in purple ink, and exercised an irresistible charm. Archie became a frequent guest at the Rives estate at Castle Hill, in Virginia's Albemarle County, near Charlottesville. Then, in April of 1888, Amelie published a novel called "The Quick or the Dead?" The plot of "The Quick or the Dead?" revolves around a beautiful young heroine whose dead husband comes to her as a ghost, while she falls in love with his cousin, who looks exactly like him. Tension arises from the heroine's struggle to choose between the living lover or the ghost. The novel created a scandal because of the orgiastic feelings that the heroine entertains for both men. (In the end she chooses the quick.) "The Quick or the Dead?" became a best-seller and Amelie became a celebrity, as did Archie, who was widely and publicly identified as the model for the identical men. This was the beginning of newspaper publicity about the Chanlers that was to disturb their socially august Astor relatives and also, in later years, perhaps to inure Mama to embarrassing exposure in the press.

Mama was born to Wintie and Daisy at Rokeby in the year before "The Quick or the Dead?" came out. At that time no one was inured.

Archie's mass popularity as the hero of a sex novel neither pleased the Astors nor fulfilled his brothers and sisters' fantasies of distinction. Wintie and Margaret were especially appalled. But then they all met Amelie and, one after another, they found that they could not but love her, and declare her brilliant. For a time, Aunt Margaret became Amelie's intimate friend and steadfast champion, a bewildering alliance given Margaret's principled puritanism, though no more bewildering perhaps than her fast friendship with Stanford White. On entering the Chanler circle, Amelie inevitably found that Stanford White was in her life as well.

Then, in June, Archie and Amelie married without notifying the family, thus devastating and infuriating them all over again. But the newlyweds visited Rokeby, and again thanks to Amelie's charm all was forgiven. After the visit, Archie took Amelie on an extended and elaborate honeymoon tour of England and Europe, very possibly paying for it out of the extra hundred thousand dollars that had been bequeathed him for the upkeep of Rokeby. The tour went well. Thomas Hardy, Henry James, and Henry Adams all fell at Amelie's feet and declared her a genius. The newlyweds returned separately, however, although they did subsequently live together at Merry Mills, an estate not far from Castle Hill that Archie had acquired. There Amelie began accusing Archie of frightening mood changes and, in letters to Rokeby, hinted at violence. There were separations and reconciliations, all highly publicized. Then, in a period in which they were together, Amelie stopped writing and instead took to her bed or, alternately, ran around in the Merry Mills woods at night in a filmy white robe. One night, she was nearly shot by a servant who took her for a ghost. It emerged that Amelie was a morphine addict. Finally, in 1894, she and Archie went to a ball in London at which Prince Troubetzkoy of Poland was present. Archie lightly told Amelie she ought to marry the Prince because he was so handsome and they would make such a handsome couple, and Amelie divorced Archie and did. All this too was well publicized.

Archie rebounded from the Amelie debacle by going into business with Wintie and Stanford. The three formed the Roanoke Rapids Power Company and also the United Industrial Company, an affiliate that would make textiles. The enterprise required not just a mill and a power plant but a whole town for the workers: it involved building Roanoke Rapids, North Carolina, from scratch. Besides investing in the company, Stanford designed everything, including housing. His two "turtletop" houses are regarded as landmarks today and are among the very few of Stanford's ventures into architecture for working-class people. The houses were fine, and the mill and the plant were handsome, but Stanford knew nothing about making textiles or generating power, so both mill and plant turned out to be useless. Rebuilding them drove costs way over budget. Pressure mounted. Archie and Wintie began to fight.

The Chanler boys had always roared at each other; indeed they rather missed their argumentative encounters when they were apart because nobody else was willing to "debate" in the same zestfully violent way. Wintie's wife, Daisy, was horrified by the decibel level at Rokeby, although she did concede in their favor that the battles were over such matters as questions of social precedence or a fine theological point. Bob's first wife, Julia Chamberlain, refused to return to Rokeby after witnessing what Bob called a mere "discussion" because she had felt that murder was about to take place. And indeed, at least once in a Rokeby discussion, knives flew. Nevertheless, the fights between Wintie and Archie at board meetings of the Roanoke Rapids Power Company, though purely verbal, seem to have been different from the start. For one thing, they went on and on, meeting after meeting, throughout 1896—with Stanford smack in the middle—in a way that made it difficult to conduct any business whatever.

In September of that year, Alida surprised everyone by becoming engaged to marry Temple Emmet, a young man from a distinguished Irish family of which Robert Emmet, a hero of the cause of Irish freedom, had been a member. The wedding took place at the end of October. It was Stanford, of course, who managed it all, who arranged for the train that would bring the two hundred guests from New York City to Rokeby, for the fashionable Hungarian orchestra, for the strolling Neapolitan minstrels, and for the tapestries to be hung from the front of the house. Grandma White had become a friend of the Chanlers and was there too. This was the first Chanler wedding at Rokeby, and Archie, as the oldest, representing their father, was to give Alida away. At the last minute, however, Archie sent a message that he didn't feel well. He also sent a gift, but this was far from enough for his brothers and sisters. They were devastated by this latest abdication. In their view Archie should have been there even if he was at death's door—as a good father would have been. Alida concluded that Archie's absence could only mean that he was dying and she cried for hours. Wintie and Bob, on the other hand, concluded that Archie was "loony," a term that got back to Archie. It was Wintie who gave the weeping bride away.

At the next meeting of the Roanoke Rapids Power Company, Archie and Wintie almost came to blows. The upshot was that Archie threatened to have Wintie's performance as executor of their father's estate audited. Wintie then declared that he would no longer speak to Archie. Archie then demanded that Wintie resign from the company board, on the ground that it was impossible to do business with someone who wouldn't speak to him. Wintie complied with alacrity, leaving the realm of free enterprise forever, to live insouciantly beyond his means as a gentleman of leisure, travelling, shooting this and that, and falling off horses and breaking this and that to the point where eventually the only company that would insure his bones was Lloyd's of London.

After Wintie's resignation, Archie had himself elected president of the company, but actually he had been losing interest in business concerns. For some time, he had been wanting to investigate what we would call parapsychological phenomena. Stanford offered to look after the business for him, and Archie gave him his power of attorney and retreated to Merry Mills to develop what he called his X faculty. Archie's X faculty sent messages to him in Ouija-board style through a planchette; it sent a reliable stock-market tip, but it also told him, erroneously, as it turned out, that he could pick up live coals without being burned.

Then Elizabeth defied expectations too, and on April 24, 1898, married John Jay Chapman, a pundit, opinionist, and literary man known alternately as the greatest master of expository prose in America and as the inspiration for Theodore Roosevelt's phrase "lunatic fringe." After Elizabeth's wedding, Margaret announced that she did not intend to marry, and convinced Alida and Elizabeth that they should therefore give her their shares in Rokeby. The unfairness of this so disturbed Chapman that he had a nervous breakdown that prevented him from leaving his bed in the tower for a year. There he was nursed by both Margaret and Elizabeth. During his illness he became convinced that he was blind, and those caring for him perpetuated his delusion by blacking out the windows because they were afraid that he would be traumatically upset if he found out that he actually could see. Margaret kept Rokeby, however.

Archie's X faculty had, in this period, told him that he could change the color of his eyes if he stood looking west out a window at a specified time, holding a pearl stickpin in one hand and looking deeply into a mirror he held in the other. Archie reported that he had followed these instructions—he was serious about his experiments and informed the press of developments—and that as a result his eyes had turned from light brown to gray. This alarmed the Astors. Amelie Rives Troubetzkoy backed Archie up by stating that when she was married to him his eyes, like those of both her heroes in "The Quick or the Dead?," had been "a sparkling, light-brown hue." Oculists, for their part, testified that they were now gray.

Wintie, who was still not speaking to Archie and therefore could not investigate the matter for himself, induced Stanford to take a trip to Merry Mills and lure Archie back to New York. So Stanford wrote to Archie saying that he would like to visit, but Archie wrote back saying that he was "ill" and did not want to be visited. Stanford went anyway, taking with him a Dr. Fuller. Archie was intensely annoyed when they arrived, but Stanford pushed right in. He proceeded to chat with Archie and try to charm him, to warm him up. He eventually succeeded, and then worked on him to come up to New York on the ground that what he needed was a plunge into "the metropolitan whirl." Archie went, speaking freely by this time about his experiments with his X faculty.

In New York, Archie checked into the Kennsington Hotel where his X faculty told him that sometime soon he should go into a "Napoleonic trance," in the course of which he would reënact the death of Napoleon. Soon thereafter, during a visit from Augustus Saint-Gaudens, Archie realized that the time had arrived. He stretched out on his bed and looked at his reflection in his shaving mirror, gasped for breath convulsively for ten minutes, and then put the mirror down and closed his eyes. The trance, in which he began to look like Napoleon, took hold. Saint-Gaudens was terrified. When Archie came out of his trance, Gus begged him never to do it again.

The next day Stanford came to visit with Dr. Fuller and asked Archie to go into the trance for them. Archie complied, and in the middle of it he heard Stanford whisper, "It *is* exactly like Napoleon's death mask! I have a photograph of it at home." Archie also invited reporters to come to his hotel room and observe his trance. He told them emphatically that he did not believe he *was* Napoleon but that the trance and the X faculty were a manifestation of a power within himself.

Next there was another visit by Dr. Fuller, who came with a man who said he was an oculist and examined Archie's eyes and asked him lots of questions. On the following day, the alleged oculist showed up with two burly attendants and informed Archie that in fact he was Dr. Moses Allen Starr, professor of nervous diseases at the College of Physicians and Surgeons, president of the New York Neurological Society and of the American Neurological Association, and Medical Examiner in lunacy. Dr. Starr said that he had a court order for Archie's commitment on the ground of insanity. Archie's X faculty, however, had warned him that danger was imminent, and in preparation he had hidden a loaded revolver under his pillow.

Dr. Starr left without Archie that day, but the next day two armed policemen came with a warrant for Archie's arrest as a dangerous lunatic with homicidal tendencies. Archie was clapped into Bloomingdale, the New York Hospital asylum for the insane, in White Plains. "I am insane because I say that my eyes have changed color," Archie wrote to an attorney in Virginia in an attempt to get released. The commitment order was signed by his brothers Lewis and Wintie.

Archie believed that his brothers and sisters were having him incarcerated because they wanted his money. The Chanlers were many things, but they were not venal. Indeed, Elizabeth concluded that Archie was insane precisely because of this belief. Still, it's possible that his brothers and sisters were angry at him for squandering the money left for the upkeep of Rokeby. Certainly some of them were still bitterly disappointed by his refusal to be head of the family. Furthermore, while subsequent generations celebrated the Chanlers for their craziness, they themselves were touchy about the idea of tainted genes. Their father had had a sister who was kept in the attic, and the Astors consequently worried that the Chanlers might disgrace them. Archie also believed that the director of the asylum, Dr. Lyon, kept him there only for the five thousand dollars a year that he brought in. In this Archie may have had a point. He mentioned the five thousand dollars to Lyon often, and when he read in the newspaper that a parrot had halted a robbery by shrieking "Stop, thief!" he pressed Lyon to obtain the bird for him.

Wintie and Lewis urged Stanford to use Archie's power of attorney to petition the court to declare Archie insane and thus deprive him of access to his money, which he was using in legal maneuvers to free himself. Stanford did petition the court successfully, though he had been unsuccessful in an attempt to have the hearing in White Plains, so that Archie could attend, "if necessary on a stretcher."

Stanford was caught in the middle again. The upshot of the hearing was that Archie was certified as insane in New York and thereby prevented from using his own money. Archie's contempt for his caretakers was not without foundation. One of the doctors who testified at his hearing later claimed that he could identify a paranoid by sight alone, from a distance of seven feet, by the shape of his head.

Cut off from his funds, Archie decided that God had placed him in his predicament so that he would champion the rights of the insane, a cause for which he considered himself particularly well suited because of a temperament that enabled him "to stay angry for life." He started to work on a tract, "Four Years Behind the Bars of 'Bloomingdale'; or, The Bankruptcy of Law in New York." He also began producing large numbers of sonnets, denunciatory in tone. Archie strove to emphasize that the sonnets were by his X faculty, pointing out that while he had never before been able to write a line of poetry, he was now producing sonnets by the hundred. (This did indeed baffle the doctors though it needn't have; sonneteering was a Chanler characteristic. Both Aunt Margaret and Aunt Alida published volumes of sonnets. Margaret wrote in her memoir, "I can rest at a moment's notice. I can write a sonnet in twenty minutes. I am often dreadfully disappointed when this chosen delight is over quickly, and I see that pondering is not going to improve the lines.")

Eventually, having conducted himself as a model patient, Archie earned the privilege of taking walks outside Bloomingdale's grounds on his word of honor as a gentleman that he would not abuse the privilege. One day, after his last legal recourse had failed, he borrowed ten dollars, sauntered through the gate of the asylum, and walked to the railroad station. Behind him he left a perfect note for Dr. Lyon.

My Dear Doctor:
    You have always said that I am insane. You have always said that I believe I am the reincarnation of Napoleon Bonaparte.

As a learned and sincere man, you, therefore, will not be surprised that I take French Leave.

Yours, with regret that we must part,

J. A. Chanler

"He pledged his word as a gentleman that he would not escape!" wailed Dr. Lyon.

At the station Archie caught a train to New York and travelled right on through to Philadelphia, where he visited Dr. J. Madison Taylor, an eminent neurologist. Using a pseudonym, he had telegraphed Taylor from Grand Central Station: in person he revealed his identity and persuaded the doctor to harbor him incognito for whatever length of time he needed to arrive at an opinion on his sanity. After nine months, Dr. Taylor told Archie that in his opinion he was quite sane, whereupon Archie suddenly surfaced in Virginia to sensational coverage in the press. He was safe in Virginia, because the court that had declared him insane had jurisdiction only in New York. Eventually, a citizen petitioned the Albemarle County court to rule on Archie's sanity in Virginia, an opportunity that Archie welcomed. Through attorneys, Lewis petitioned Archie to delay the proceedings so that Wintie could return from Europe, and Willie from Mexico, where he was adventuring. Archie gladly did this, looking forward with joy to a reconciliation with his family and firing off telegrams to all, declaring it time to let bygones be bygones.

When the great day came, Dr. Taylor and other eminences testified to Archie's sanity. His witnesses included officials of the Roanoke Rapids Power Company. Among the letters from experts writing in Archie's behalf was a strong statement from the philosopher William James extolling Archie's interest in the unexplored field of automatism.

On November 6, 1901, almost without contest, Archie was declared sane in Virginia. All of this was reported in the newspapers, with Archie identified in most of the stories as "the former husband of Amelie Rives." And so he became known as the man who was insane in New York and sane in Virginia. Endless quips about this peculiar status would follow him all his life and beyond, right into the Box Hill library, where I would hear about my great-uncle Archie, insane in New York and sane in Virginia—a splinter of a story with no context. Certainly no mention was made in the library that Archie's brothers and sisters failed to show up at the Albemarle County hearing.

Archie was so wounded by the failure of his brothers and sisters to attend that he changed his name to Chaloner—what the name Chanler had been originally—and began referring to his "ex-brothers and sisters." Their continued hostility to him was further made plain when, immediately after the Virginia verdict, he instituted proceedings to regain his rights in New York where most of his wealth was located. Again his brothers and sisters obstructed his efforts, as they would until 1919, when he finally prevailed.

Archie continued to write, channelling "his surging energies through the typewriter," as a Virginian friend put it in a memoir. He published the results with a new company that he had set up, the Palmetto Press of Roanoke Rapids, South Carolina. His works include a play called "Robbery Under the Law," in which Wintie had become a character called Winston Blettermole and Stanford White had become James Lawless. He completed "Four Years Behind the Bars of 'Bloomingdale'; or, The Bankruptcy of Law in New York," which included verse as well as prose. "Scorpio," a book of sonnets, had a purple cover that showed the strands of a cat-o'-nine-tails terminating in scorpions and dripping blood. One reviewer called "Scorpio" the "anchovy paste on the buttered toast of our literature." The sonnets in "Pieces of Eight" were, according to the New York *Tribune,* of a "rare and awe-inspiring violence"; so vituperative that their author exhausted the Anglo-Saxon store of invective and had to turn to French. Archie was, in this prolific period, still fighting for his money that was locked up by the insanity decree in New York.

*   *   *

While Archie was incarcerated, the Spanish-American War had been taking place. This was the Chanlers' war, as it turned out. Margaret, as a nurse on a typhoid ship, became known as the Angel of Puerto Rico—forty years after the war her services were recognized by Congress with a special medal. Willie and Wintie charged up San Juan Hill, in groups supporting Teddy Roosevelt. Alida became known for having driven into a base camp in Florida in a buggy and said to her husband in a carrying voice, "You must come home, Temple. I find that this war is dangerous." (Temple complied.) After the war, Willie was elected as a Democrat first to the State Assembly and then, from the solidly Republican 14th District of New York, to Congress. (It was his swashbuckling image as a war hero that carried him.) Margaret went to both Albany and Washington with Willie, and served as his hostess in both those cities. She became involved in a number of political movements on her own, including temperance, this last a direct result of experiences with Willie.

Both Lewis and Bob made unsuccessful runs for office in Dutchess County, and then, in 1906, Lewis ran for lieutenant governor of New York with Willie as an adviser, and Bob ran for sheriff of Dutchess County, campaigning on horseback in a ten-gallon hat and wearing a six-shooter. Aunt Margaret was the manager of both campaigns, and Rokeby was the headquarters; indeed, Rokeby became, in this period, the Democratic headquarters for the whole state. Bob announced his candidacy at a clambake that he gave at Chanler Park, an amusement park he had set up near Rokeby as a business enterprise. The clambake, supervised by Aunt Margaret, was attended by five thousand people who were entertained by the Chanler Brass Band, the Chanler baseball team, the Chanler Drum Corps, and the Chanler Hook and Ladder Company (actually the volunteer fire department of Red Hook, New York, but organized by Bob). The guests were served sixty-five thousand clams, twenty-two hundred pounds of potatoes, twelve hundred chickens, six thousand ears of corn, three thousand bottles of soda pop, three thousand bottles of beer, and five thousand cigars. The Chanler baseball team beat the team from Chatham. Lewis accepted the nomination for lieutenant governor in a speech on the porch at Rokeby. Lewis liked to make lengthy speeches. Alida, who had become a suffragette, regularly turned up to heckle Lewis when he was making a speech and then, when he was finished, to get up on a soapbox and make a speech of her own. Archie contributed to the campaign by lambasting Lewis's running mate in Palmetto Press publications. In the fall, in the middle of the campaigns, Aunt Margaret, to everyone's shock, married Richard Aldrich, the music critic of the New York *Times*. In November, both Lewis and Bob won.

But in June, before those events, Stanford was shot. In the storm of scandalous allegations that followed, Aunt Margaret, champion of abstinence and monogamy, boldly and firmly placed the following plaque in the front hall of Rokeby, of which she was now the sole proprietor:

STANFORD WHITE
Architect and Friend
1853–1906

As a child at Rokeby, I was naturally struck by the evidence everywhere of the past presence of children. There was a rocking chair for a one-year-old and an armchair for a two-year-old in the library, for example, dark little wooden chairs with plush pillows. Upstairs were children's beds, also of different sizes: a bed for a five-year-old next to a bed for a seven-year-old, and a third, a bit larger, for a child of nine—all in one room, with matching ornate headboards. There were children's desks all over, and rocking horses, their horsehair manes worn to a nub in the way only a child's hard-used toy gets worn, the long hair of the tails pulled and mauled to stubble. On the attic floor, elaborate Edwardian toys—a little coach, a fancy well-sprung pram for a doll—stood alongside the trophies of Willie's African expeditions.

When I was at Rokeby with Mama and Aunt Margaret, the tone of life from day to day was quiet, the quietness enhanced by the largeness of the house and Aunt Margaret's manner of sitting on the porch or in the small drawing room and sewing while she talked to Mama in a formal way that seemed to dissolve linear time and contiguous space, as if there were no newspapers, or road to New York, or even progress in life such as moving from second to third grade. Yet the very air was dense with impacted emotions of a past time. Under high ceilings, the darkness of many portraits stood out from the softness of the old plaster like burned-through places in the ordinary texture of the world. Unlike Box Hill, Rokeby had no garden, just a bit of lawn and then the land rolling away, pitching down to the Hudson River in a slightly violent yet poetic motion that had the intensity of a demented aria.

Down among the barns was a shed in which enormous iceboats were piled on top of each other, their long blades conveying ferocious speed, their racy but broken-looking frames filmed with dust, caked straw, and bird droppings. There was talk of a pony that among the vast barns was nowhere to be seen. The problem was to get Cousin Dick to hitch the pony up to a cart so I could have a ride, but Cousin Dick did not appear. Cousin Dick was Aunt Margaret's son, and he was somewhere in the house; Mama told me in private that he was an alcoholic, and that he drank somewhere on the third floor. Eventually he did appear, and the pony and the cart were hitched up. I don't remember the ride. What I do remember is Aunt Margaret taking a snapshot with her Brownie camera, and the snapshot itself, which she later sent on. The photograph was black-and-white and a little washed out, on thin paper with serrated edges that were inclined to curl. Cousin Dick was holding the pony's reins just below the bit, with his chest stuck out absurdly in mock pride, and with a big grin, a grin full of fury and blind-seeming eyes behind glasses. He was wearing plaid Bermuda shorts. I can't remember myself, but Mama I see clearly, with my adult eye. What I surely must have seen then in some way was a Mama who was not at all the long-shinned Mama who had sped me to Rokeby over jumps. I saw a Mama who was a little overweight at the hips, leaning to one side in her summer dress, smiling in her elegant, slightly lupine way, but sad, empty, at a dead end, having come up empty, perhaps, on our trip to Rokeby, where she'd been looking for her family, for Wintie, her father, for the Chanlers, looking for her cradle, and finding that Rokeby was only Aunt Margaret with Cousin Dick all alone.

The convergence of the Stanford White and Chanler lines is a crucial nexus in the ancestry of the Place. In Rokeby there were screens, statues, paintings of predators assaulting prey, many of them by Uncle Bob who became an artist of distinction. In the back hall hung one of his works, a large painting on wood called "The Dance of Death." There skeletons swarmed up a black hill as fish swam in schools in the ocean beneath the hill, and a flock of cranes flew in the sky. The room that had been the nursery was called the Crow Room, because when Bob was a teen-ager he had painted a fresco on the wall: black crows blown helter-skelter over fields of red poppies against a dark-gray, stormy sky.

ROME

Mama used to tell a story of her childhood blithely, though with a barely perceptible undercurrent of agitation that suggested she was seeking to resolve something troubling in the tale. One day, when she was seven, she would recount, she was galloping with her mother, Daisy Chanler, in the Roman Campagna, and her horse, an eighteen-hand hunter, tripped. As Mama flew off, her skirt caught on the pommel of the sidesaddle in such a way that she was dragged along the ground, and as she was dragged she was kicked in the head by the horse. The horse then tripped again and fell on top of her—fortunately in a ditch, so she survived. When she came to, she said, her mother was far above her on horseback, looking down and instructing her on what to do. When asked why her mother had not dismounted to help her, Mama explained that Daisy had also been riding sidesaddle and it would have been impossible for her to get back on her horse without a mounting block.

By chance, a Roman nobleman was riding nearby and came galloping to the rescue. He got the seven-year-old back on her horse and they started home. Mama's mother and her new friend rode ahead conversing, and Mama rode behind. Suddenly, her mother turned around and chided her sharply for interrupting her conversation with the Roman nobleman by talking in a loud way. This was the point of the story. Even when Mama was very old, she was stung by that chastisement. The criticism was unfair she would say because—as was later discovered—Mama had a concussion: she hadn't even realized that she was talking. How awful it was to Mama, even when she was in her nineties, to think that her mother could believe she would knowingly babble in that way.

In the family we called Mama's mother Grandma Chanler; her name was Margaret Terry Chanler, but here I call her by her nickname, Daisy, to distinguish her from Aunt Margaret and also from Grandma White. Daisy Chanler and I overlapped—I was eight when she died, in 1952—but the times when I saw her were relatively few because she lived in New York City and upstate: she was, in any event, not at all a cozy great-grandma. With big ears, a big nose, and tiny bright-blue eyes (she looked a little like a superlatively intelligent elephant), her face was brought into focus by sensibility and thought in a way that made one think of a liquid jewel, of wine.

Daisy numbered modernists among her close friends—Alfred North Whitehead was one of them—but when she travelled she took with her a relic of the True Cross. She was not much interested in children, but a child entering a room where she was holding court might be invited to cross the room under the eyes of all the adults present to kiss the relic as Daisy, sitting in state—as if on a throne and with wings—held it in her hand. She had acquired the relic through special connections with the Vatican for a private chapel she had had built at Sweet Briar, her Genesee Valley estate.

It was because of Daisy that we, on the Place, with the exception of Papa, were Catholic. She had been born and reared in Rome, the daughter of American expatriates who remained staunchly Protestant, but in her the nineteenth-century Protestant contempt for Catholicism did not take hold. The idea on the Place about Daisy and Catholicism was that she had been overwhelmed by the irresistible seductiveness of Catholic Rome and we, her descendants, had continued to be seduced in the same way. Daisy's life was marked by autonomous choices—in this creating the great female narrative in the family—and her conversion to Catholicism was the most dramatic of those choices. With it she separated herself from her parents' values as well as from Protestant America, and laid a foundation of her own. "Her life had a plan to it, like very good architecture," my mother has said. "But it was one-way architecture. You had to go in, you had to be in her choices."

Rapture was an aspect of Catholicism that attracted Daisy and yet there was a coolness about her too: "She was not tortured, not one bit, and all her children were," my mother has said. She came from disturbance—there was trouble in the Terry family—and in marrying a Chanler she married disturbance; but she herself was undisturbed. In the family in my time, Daisy and her choices were at least as influential as Stanford was, and her idiosyncratic Catholicism was the principal medium of her legacy. Through it she remained present in our atmosphere long after her death; breathed in and out.

Even in my time, the family Catholicism retained a tinge of Daisy's rebellion, principally in the form of feeling different from an American upper class that was perceived as philistine and xenophobic. Through Daisy the family was connected to Rome, where darkness was sophisticated and bloody and the light was deceptive and baroque—in contrast to our neighbors and cousins in their airy Episcopal church, so plain with a service in English and no gore.

Like Daisy, Mama maintained an active practice of devotion. She often went to daily Mass, and habitually read the office, a daily liturgy followed by contemplatives, as her mother had done. On the wall above her bed there was a crucifix by Giambologna, a bronze figure on a wooden cross set against red silk in an old leather frame.

The objects of Mama's private practice—her missal and a small silver crucifix, placed on a little table in a certain way—had the charisma of objects in medieval illuminations, and they projected a feeling of privilege too. An aristocratic style of spirituality, a European style, was a direct legacy from Daisy, who had moved in that portion of the Roman nobility which made up the Papal Court. Mama was never more the duchess than at Mass, first striding to the very front pew, genuflecting slowly, and taking her place on the aisle, the most conspicuous place in the church, with a rightful gravity. She was always the first to take Communion, not because the rest of the congregation necessarily accorded her first place but because from her seat in the front pew she was advantageously positioned.

Mama's Catholicism was a medium of closeness to her mother, and as an adult I recognized that for me Catholicism was a territory in which I felt closeness to Mama. It was in this territory that I could see in her a passion for her life which, in her case, was the passion of her love for her mother. There were times when she was very old such as early mornings while she was still in bed, and had just put down the Breviary in which she had read the office—times when, coming in for a visit at such a moment, I would find her in a kind of awake repose, and I would feel her presence and my presence in combination deeply. It was not that she would be in a religious mood—it was not that at all. Rather, she was apt to be thinking about an event of the past that had come to mind, or perhaps about current events: it was that she was present on a variety of levels. Once, for example, she said, slowly, looking out the window at a spring day, "My great-uncle Sam's father grew up on a farm in Jamaica, Long Island, and, when he was fourteen, joined the Army and fought under Washington in the Revolutionary War. It hasn't been so long." In these instances, it was not what she said so much as the ruminative way she said it and how that conjured up time as a space in which one could move backward and forward, rather than as a one-way, linear condition that was running out. Or she might be thinking about Richard Nixon and the Watergate fiasco. Or she would blend memories with reflections on contemporary affairs, comparing the experience of waltzing with a count in Vienna, for example, with the popularity of the Beatles. At such times, she seemed to float in her life—to be searching for the continuousness of the historical line with that of her own life, or for the continuousness of her life and mine, or for the connection between public events and private life.

In the atmosphere of repose that filled the room when Mama travelled back and forth in time, the hierarchy of age was dismantled and I felt an equality between us that was intimate. For some reason—perhaps having to do with her mood on those mornings—I associate that intimacy with Catholicism; I think of it as the equality of souls.

Catholicism was the one domain outside the family into which our family circle truly opened. And the Catholic idea of the soul lifts identity out of the web of familial relationships, affirming a person's worth independently of their ordinary status in the family. It can make possible a kind of encounter that familial roles rule out and this was true in our family, even though our Catholicism was so separate from the wider world of contemporary American Catholicism that it was almost a cult.

In both the Red Cottage and the Bobby White household, the aristocratic charisma of Mama's Catholic style was translated into a bohemian style of aesthetically pleasing austerity, a style that was also in its own way privileged; it was different from the way others lived. The liturgical year was woven into our lives: there was fish on Friday and delicious penitential food in Lent and Advent (lentils on a blue plate, brown bread on a board). Perhaps the Catholicism was deepest in our lives through a vision of a sacramental alchemy in the quotidian:

> In the window and out the door,
> The Lamb and the Dove on the tiled floor,

as my aunt Claire Nicolas White wrote. Claire was the eloquent
bard of the quotidian vision:

> When the key, turned in the lock,
> Stops the treading of the clock,
> Mirrored in a copper pot
> Lies the open hand of God.

My mother's gift for the accessories of love flickered with unusual
brightness at christenings and First Communions: a tiny gesture
with her hand would capture the breathtaking sanctity of an infant; a
shift in tone would convey the heartbreaking purity of a little girl in
her veil. She was also deft at turning a holy day into a circle of
arrested time, principally through the meals that she cooked, which
were rarely traditional; we might have bluefish on Christmas, for
example. It was precisely their unusualness that made the meals
sacred: the honoring of the humble bluefish accentuated its holiness,
its aspect as a gift from our beloved local waters, and through this
association we touched a quick of meaning that we could never have
reached through a turkey or a ham.

In her memoir "Roman Spring" Daisy wrote that she disliked
Protestantism, pure and simple, but in particular its insistence that
God intervened in human affairs only in the time of Christ, "thus
denying revelation and the miraculous to the present." Therein lay
the origins of our epiphanic daily life on the Place. She also recorded in her memoir that her good friend Giovanni Borghese had
told her that to whatever he said in the confessional his confessor's
response was *"Troppo naturale, Principe!"* We on the Place too had a
cavalier attitude toward the Catholic rules—the idea being that for
sophisticated people the rules don't apply. The interpenetration of
culture and religion in Rome had swept Daisy toward Catholicism;
she first knew music, for example, through hearing the sacred music
performed in churches all over Rome. In "Memory Makes Music,"

another memoir, Daisy describes the quality of an exceptional performance of secular music by writing, "We were in the presence of the Great Spirit." This connection of art with the sacred was continued in the family, principally in the form of a distinction made between responsiveness and connoisseurship. In Mama's view, Papa could not really understand Dante, because he was Episcopalian. (Her opinion was unchanged by the success of his translation of "The Divine Comedy.")

Catholicism was connected to the most serious things in the family—it was as serious as class, it was as serious as art—and yet there was a lightness about it too. My mother was regularly moved to hilarity by the ways in which a Long Island accent surfaced in the Latin Mass at our local church. Jokes about holy cards, or even about doctrine, were commonplace in the gatherings in the Box Hill library. Vatican gossip of a cynical cast was a favorite, either contemporary or ancient scuttlebutt passed on through stories about Daisy. Daisy had liked to have powerful cardinals as her confessors. One to whom she went in a period when she and Wintie were living in Rome was Merry del Val, a right-wing Spaniard who was Secretary of State of the Vatican. At that time, an Irishman called Mutts was hanging around the Vatican, and Wintie found Mutts unattractive and refused to have him included in social events at their house. In the only instance in which it is known that Daisy was reprimanded in the confessional, Cardinal Del Val told Daisy that she had to invite Mutts.

Stories like this were on a continuum with Chanler stories, and some of them actually were Chanler stories—for example, the story of how, when Daisy and Wintie were about to be married in Rome, three major dispensations having been required, the cardinal who was to officiate then balked because Daisy's father's name was Luther. "His brother's name is Calvin," Wintie volunteered and, for some reason, his remark dissolved the tension and the marriage went forward. Aunt Margaret, of course, was not so easily placated. When Daisy had the private chapel built on the grounds of Sweet

Briar, her and Wintie's estate in the Genesee Valley, Aunt Margaret wrote to Daisy:

> I have been crashing about half alive since October conscious of my brother's humiliation at the hands of those who owe him everything. In your direction all is dark. Here love lies bleeding.

On the Place we would sometimes have Mass in the Parlor at Box Hill with the Whoopsie Girls—the gilded, half-nude, androgynous women who stood nude holding lanterns by the fireplace—looking on. One of our Smith cousins had become a convert to Catholicism, and then a priest. He was our own exquisite priest who understood us. He would say the Mass in the Parlor, and in lieu of a sermon he would tell cozy anecdotes about relatives and forebears and usually in some way flatter Mama. Daisy had been our Pope, and Mama had become our latter-day Pope in turn, though in this respect, one could tell, she felt herself to be a proxy, a mere shadow of her mother.

A related kind of hoedown that Mama enjoyed was drinks with Tommy Emmet, one of Aunt Alida's sons. Tommy, who had been known to get drunk on more than one occasion and wrap himself up in robes and pretend he was the Pope, shared with Mama an interest in that portion of the Roman nobility known as the Black Romans— the portion that made up the Vatican court, "black" being the clerical color. The Blacks stood in contrast to the much despised Whites, the nobility from the north that had come in with Garibaldi. Black Roman families have about them an atmosphere of antiquity, dark violence, and labyrinthine treachery combined with a kind of stultifying snobbery possible only in the Old World. There is a sickly-sweet perfume to it. Daisy had had close friends among the Blacks, and Mama too, in her young womanhood, had moved in that world and that perfume lingered about her. You might not notice it on an ordinary day, but when she settled in with Tommy and cocktails for a Black Roman binge, and they started unearthing old rumors of scandal, the perfume would become strong and shocking, as the two of them began to look as if they were salaciously opening a rotten fruit, or stirring a witches' brew.

Not only were the Black Romans probably the most reactionary circle in Europe at the time of Daisy's conversion but the Church to which she, a young intellectual seriously engaged with modern philosophy, had converted was in what may have been the most reactionary period of its history. In the eighteen-seventies the Catholic Church, stripped of its worldly power by Garibaldi and the formation of the democratic nation of Italy, not only favored the tottering monarchies of Europe but opposed democracy so vehemently that voting was declared a sin. In this period the Vatican refused to have diplomatic relations with the nation of Italy. Indeed, after Pius IX lost control of Rome in 1870 he refused to leave the Vatican— refused to set foot in the new nation of Italy (in solidarity with him, some Black Roman families sealed up the front doors of their palazzi). It would be sixty years before Mussolini would coax the Church into reëntering the world. (One Black Roman family, nevertheless, still has its front door sealed.) Mussolini was a great favorite of the Black Romans. One of Tommy's fondest memories was of dancing with Mussolini's daughter at a Black Roman ball, though this came out in his sessions with Mama only when the evening had progressed to a point.

It is a paradox of Daisy Chanler's life—creating an inversion that lived on in the family—that her greatest act of independence, her choice of Catholicism, was a movement toward the reactionary. However, the choice should be seen in the context of an irony of feminist history: in many aspects feudal society offered more scope to upper-class women than did the democratic Enlightenment society of the nineteenth century. In feudal society the aristocratic woman had power—or, at least, the aura of power. She was recognized to have an interior life of importance; she was understood to have a soul. Daisy, who found her own mother's life drearily constricted, even pathetic, moved backward strategically into a cave that was spacious and gorgeous but was not connected to the future. She developed a backward-longing tropism for a luminous past that had largely vanished from the world even in her time, the cozy Renaissance Rome, for example, that was destroyed in her childhood by both real-estate development and the archeology of ancient Rome. But that past burned in her heart, illuminating it, making of it a kind of vigil lamp. She engendered in her children a feeling of exclusion from an unattainable world that was to be quested after, and they did quest after it, reaching for a mirage in their mother's heart—a mirage of a past where they could not go in a heart that was unattainable to them also.

Daisy did not become a political reactionary. She simply disregarded the political character of the Church in her time in much the same spirit that she ignored Church censorship of reading material, or told the joke about a cardinal confessor who had let her off the hook when she smuggled some jewelry into Italy on the ground that "smuggling didn't count." She dwelt in a reactionary atmosphere but was unaccountable for it. "She was able to overlook much," my mother has said, and so were we, in my time, in the "floating paradise" (as my aunt Claire describes it in a poem) of the Place.

Catholicism in the family mind was, in many ways, one and the same as Rome—not "Rome" taken to mean the Vatican but the entire city. This was a direct legacy from Daisy, who remained so deeply connected to Rome throughout her life that she developed a habit of bilocation. She wrote in her memoir "Autumn in the Valley," which purportedly expressed her attachment to the Genesee Valley, that if she had been, at any time in the valley, stopped and asked, she could have told you where exactly she was in Rome at that moment. We on the Place were, in a vaguer way, bilocated too. We were not Americans exactly, and we were not Catholics, exactly, in the normal American meaning of that word. Our ancestry reached back to the founding of the Republic, but we were not at home here. We identified ourselves so fiercely with our local countryside that we felt any shift or change in its landscapes or its character as revelatory, yet we lived like a person with a lover elsewhere.

The world of the Place was a perverse one, in that what appeared on the surface ran in a direction opposite to what was happening underneath. Catholicism added to that perversity in ingeniously deceptive ways. The epiphanic visions in the kitchen, along with the south wind in the hickory, the mourning doves in the garden, the bread rising—on the bookshelf next to "Lady Chatterley's Lover," banned by the Church—my mother skylarking through her scales in the morning, and the signature of the rose on the dining-room wall in the evening: all these were true, and all these enriched our lives and even awakened us, and all these also thickened the slick that was concealing from us the truths of our lives together and alone.

At five I began attending the parochial school on the far side of the potato fields that stretched out south of the Place. My school was overcrowded—two grades to a classroom in which seventy children or so were ruled through terror by an ignorant, overworked nun. We students were crowded together, yet to me parochial school seemed lost and far away, like Dad's dusty California. The farm boys cracked their knuckles. The goody-goody swanned around, with light-brown hair that swung from side to side. Boys and girls were separated at recess. There were stories you heard, such as that boys might look in your patent-leather shoes to see a reflection of your underpants. The nuns administered beatings regularly, but only to the boys. The girls would have their ears boxed or a wrist slapped with a ruler, or would be made to stand in a briar hedge during recess.

I easily became attuned to the nuns' fascination with details of the Crucifixion which, in retrospect, seems sadistic, as do their vivid imaginings of the experience of burning in Hell. For me as a child, however, these violent fantasies were pacifying. So was the drama: "My God, my God, why hast Thou forsaken me?" The physicality of Transubstantiation—"This is my body . . . This is my blood"—was gruesome to a child, but corporeal mysticism came naturally to me: soon I would be sensing the St. James landscape as a body. School was merged with church as we learned to go to Confession, had First Communion. The Mass took on meaning. The extremes of experience were represented in the Mass: its images and its messages were passionate. The Mass also afforded extreme privateness in combination with the commonality of a public ceremony and in that I discovered inclusion, as well as an interior space. It was Communion that drew me directly into that space where I sensed vastness and also *something:* a self, perhaps—a horse shifting in the dark.

In contrast to the false spirituality of lust and the terrible glamour of an eclipsed soul which underlay the brightness of the Place, this religion openly addressed violence, sadness, and abandonment; had forgiveness as its hallmark; and in full acknowledgment of suffering envisioned a cosmos powered by love. Here the spectrum of spiritual experience, from ecstasy to despair, was affirmed. Only when shadow is admitted can there be connection: otherwise, I have come to understand, we are truncated beings who are not wholly present, who like ghosts cannot achieve touch. The Catholic Church was a precious matrix of intimations of connection for me.

In 1952, when I was eight, Dad got a Guggenheim and the Rousseau family—there were four of us girls at this time—went to Rome. We arrived in October. I was slapped late into an Italian school and went into an almost total blackout from which I awoke a month later not only speaking Italian but dreaming in it. Soon, too, I felt that I knew the city like the palm of my hand: in recollection it seems as if I travelled all around constantly on my own. Since I was only eight, this cannot have been the case, but the sense of mastery was real. When I returned to Rome forty years later I knew the relation of parts of the city to each other—the Janiculum to the Spanish Steps, the Colosseum to San Giovanni—and found the placement of the booths in the Piazza Navona where figures for nativity scenes were sold, or of the Pietà in St. Peter's, to be exactly as I expected.

We lived outside Porta San Giovanni, on the Via Sannio, in a vast apartment with long halls, terrazzo floors, and chandeliers. Though the apartment was palatial, there was no place for us in a way. The piano was in the living room, so that became my father's studio, leaving bedrooms and the very formal dining room for the rest of us. (The kitchen was cold and dark and had only one chair at the marble table.) Footsteps rang out—click, click, click—on the terrazzo floors, especially in the halls: as winter came the cold of the kitchen spread out, as did—after our first electric bill—the dark. I remember little of life in the apartment, though in what memories I have I sense myself as a child there—small, dependent, unknowing—in contrast to my sense of myself in the city. The city engaged me with its colors and its light and its scents, and the aural texture created by the bells near and far. I absorbed Italianness. I learned an attitude and, with it, the street dialect, Romanaccio, beginning with lessons from our maid, Marcella, in what the right obscenities were with which to retaliate against insults at school. My mother had great faith in Marcella's tutorials. She felt that I was learning something useful at last.

In addition to the liberating effect of living, for the first time, outside the cocoon of the Place it was the manifest layeredness of Rome and the complexity of its imagery that empowered and awakened me. Here, at last, was a metaphor that was the equal of my situation. The confusion of different periods, sometimes even in a puddingstone way—ruins growing out of the back of the Pantheon—was profoundly satisfying. I loved how the Forum was at a three-quarter depth below the contemporary street and the tops of the ancient columns showed above ground level, intruding partly into contemporary life in a way that made ambiguous whether it was the street or the Forum that was ghostly. A stony mustiness and darkness in certain churches seemed to be qualities I already knew. A contrast between oppressive monumentality in the city and then intimacy in an ancient place seemed to be something I had foreseen. Joy (the Castel Sant' Angelo, the Campidoglio) and horror (holes in the ancient walls in which people lived) opened up in me registers of response that seemed to have been merely dormant. In Rome I was becoming myself. Here Christian churches sat frankly on pagan sites. Here the gruesome was everyday: mummified saints, with hair still on, in glass coffins; the rotten darkness of the catacombs; the old bloodiness of the Colosseum. In St. Peter's, rotund, raspberry-hued prelates in bright silks scurried, looking like personifications of the seven deadly sins.

Mama and Papa came to visit us when we were in Rome. They stood out in their tweeds—Mama with her "bag"—and their solid shoes: they were elegant but with the air of good Republicans with a *Social Register* apartment on the East Side of Manhattan and orchestra seats to "My Fair Lady." With them I went to smaller churches, like Santa Maria in Cosmedin, San Lorenzo Fuori le Mura, and San Pietro in Vincoli (all these names stayed vividly in my mind) where there was that duskiness of worn stone which was tough, which gave no quarter and had no softness: that I liked. Mama and I would kneel in the pews as Papa whizzed around the periphery gobbling up things to see. We would pray a little pointedly, perhaps, emphasizing the superiority of our entrée.

Mama in Rome on that visit had something about her of the hungry outsider. When she spoke of Rome on the Place she would get a look of her mother's that was like a liquid jewel, or like wine, but when actually in Rome she was an American Wasp lady with a handbag. In Rome it was as if she had knowledge of a vision but no access to it. It was as if she were taking me to the edge of a territory that she could show me but could not enter herself. Mama systematically showed me the territories of her heart, filling me to the brim with the feeling of things, with the timbres of meaning, with the allure.

I didn't see the Chapel of St. Felicity that Daisy had built for herself upstate until, in my mid-thirties, I took a trip with Mama to Sweet Briar, then owned by my great-aunt Gertrude Chanler. The chapel overlooked the wheat-filled Genesee Valley and the long lines of the hills that enclose it. On the outside it was plain white-painted stucco. Inside the walls had been frescoed by Mama and her sisters Hester and Gabrielle in a pagan bacchanalia of pomegranates and grapes. Even more shocking, perhaps, was finding there that uninnocent Roman austerity of dankness and dim light in which there were gleams (the gleam of the gilt on an icon, the metal of the incense boat). It was an austerity of whispers and glints, a stillness full of innuendo, a bareness that was stony. The chapel also had something about it of a playhouse.

Throughout the nearly forty years that our lives overlapped, I encountered Mama far inside her dream of her mother's love—that is where one found her. When I ask myself what in that mirage-ridden world it could have been that she gave me which was real, which I could carry out, I think of a large solid jewel. It's as if we had lived inside a complicated, dangerous court, run by a despot—that would be Daisy—where all transactions had been stylized to reinforce the despot. And yet, by an ingenious use of those very transactions, we'd devised a gleaming, faceted, deep-colored, and durable exchange of our own. That was the jewel. It's simple really. She gave me love and attention. She had it to give by that time.

And there's this. When I was in Rome as a child, a special family priest at San Clemente took us down through layers of older San Clementes, each more fragmentary, more obscure, blacker and more rotten. In the bowels of the earth near the bottom of our descent we came upon a dimly perceptible Roman arch: that was the earliest church. One could just make out a piece of the line of the arch, and get from it a feeling of a larger structure in the dark—but we went still farther down to an iron railing around a pit. There, after a while, we could discern, below and across from us, a pedimented window, a part of a Roman villa from pagan times. A house. Nor was this all. The surfaces dripped, and in the darkness below was a sound of rushing water.

And this. From three o'clock on Good Friday afternoon, the time of Christ's death, until noon on Holy Saturday, when Christ rose, all the bells of Rome were silent. In this time, also, the door of the tabernacle in every church was left open, and there was no Host inside. This emptiness would be existentially brutal in any church in the world. But in Rome, where the bells were integral to daily life, their silence made the absence in the tabernacle not secret inside churches but as big as the city, as big as the sky.

There was a place on the Janiculum I think—it was on one of the hills—from which it was said that every bell in Rome could be heard, and on Holy Saturday that year we went there for a picnic. From the hilltop you could see all of Rome with its domes rising out of a patchwork of mellow hues in a golden haze, but I was lying on my side, a child, fingering some small wild plants, when the bells broke. One clang, a little hoarse, was the leading edge, and then came an explosion. Glory can burst forth from barren grief. The world can break open like a pomegranate.

DANGER

O N T H E E V E N I N G of June 25, 1906, Papa, who was eighteen at the time, had been with Mama, who was also eighteen. It is
possible that later on in the evening Papa and his college friend
Leroy King had dinner with Stanford, as Papa told the press. Since
Mama and Papa had sandwiches with friends before Papa put her on
a train for upstate, it seems unlikely—she certainly always assumed
he made the story up to keep her name out of the public eye. What
is certain is that Stanford went to see "Mamzelle Champagne" at
the Roof Garden alone, and that it was quite late when Papa got
home—alone—to the house on Gramercy Park. It was then that he
learned of his father's death from reporters who were lying in wait
around the front door. The reporters asked him about Evelyn Nesbit

and Harry K. Thaw. He said that he'd never heard of either of them, and rushed directly to Madison Square Garden, not out of concern for his father, who was beyond help, but to look for his father's chauffeur. When he found him he had the man drive him immediately to his mother at Box Hill. Arriving in the wee hours of the morning, he then decided not to wake his mother. Instead, he got a chair and sat outside her door until he heard her stirring in the morning. The image of this vigil floated around in the Sargasso Sea of pictures, anecdotes, and information bits about the past in which I swam when I was a child.

I used to search the picture of this vigil for the story of Stanford and Bessie and Larry. I used to search the scene of Papa sitting in a chair outside Grandma's door in the night for the family story inside the public one which was so big and yet elusive. Certainly there was drama in the fact of Papa sitting there, containing the shock of the murder until his mother woke. The picture perfectly captured the selflessness in the form of good manners which structured Papa's life—it captured Papa's character—but it also suggested an imminent climax in which the pent-up truth of Stanford's dangerous and destructive character, a hidden family truth, would burst into the open with the news of his violent death reaching Grandma. But that sense of impending drama was forever unsatisfied, because my sense of what happened next was that when Papa finally spoke to his mother she took the news in a resigned way. The idea that came down to me was that even Papa himself, though he was in turmoil throughout the night, was not completely surprised by what had happened either. My impression of the moment when he told Grandma was of calm, like the calm after a hurricane has passed and the damage can be finally assessed. Over the years, that calm translated into a strange indifference to Stanford's death. A major figure in the family had been slain and yet about that violent ending of an important life the family was numb. That Stanford had been murdered did not seem to rate as a story in the family. Certainly there was no resolution of this terrible incident—none at all.

Others were unsurprised by Stanford's end as well. A Gramercy

Park neighbor said that the shooting, in itself, was not a tragedy but only the culmination of an ongoing tragedy. A taxi-driver was quoted in the newspapers as saying, "I knew that fellow would be killed sooner or later, but I thought that it would be a father rather than a husband." Many taxi-drivers of the time seemed to know quite a lot about Stanford's private life. *Town Topics,* a gossip sheet that Stanford had paid regularly to refrain from reporting on his private activities, took the occasion to observe that "some such deplorable incident has been anticipated." Similar sentiments were expressed among friends. Henry White, a diplomat and friend (not related to Stanford), wrote to Charley McKim that he was not at all surprised Stanford had come to "an untimely end," though he had not expected the circumstances to be so dramatic.

At the time of the murder, the revelations about Stanford's life were generally received as morally reprehensible—and Stanford was perceived as having gotten his just deserts. However, as the decades passed and times became more and more permissive the public story changed. Stanford became a glamorous, sexy figure, whose murder was an iconic event—almost in itself glamorous—at the juncture of the centuries. The idea became established that censorious judgment of Stanford at the time reflected prudery, hypocrisy, and naïveté. Yet it was a curious feature of Stanford's posthumous life in the public eye that, while he remained well known—more widely known for the circumstances of his murder than for his architecture—biographers who sought to dig deeply into his life faltered. An exception was a biography by Charles Baldwin, published in 1931, that focussed principally on his professional life, but after that, though many attempts were made, for half a century no new biography was completed. Aline Saarinen, an art historian, and the wife of the architect Eero Saarinen, was one of those who made the attempt and her papers reveal the process that brought her efforts to a halt. Ms. Saarinen began her project with the almost dogmatic preconception that Stanford was a charming, charismatic figure who had had affairs but had been no worse than many—had been nothing that a mid-twentieth-century sophisticate would find untoward. Her notes, and especially her correspondence with her agent and publisher, reveal that what she found instead, as she got deeper into her research, was a "mechanical" progression of compulsion that gradually destroyed her liking for Stanford and, with it, her will to continue.

The only fruit of Ms. Saarinen's two years of work on Stanford was an article published in *Life,* in 1966—many years after she dropped the project—in which she not only portrayed Stanford as the admirable, glamorous man she had initially surmised him to be but also stated that there was no substance to Evelyn Nesbit's allegations, although it's clear from her papers that this could not have been what she believed. The article was accompanied by photographs of Stanford's architecture with some of my younger sisters and cousins posing in it (I was twenty-two by this time), either in romantic costumes or in the type of clothes that royal English children wear. The feature, in other words, was from start to finish a fantasy. Ms. Saarinen had got herself into a fix. In the course of researching her biography she'd become especially close to Mama— she spent a week at Box Hill at one point—and in letters had reassured Mama repeatedly of her great liking for and understanding of Stanford. She conveyed that she had an intuitive grasp of what he was like which would allow her to set the record straight at last. It is clear from Mama's letters that she was profoundly engaged in and enlivened by this opportunity to discuss her beloved Stanford in depth. What was Ms. Saarinen to do? In her article in *Life* she confirmed what she imagined the family's fantasy about itself and Stanford to be, making of the piece a form of love letter, perhaps an apology for having—inexplicably, to the family—dropped out.

Brendan Gill, another quondam biographer of Stanford, wrote— in a review of a biography of Stanford that was successfully completed in the late eighties—of the difficulty of reconciling "the authentic White, the big, bluff, open, lovable man of superb talent, and the predatory . . . satyr." He wrote that biographers became repelled by White's monstrous insatiability, and that their projects ground to a halt because they "came to dislike him" and because they had a "reluctance to admit that his amoral multifariousness had defeated them."

The biography under review was Paul Baker's "Stanny: The Gilded Life of Stanford White," published in 1989. This work, which had taken seven years to complete, coherently documented for the first time both the course of Stanford's compulsions and his professional achievements. As Papa had done his best to erase the record of Stanford's private life, Baker's resources were limited. (Another hole in the record had been created when Grandma had thrown out all Stanford's letters to her—not that they would have told much about his secret life, but they would have been a substantial part of the record.) It is nearly impossible to wipe out entirely such a wide and lifelong trail as Stanford left, however, and so, despite Papa's efforts, Baker was able to find sufficient materials to construct his painstaking, sober account that by the end leaves a reader in little doubt about the nature of the hidden side of Stanford's life.

Though Baker's biography was the first one to unfold the facts of Stanford's secret life—facts at which so many biographers had balked—nothing in his account surprised me utterly. There was a good deal in the biography that I hadn't known in detail, and much of that was shocking, yet the experience of reading it was anticlimactic in a way that, perhaps, was similar to Grandma and Papa's reaction after Stanford was shot. In some part of me, I had known these things: the story had been there on the Place all along. It was a relief, though, to see the information spelled out. It put to rights small matters, such as my queasy and confused feelings about Ms. Saarinen's article in *Life* when it appeared. I thought I should be proud, and my friends thought so too, but in truth I was disoriented by the article and weirdly indifferent to its contents.

To judge from Baker's account, Stanford's sexual voraciousness was probably full blown even before he married, in 1884; there is the remark of Joseph Wells, for example, that he lost interest in a woman as soon as "all new sensations were exhausted." Whether Stanford suspended his activities for a while after he married is not

known, but in 1887, the year Larry was born, he started the Sewer
Club—the sex club that grew out of the concert evenings—with
Wells and the artists Frank Lathrop, Thomas Dewing, and Augustus
and Louis Saint-Gaudens. Stanford eventually belonged to more than
fifty men's clubs, but among them the Sewer Club was unique. It
met in a rented room in the Benedict, the building designed by
McKim, Mead & Bigelow on Washington Square where Wells lived,
and though there is no record of its activities, it seems close to
certain that the principal activity was sexual. "Scenes of mirth and
physiological examination" was how Dewing described the Sewer's
successor club, which involved largely the same membership and
was called the Morgue. The Morgue's headquarters were in the
Holbein Building on West Fifty-fifth Street where the club maintained a number of hideaways for use by members. That Wells, who
was a part of all this, was nevertheless critical of Stanford's pattern
in the Sewer Club days is an early indication that Stanford's tendency toward sexual excess was out of the ordinary, even in that
crowd.

By the late eighties Stanford was also regularly going out on the
town for evenings of sexual adventure and going to establishments
where sex could be watched, accompanied by his bohemian cronies
and also by new, rich friends he had met as clients. There was a lot
of drinking—these were very late nights—with rich food thrown in,
and a boxing match perhaps, or a visit to a music hall to see the
Florodora girls. Or there might be a bit of opera and several stops at
regular men's clubs, or sexual intervals in one or another of the
private hideaways that Stanford kept in addition to his secret club's
hideaways. It's an indication of the pace at which Stanford lived that
his night life often included late-night stop-offs at the office. There
are several descriptions by colleagues of Stanford dashing in, sometimes dressed in evening clothes, and brushing everything aside to
jot down a design that had come into his head, commandeering any
draftsman who happened to be around doing late-night work and
forcing him to focus on Stanford's project. When Stanford was
done, the draftsman would be likely to find red mustache hairs and

bits of chewed and splintered pencil all over the work—Stanford would twist his mustache furiously as he drew—and a sea of crumpled paper on the floor.

The process of seduction was a major feature of Stanford's obsession with sex, and it was an inexorable kind of seduction which moved into the lives of very young women, sometimes barely pubescent girls, in fragile social and financial situations—girls who would be unlikely to resist his power and his money and his considerable charm, who would feel that they had little choice but to let him take over their lives. There are indications that Stanford would sometimes adopt the role of a paternal benefactor, and then would take advantage of the trust and gratitude that had been built.

Elaborate seductions notwithstanding, the indications are that Stanford got bored quickly with the girls he seduced, and that he frequently had several affairs going on at the same time. Nevertheless, he often seduced deeply—so that his quarries fell in love with him, and even thought he was going to marry them. When it didn't work out that way, his ex-girlfriends sometimes sued him for breach of promise. The notorious attorneys Howe & Hummell became a part of Stanford's backup system; he very likely had this disreputable firm on retainer but we will never know, for although it was one of the largest and most prosperous firms in the city, it kept no records at all. The offices of Howe & Hummell were situated across the street from the Tombs, a New York City prison, and were open twenty-four hours a day for the convenience of clients, who might be taking unofficial leave of the Tombs at odd hours. (Howe & Hummell were famous for having represented many famous criminals.) Changes of clothes as well as legal advisers were kept on hand. Howe & Hummell were also well known as experts in the legal ramifications of shadowy romance—the area in which they were of use to Stanford. At the very time that Stanford became involved with Evelyn Nesbit, for example, he was fighting off a breach-of-promise suit by the young actress who had introduced Evelyn to him in the first place. Not only did the plaintiff lose her suit but she and her mother, who was also an actress, found that thereafter they could not get work in the theatre.

Boys may have been a part of Stanford's nocturnal life too—it's hard to say. Though there were certainly men of a homosexual tendency in his inner circle, where Stanford was concerned there is a great deal of smoke but no fire that can be detected from this perspective in time. Saint-Gaudens and Stanford regularly addressed each other in letters as "Darling" or "Dearly beloved," and signed off with "KMA," meaning "Kiss My Ass." The phrase was a part of the currency of the friendship; indeed, a large bronze medallion by Saint-Gaudens, which commemorated the 1878 European trip and was kept on a cabinet beside Papa's chair in the Box Hill library, included the initials "KMA." In a recorded interview Papa explicates the initials astringently but quite openly: unlike the rest of the family, Papa, I think, was unflinching in his awareness of Stanford's nature. He did not wish to advertise it—he culled the office files—but he saw it plainly himself in a way that the rest of us did not.

I can vividly recall that Saint-Gaudens medallion, especially the visual softness of a surface that seemed to absorb rather than refract the light and its cold silkiness to the touch too. But knowledge of the meaning of the initials was not a part of that familiarity, and to learn it was to uncover once again something that was present but hidden, or cryptic, in my experience of the life of the Place. To Papa, in contrast, the initials on the bronze medallion, sitting by his chair, were not cryptic at all. Papa, in some ways, was a sealed-off man, and yet he also inhabited a whole world in a way that the rest of the family did not.

In letters Saint-Gaudens would sometimes spell out "KMA," or put it in French or Italian, and once Stanford modified and expanded the usual "KMA" to "SMA-SsssMB-SMC." Once, Saint-Gaudens wrote Stanford, "I'm your man to dine, drink, Fuck, bugger or such, metaphorically speaking." Saint-Gaudens often signed letters to Stanford with a phallic-looking "A," and on one occasion he expanded it into thirteen phalluses. One can add to this that, according to Baker, Stanford once confided to a friend that he regarded the most beautiful body to be that of a twelve-year-old boy. But Stanford's private world was so fraught with lewd excess, so scrambled and unbounded that distinctions lose meaning. In this atmosphere of untrammelled indulgence, the question of whether Stanford was bisexual seems irrelevant. In some ways, his activities don't even seem to be sexual, in the usual sense. They were more like a form of compulsive consumption. Stanford was merely all over the place, sexually. He was out of control.

Through all this Stanford never stopped working and, as Baker documents, this demand on himself, in combination with the high life he was leading, was taking its toll as early as the nineties. In 1890 he was sick with a succession of severe colds; in the next year a bad attack of grippe put him out of commission. The following year a severe bladder and urinary infection plagued him and required minor surgery twice. And yet his pace continued to accelerate. He continued, also, to be grandiosely generous, giving away money when he himself was plunging into debt, and giving away his services when he was already staggering under his workload; he moved toward the point of collapse almost routinely, and at the same time kept his supply of girls flowing—sending notes and gifts and flowers, courting, luring, drawing them in.

Whenever Stanford was not sick, it seems he was on a roll, sweeping everything before him, commanding the center of attention in a sometimes abrasive way. His nickname in the office was "the Indian," and his telegraph code name was Giddydoll. For workmates his relentless energy was exhausting to be around: he caused a disturbance wherever he was. He could be intimidating, brusque, and sarcastic: even friends found him, at times, obnoxious. Thomas Dewing once advised the art collector Charles Freer to avoid visiting him in New Hampshire on a weekend when Stanford would be there because Stanford was such a noisy presence. When telephones came into use, Stanford had one installed in his office and one day, when it didn't work the way that he wanted, he ripped it out and kicked in the side of the booth where it had been kept.

The draftsman Henry Magonigle recorded in a memoir a day he

spent with Stanford during which two startling incidents occurred. Magonigle was assisting Stanford in the renovation of the interior of Ophir Hall, the latter-day Norman castle in Westchester County owned by Whitelaw Reid, the editor of the New York *Tribune,* and Elisabeth Mills Reid, the heiress to a Western mining fortune. (It was the Reids who had bought the Villard Houses when Henry Villard went bankrupt.) As a part of his job, Magonigle regularly travelled to Ophir Hall to inspect the ongoing work. In the period in question, the work that he had been overseeing was in the mansion's front hall, which Stanford had redesigned as a series of interlocking spaces to be finished in a lush pink marble and topped by a plaster ceiling with plaster rosettes placed on it as intervals.

Routinely, Magonigle would go by train to White Plains and there hire a horse and buggy from a livery service and drive himself to Ophir Hall. He often got the same horse, whose name was Walter, and who had a passion for galloping downhill. This is a terrifying trait in a horse, especially when a buggy is involved, and there were many hills between the railroad station and Ophir Hall. Magonigle had got to know Walter, however, and always restrained him aggressively as they approached a hill. Whenever they came to the first hill—an especially long and fairly steep one—there was a particularly pitched struggle between Magonigle and Walter.

After the work in the front hall was finished, Stanford wanted to take a look for himself, and went out to White Plains with Magonigle. When they got to the station, they hired a horse and buggy, and as usual the horse was Walter. Stanford took the reins, and everything was fine until they reached that first, very long hill. Walter began speeding up, and, according to Magonigle, Stanford, far from restraining him, "gave a wild yell, rose to his feet and leaning far out over the dashboard urged Walter on with whip and voice." They plunged down all the hills on the way to Ophir Hall in this fashion.

Upon arriving, Stanford, flushed from the ride, charged in, took one look at the rosettes on the ceiling, and, as Magonigle recorded it, said:

Well if that isn't the goddamndest lookin' ceiling I ever saw—gimme a hammer! gimme a hammer!! gimme a ladder!! Gimme a ladder!!!

Magonigle's account continued:

When these were hastily provided he seized the hammer, climbed the ladder like ascending smoke and proceeded to lay about him, knocking off rosettes; they fell with satisfactory crashes; White gave a whoop of delight, and knocked off some more, each with a yell, until he had cleared a space leaving certain ones sufficient for accent. He came down and handed back the hammer, saying "There! Take off the rest of 'em."

Magonigle went on to report that the ceiling looked better with fewer rosettes but that Stanford had done a lot of unnecessary damage while knocking them down. The workmen had thought Stanford was "loony," he said.

As it happened, Ophir Hall later became the administration building of my college, Manhattanville, then a Catholic college run by the Religious of the Sacred Heart. I knew that Stanford had designed the interior of the Castle, as we called it, but typically the knowledge remained, at best, crepuscular to my conscious mind. We students used to snicker about the pink marble. It embarrassed us, I think, because it was so unrestrainedly sensuous, so soft-seeming, with an alternately swirling and mottled grain. Even without the connection to Stanford, how amusing, how disturbing, the contrast was between that voluptuary pink and the nuns gliding through it in their floor-length black habits, their faces narrowed by starched white bonnets. With no duplicity I could joke with my friends about the nuns and the pink marble—forgetting who it was that that choice of material represented.

I went to the Castle as rarely as possible. On the few occasions when business forced me there, the perversity of the nuns in that quasi-bordello environment would dizzy me, and yet it would steady

me, in an odd way, with its familiarity: the combination was similar
to Mass in the Parlor at Box Hill. The breathtaking splendor of the
pink marble—because, for all its absurdity, it was beautiful—generated that seductive effulgence, the Stanford spell. There was in
addition the rational pleasure of Procession, of spaces opening from
one into another, a rightness of measurement holding overrichness
in tension. The tension between the rightness and the richness situated a person in stillness and lightness, as if poised on the edge of
flight.

As the eighteen-nineties progressed, Stanford's secret life became
less secret. In 1895, when he was forty-one, he boasted that at a
wedding at which he was an usher he had "kissed the bride and two
bridesmaids and acted in a most scandalous way generally." In the
same year, he held the Pie Girl Dinner, organized to celebrate the
tenth wedding anniversary of his friend John Elliot Cowdin. Before-
hand, Stanford had said about the dinner, "Hell is going to break
loose but don't tell anybody about it." Stanford took a juvenile
pleasure in the idea of being shocking. In 1897, he shocked the
swashbuckling journalist Richard Harding Davis by behaving in a
"drunk and crazy" fashion at the Bradley Martin Ball, a great binge
for which the Waldorf was transformed into Versailles: there he
made a spectacle of himself by blatantly pursuing a beautiful young
woman called Mrs. Starr.

His spending went still more seriously out of control in this
period, and in order to catch up with his debts he began to speculate
recklessly, looking for the big killing that would pull him out of his
financial difficulties in one swoop. Among his growing expenses
were the costs of his "girls." He did pay their dental bills: as if his
girls were works of art, he would try to perfect them. According to
Baker's biography, there were also steep debts to jewellers and
florists. When Stanford ordered champagne, there would be three
deliveries at least: one to his home, one to the studio in the Garden's tower, and one to a hideaway. Just the rents he had to lay out

for his various establishments must have amounted to a considerable expense. In 1897, when he was in particularly difficult financial straits—and also wrestling with the Archie affair—he ordered extensive improvements to a hideaway a few blocks from his home, above F. A. O. Schwarz on West Twenty-fourth Street, not far from Madison Square Garden. He had a furnace and heating ducts put in and a marble mantel that had to be hoisted up the front of the building by rigging and brought in through a window. As was his wont, he created a fantasy interior there; this one included a swing attached to the high ceiling by red velvet ropes. He would not meet Evelyn Nesbit for four years: she was not the only girl he pushed on the red velvet swing.

Bessie gradually began spending more and more time at Box Hill, leaving town in the spring and returning in October. Her life with Stanford in the city entailed the kind of frenetic public socializing that she did not enjoy—combined, no doubt, with being left at home alone for stretches. Stanford still came out to Box Hill for weekends, however, and he continued to expand the Place.

Stanford and Bessie did have something of a life together. They enjoyed playing golf on a course Stanford had had made on the hill going down to the harbor, and sometimes on weekends Stanford, Bessie, and Larry went fishing for trout on the Nissequogue River. This activity gave Stanford the idea of establishing a trout club there. Papa wrote in one of his memoirs:

> For a club-house my father had bought the Javanese exhibit at the World's Fair: a most picturesque affair, with columns of huge trunks of bamboo, and walls of palm-leaf matting picked out in black and white. There we often went down for weekends in the Spring, and had excellent sport for many years, until the trout all died of an incurable and contagious disease.

If there is an idyll, Papa always includes the detail that poisons it. But it seems likely that Papa knew his father had, in a way, poisoned this idyll before the first trout got sick. One of the club features was round-the-clock kitchen and bar service—not an amenity that one would expect to find on the banks of this obscure estuarial river, but convenient for a love nest. A long-term inhabitant of the neighborhood told me that her mother had told her that many of Stanford and Bessie's neighbors knew that Stanford would bring his New York friends down to the trout club for illicit sexual episodes.

I was startled once by a different manifestation of Stanford's private life in the heart of St. James. In the course of my research I had learned that, at one time, Stanford had gotten into trouble with a woman in Paris—exactly what kind of trouble is not known, but it was a bad kind of trouble that had to be kept secret—and, whether because of the international aspect of the situation or for some other reason, Howe & Hummell were not of use. Instead, Stanford turned for legal help to Nellie's husband, his brother-in-law Prescott Hall Butler. Whatever rescue it was that Prescott engineered, Stanford's gratitude was considerable, for it was measured in a large bronze relief portrait of Prescott's two small sons, Lawrence and Charles, by Augustus Saint-Gaudens.

Prescott had a grandson, also called Prescott, who received as a wedding gift from Nellie, his grandmother, a vineyard with a farmhouse and outbuildings on a promontory on the harbor called Rassapeague—as enchanted a piece of old Long Island as one could hope to find. The waters are dark and the tide runs fast there, the light falls like honey on the meadow that was a vineyard, and the family that lives there—Prescott, Jr., until he died, and at this time his widow and some of his grown children—is prosperous and upright and golden. There is no trace of the Gilded Age there, no volcanic dust of plundered objects, and certainly one does not associate Rassapeague with scandals or shame.

One day I was having tea with Prescott's widow, whom we call Cousin Sarah in the family, a patrician woman and an emblem of probity, illuminated with inner vision. When the topic of Stanford came up, Cousin Sarah mentioned the incident in which Prescott, Sr., had helped Stanford out in the murky matter of the woman in Paris—I was amazed that she talked about such matters so easily—

and then she rose and led me into a bedroom where from under the bed she dragged out something wrapped up in sheets which turned out to be the Saint-Gaudens relief. The likeness of two little boys— two profiles looking in the same direction—set in timeless bronze, was beautiful, but also heavy, with sharp edges and corners. The relief was kept under the bed, Cousin Sarah said, because it was too valuable to hang on the wall, but it seemed to me that it was also awkwardly hard and cold, and altogether impossible to assimilate into the soft Rassapeague charm.

All through the nineties, Grandma and Stanford took family trips. In 1893, they took Papa, who was five, to Egypt. Papa's aunt and uncle Ella and Devereux Emmet were along as well. There was a stopover in Paris for Bob Chanler's wedding to Julia Chamberlain and, for Papa, a vividly remembered ride over the city with his father in a hot-air balloon. When the Pie Girl Dinner scandal broke, in 1895, Stanford went abroad with Bessie and Larry again. On shipboard their cabins were a few doors down from the cabins of Archie, Margaret, and Elizabeth Chanler. Archie had been at the Pie Girl Dinner: the ordeal of Bloomingdale had not yet begun.

As the years passed, however, Grandma and Stanford led lives that were still more separate, with Box Hill increasingly acknowledged between the two of them as her domain, though it was known publicly as Stanford's showplace. What letters between them have survived are polite but distant, almost formal. Grandma took to compiling scrapbooks, in which she collected clippings about Stanford and all sorts of other matters of interest, including adages and bits of advice; one of them was "Laugh heartily at least once a day." She also compiled lists—lists of the English kings, lists of the wonders of the world, lists of the trout caught by herself, Stanford, and Larry at the club on the Nissequogue River.

According to Baker, in 1898 Stanford was out sick again for a substantial period, and in the following year insurance companies found his health to be so bad that the best medical coverage he could negotiate was a fifty-thousand-dollar policy at a premium of five thousand dollars a year. He was forty-six years old. He suffered a serious financial setback in 1898, followed in 1899 by a speculation in sugar that failed, leaving him four hundred and thirty-eight thousand dollars in debt to brokers (more than twenty million dollars in 1996 terms). Sores and carbuncles were then breaking out on his arms. Nevertheless, he continued negotiating for the lease to a far grander town house on Gramercy Park than the one he and Bessie had been living in. When he got the lease, he decorated the house opulently with plunder from Europe and threw a Vaudeville Party for hundreds, catered by Sherry's, where his tab was already in the thousands and was mounting steeply. In 1899, he invested in a flooded copper mine in Cuba, in partnership with Prescott Hall Butler and Willie Chanler, who had greatly enriched himself through ventures in South America and could afford to have Stanford design a mansion for him at Sands Point, Long Island. Stanford couldn't keep up the assessments required by the Cuban project, however, and had to borrow his portion from Willie. In 1900 he had to withdraw altogether. "Matters have been going from bad to worse," he wrote to Willie that year. "I find my affairs in a desperate state with unexpected calls for money . . . but what makes me madder is that the money is simply thrown into the sea. Every attempt I have made to recover myself has proved disastrous and only an additional source of worry and anxiety and outlay. I am at the end of my tether and must chuck everything overboard." Still, in these years of financial disaster he continued expanding Box Hill with extensive landscaping, and added the barns and the stables, the icehouse, the pump house, and planned a fancy pergola for the box garden. And it was in 1900 that he carefully sited the exedra seat on the knoll and placed Diana on her pedestal overlooking the Sound.

In the six years left to him after the turn of the century, Stanford's compulsions acquired a cyclonic velocity. The hideaways proliferated, the liaisons increased, and the financial maneuvers became even more desperate. In order to pay brokers, he borrowed from friends, and then lost more on the stock market. By 1903 he was seven hundred and nine thousand dollars in debt—more than thirty-five million in today's dollars. As Baker documents, in 1904 he owed his Gramercy Park landlord fifty-three thousand dollars in back rent, he owed Prescott Hall Butler sixty thousand dollars, he owed Bessie a hundred and twenty-one thousand dollars, he owed his client Henry Poor ninety thousand dollars, he owed McKim, Mead & White sixty-three thousand dollars—all these sums approximately fifty times as great in contemporary dollars. Nevertheless his high living went on, almost entirely on credit from tradesmen by this time. In his office he had a mirror installed in which he could spot creditors arriving in cabs on the street below and thus evade them when they got upstairs. Out at Box Hill, the laborers were not being paid and threatened to sue.

Baker documents a precipitous decline in Stanford's health in these years. He was plagued with bowel trouble and crippling attacks of sciatica. He knew that drinking at night was making his health worse, but he did not stop unless he collapsed—as he did periodically, sometimes for weeks at a stretch. By 1903, his debt to McKim, Mead & White had risen to seventy-five thousand dollars, and an agreement was drawn up among the partners establishing a lien on Stanford's share of future profits. Around then he wrote in a letter that he was "hopeless and desperate," so much so that it was "hard to work at all, to stick to my affairs and to stop myself ending the whole business." Still he did not cut back on his spending. From January through April of 1905 he sublet the house on Gramercy Park for a goodly sum and moved into McKim's apartment on East Thirty-fifth Street, while Grandma stayed out at Box Hill.

Work continued to flow from his drawing board—some of it reflecting the excess in his life. One plan was for a monument to commemorate the bicentennial of the founding of Detroit which would consist of a two-hundred-and-twenty-foot Doric column supporting a huge torch and surrounded by sculpture and a vast colonnade. In keeping with the hyperbole of this design, the mayor of

Detroit compared Stanford to Michelangelo when he presented the scheme, but in the end the city government balked at the expense. Another project never taken to completion was a mausoleum for James Bennett, the publisher of the New York *Herald*. Stanford had already designed the *Herald*'s offices, a four-story building at Herald Square, in the style of a Venetian palazzo, with four-foot-high bronze owls—the symbol of the paper—placed at intervals along the roofline: the owls had electric eyes that winked at night. The Bennett mausoleum, to be situated on Riverside Drive, was, in its turn, to be an enormous bronze owl, on a scale to rival that of the Statue of Liberty. Visitors were to be able to ascend to a viewing platform in the head of the owl, and Bennett's sarcophagus was to be suspended in the interior. Stanford was shot before the project could go forward.

A seventeenth-century château in Roslyn, Long Island, which Stanford designed for Clarence Mackay, heir to a five-hundred-million-dollar silver fortune, and his wife, Katherine, was completed in 1902. It was the largest private home he ever created. Here is part of Baker's description of it:

> From the front entrance hall guests might move directly ahead into the huge main hall of the house, 48 feet wide and 80 feet long, the walls of dark paneled oak, partly covered by large Gobelin tapestries. The 38-foot-high ceiling was of molded plaster, and a musicians gallery projected from the floor above. The salon-drawing room to the left of the hall, decorated in Louis XV style, had cream-colored walls and a molded ceiling, and was dominated by a large portrait of Mrs. Mackay over the French fireplace. Extending beyond the salon was a glass-enclosed conservatory. The stone room, with a plethora of carved stone surfaces and an antique coffered ceiling, served as a second drawing room and for display of some of the Mackays' remarkable collection of Italian Renaissance painting.

Mrs. Mackay was not at all intimidated by Stanford, and often overruled him on aesthetic matters. "Listen and *think*," she wrote to him once about an aspect of his designs. She freely criticized his work, but then, in another letter, she promised him a "special girl" when he came out to survey the progress on the house. Stanford was able to goad the Mackays on to extremes of opulence, although Mr. Mackay helplessly protested that he would be ruined. According to Baker, on one occasion when Mackay scolded him about the expense Stanford assured him that he would be getting a very fine house, "although it may be a calamity for you." Amidst the disasters taking place in his own life, Stanford visited Naples, Palermo, Malta, Marseilles, Córdoba, Seville, Lisbon, Oporto, Bruges, Bordeaux, Paris, Turin, Vienna, Munich, Dresden, Berlin, and London, looking for objects suitable for the Mackays' Hall of Armor. (He collected a commission of ten per cent on these buys.) "I don't want another thing," Katherine Mackay wrote him, but she got another, and quite a few more.

Harbor Hill, as the Mackays' residence was called, eventually also became known as Heartbreak House, not only because Mrs. Mackay, in time, divorced Mr. Mackay for alienation of affections and because he suffered a terrible financial failure but because their daughter Ellin married Irving Berlin and, because he was Jewish, found herself removed from the *Social Register*.

The palace that Stanford designed for Payne Whitney, son of a streetcar tycoon, between 1902 and 1906, was the most expensive private home he ever created. A five-story, forty-room house, on Fifth Avenue at Seventy-ninth Street, in High Renaissance style, it cost a million dollars—approximately fifty million today. In 1905 alone, Stanford spent the equivalent of fifteen million dollars on European purchases for the interior. (It was in that year that he purchased the recently discovered statue by Michelangelo.) The spending and acquiring exhilarated him. In 1905 he visited Henry Adams in Paris; Adams describes him rushing in and announcing, "with huge excitement," that he had just bought a Clouet portrait of Henry II for the Whitneys. Adams wrote to a friend that the New

Rich were unappeasable, and that "Stanford White is their Ma-
homet."

Not all the work Stanford did in this time reflected excess. In
fact, as he became ever more disaster-bent a stream of buildings
came from his hand which were ever more refined. In his final years,
when the disorder in his life was at its worst, he produced several
masterpieces, including, in 1906, the Madison Square Presbyterian
Church. His very last work was a church in Roslyn, Long Island,
subsidized by Mrs. Mackay. Modest in size, and of brick on the
outside and stucco inside, the church is elegant, simple, and cozy.

Though his own spending continued right up to his death, Stanford maneuvered frantically to keep his debts from sinking him—
principally by borrowing from friends to pay brokers and putting up
art work as collateral. Besides holding the lien on Stanford's profits,
the firm found it necessary to sever Stanford from the partnership in
order to avoid becoming liable for his debts; on May 1, 1905, he
became a salaried employee. For a similar reason, Stanford saw to it
that Box Hill and the furnishings there were put in Grandma's
name. (He "sold" the furnishings to her for eighty-one thousand
dollars.) Although most of the furnishings of the house on Gramercy
Park had by now been indentured as collateral for loans, Stanford
still had objects of value stashed in his hideaways, in the tower at the
Garden, and in various friends' houses and studios. In 1904, he
started gathering these objects—paintings, furniture, tapestries,
statues—into a warehouse on West Thirteenth Street for catalogu-
ing in preparation for a sale. This sale represented the only remaining hope that he could significantly push back the mounting debt.
The objects for sale were completely assembled by early 1905, and
the sale was to take place on February 27th. On February 13th,
however, a short in the electrical wiring at the warehouse started a
fire, and the fire quickly got out of hand. Everything except some
bronze pieces and some ironwork was destroyed. The contents of
the warehouse had not been insured.

The loss from the fire was estimated at between two hundred and
fifty thousand and three hundred thousand dollars—approximately

fifteen million dollars today. Stanford went to McKim's house and sat there in what McKim described in a letter to Bessie, who was in Europe, as "stony misery" for two days, and on the third day he "broke down and sobbed at the breakfast table like a child," Charley's account continues. "Then he made his mind up to it and threw it off so that one would think he had forgotten all about it." There is a sense about Stanford that, though he had moments of desperation, he did not deeply grasp the desperate nature of his predicament.

When the fire occurred, Stanford wrote to Larry at Harvard not to tell Bessie about the scale of the loss, and wrote to the wealthy photographer Jim Breese, his companion in nighttime adventures, in Naples—where Grandma was—to "say nothing but to make light of it," even though the situation was "about as bad as it can be." (He also asked Breese for another loan.) Grandma found out about the extent of the damage, of course. She must have looked up back newspaper issues, because she included in one of her scrapbooks a newspaper photograph of the charred wreckage of the warehouse, dripping with icicles where the water from the firemen's hoses had frozen over it. There was no need to protect Grandma from bad news of this sort. If something happened like the warehouse fire, she would regard it as a family event, and would want to be with you in that. She would feel the disaster of it, and groan, and stick with you—and put a picture in her scrapbook—and soldier it out.

Most of Stanford's major creditors were friends and the pressure on him to repay his debts to them was not as severe as it might otherwise have been. His landlord, however, was not so accommodating. Baker records that after the warehouse fire his landlord threatened to take him to court. Stanford calculated that he still had objects worth seventy-five to a hundred thousand dollars—in the neighborhood of four million dollars today—in storage elsewhere, as well as in his home. To fend off the landlord, he took out a new loan from Charles Barney, president of the Knickerbocker Trust Company and a crony in nocturnal sprees, who had been helping

Stanford consolidate his debts. This time, what they did was to identify *everything* of value in Stanford's house—as well as every-thing that he still had stashed away—as collateral for his consoli-dated debt, so that the landlord could not appropriate those objects. Of the objects in the house, the collateral included mantels and newels, columns, doorways, tiles, a fountain, and, in the parlor and the dining room, two antique ceilings that Stanford had bought and installed. Surely it is a perilous refuge to have the doorways, ceil-ings, and mantelpieces in one's house made hostage to one creditor in order to escape the claims of the owner of the house.

Evelyn Nesbit was one of the young women who fell in love with Stanford and thought that he would leave his wife and marry her, or thought, at the very least, that she was his only extramarital affair. She was so disturbed to discover that Stanford had other liaisons that, even many years after his death, she could still fall into baldly denying that fact. She remained in touch with Stanford after their affair ended, in 1902—and ostensibly remained friendly with him—but in 1905 she married Harry K. Thaw, who was obsessed with hatred for Stanford. At the time Thaw had private detectives follow-ing Stanford to try to catch him out in his predations of underage girls. This Stanford knew. He also knew that Thaw carried a re-volver and was threatening to kill him. Stanford had booked passage to Europe on the *Lorraine* on June 29th. As he ascended the gang-plank, the entire McKenna detective agency jeered at him: they had been hired by Thaw to do so. Thaw also repeatedly pressed the New York Society for the Suppression of Vice to expose Stanford as a pervert who had corrupted many young girls. Officials of the soci-ety responded on one occasion by putting really little girls—seven and eight years old—directly in Stanford's path: they were disap-pointed when he only brushed the children aside, mildly irritated by the obstacle they presented.

Although Stanford made light of Thaw's threats, a detective whom he hired to follow Thaw's detectives later described Stan-

ford's spilling the whiskey in his glass while telling of Thaw's harass-
ments. He was nevertheless seen speaking to Evelyn in public after
her marriage, and told a friend that he wanted to go out with her
again.

In April 1906, the famous San Francisco earthquake took place,
and Stanford plunged into this larger calamity by working day and
night to think up ways that structures could be made to withstand
seismic activity. This was a self-appointed mission: he made sugges-
tions to the Chicago architect Daniel Burnham, who was working
on a city plan for San Francisco. At the time, Stanford wrote to a
friend, "The San Francisco disaster has added so much to my labors
that I have hardly had time to think." His health continued to
collapse: he had bowel trouble again, and now terrible pain in his
joints drove him constantly to take a variety of treatments. He was
aging rapidly and was often puffy and tired-looking but, as his involvement in the earthquake reveals, was continuing to accelerate,
to hurtle, to pack in more. By 1906, though he may not have known
it, he had Bright's disease, or fatty degeneration of the liver, and
incipient tuberculosis; within a year he would probably have died of
one or the other of them.

On the evening of June 25, 1906, during the intermission of
"Mamzelle Champagne" in the Roof Garden restaurant and theatre,
Stanford went backstage to get the phone number of one of the
actresses—there are indications that he was already involved with
two others. During the second half of the show, when Harry K.
Thaw came up to him in a highly agitated state and wielding a gun,
Stanford simply stared at him. It could be that he felt invulnerable.
It could be that he recognized inevitability. Or it could be that in
the stillness, the unendingness of that moment he chose not to
move.

In her memoir "A Backward Glance," Edith Wharton describes
how for a long time she was unable to develop a plot about Gilded
Age society in New York, because of the extreme thoughtlessness of

the people in that world. The problem was solved only when she understood that in such an environment meaning can be discovered only through the good that such people, in their thoughtless courses, destroy; she was then able to arrive at the tragedy of "The House of Mirth." Although Stanford's destructiveness was combined with creativity and enormous productivity, and he thus cannot be compared to the kind of empty people of whom Wharton was writing, the search for meaning in Stanford's life presents some of the same problems. The acceleration toward disaster was mechanical; that is to say, because Stanford was in the grip of compulsions whose course was foreordained, the course of his life was predictable. I, for one, have searched for an indication of a moment of thought, of awareness, of consideration of the consequences to others—of realization, even, that a different course might be chosen. I have surmised that Stanford's abdication of responsibility was complete. As the moral custodian of his own life, he simply wasn't present. Because of this, there is no story. Without awareness, without at least an attempt to exercise choice, there is no drama. How can there be drama if no one is there? In itself, a cyclone is not interesting. It is just a blind force. The story of the cyclone can emerge only through telling of the damage it wreaks. Only then does a moral universe, a universe in which there is sense and meaning, appear.

I know so well the spot on the second-floor landing at Box Hill where Papa sat outside Grandma's door, waiting for her to wake. It is like a deck—a narrow space between a wall and the railing at the edge of the stairwell—and when I was a girl, paintings of clipper ships hung on the wall there. The stairwell was open from the third floor, above, to the first floor, below. Hanging from the ceiling of the third floor was a long chain, connecting objects such as a lantern with glass doors—to light the second-floor level—an iron curlicue and, at the bottom, hanging by three lighter chains from the main one, an exotic brass lamp with a bellied base. This extraordinary contraption of floating objects, engraved on my imagination from childhood, was surely the model for my dream of Box Hill in which things from all over the house spiralled slowly down the stairwell in an atmosphere of catastrophe that was so familiar that it was safe-feeling and serene.

BOAT

WHEN WE RETURNED to America from Italy in 1953, I was nine years old. In my mind Rome was folded in to my world, mixing with the Propylon and the temple; the blackberries and the rabbity thickets; the cabbage and potato fields south of the Place. There I was once again, bicycling to parochial school. The fields and the lanes and hedgerows between them belonged to Grandma White's landscape, the older landscape of uses which had preceded the landscape of leisure and aesthetic effect. There was a storied feeling in the lane light: a tale of a hedgehog perhaps, or of a field mouse and her family. This landscape was domestic, but it could be bleak out there. Sometimes dust blew steadily off the surface, and once, when I ran a fever at school and had to bicycle home at midday, I took a shortcut along a tractor track right through the middle of the fields. There was a tiny shack out there that I had never seen anyone go into or out of, and just as I pedalled by a black man came out and looked at me with unmasked hatred, startling us both, I think, as if I had surprised him when he was naked.

It was after Rome that I started shooting with a big bow—a hunting bow that curved back on itself, like Bobby's. Claire made a little book of drawings of our family, in which I was poised on one foot on my bicycle seat, shooting with my bow. I started wearing bluejeans rolled up under my school uniform, with a hunting knife like Bobby's on my belt, making a lump. At lunchtime I'd play hooky, taking off for the rest of the day. I read "Huckleberry Finn" and began to see myself as a boy without a family who could just take off into his life on a raft.

When I was ten Papa bought me a boat. I recall no moment of connection with him about this, however: I do not even remember thanking him. All I remember is Mama telling me that he had said, "Suki needs a boat." He would pay for it, the idea was, while Mama did the footwork. Even today I am dumbfounded by the thought that Papa would think of me to that degree: that he saw me at all, let alone that he perceived I had a need, and, furthermore, was moved to fill it. My boat was a wooden pram, white on the outside, light blue inside, with three varnished seats and a set of oarlocks and oars. I kept it beneath the windmill, tied to a beech tree that had slid down the bank and continued to live horizontally, forming leafy caves.

Rowing out onto the water, I learned how the shore of the harbor changed from different vantage points, and how some parts not easily accessible from land were virginal and wild. From the middle the harbor in general looked wilder than it really was, because the houses were nestled in trees. The windmill was prominent, however. From the far side of the harbor, it had the look of a woman in a cloak that fell straight from her shoulders, a woman with a ponytail (the rudder projecting from the vanes) that stood straight out in the wind.

I felt both free and safe out there on the harbor in my boat. I imagined I was in a wild place, yet if I looked carefully at the crest of the hill just to the left of the windmill I could make out the Box Hill gables through thin places in the cuddly surf of trees. Just to the left of the gables, and a little higher, was the sawtooth edge of the pines around Diana. Three of Grandma's sisters had lived on the harbor too. Bytharbor, Nellie's place, was above the windmill; Kate's house—its Maltese cross four stories high and shingled— stood on a hill at the southeast corner; and Ella's Sherrewogue was on the eastern shore. Rassapeague, the homestead that Nellie had given to her grandson Prescott, overlooked the harbor on the northern side. With the exception of Rassapeague, Stanford had had a hand in all of these. The temple, which stood on a knoll above the harbor, was his too, though I associated it with Papa who fussed there. So although I was not directly aware of it, Stanford's harmony with chaos underneath—that irony—was there on the harbor, as was Papa's sorrow, like a pentimento in the frivolity of the temple. Aunt Alida's house—Stony Brook, as we called it, thereby appropriating an entire village—was on the south shore of Porpoise Channel, which ran northeast beyond Sherrewogue Point to the Sound. Stony Brook added the frisson of the Chanlers—that questing hope that went with the Chanler stories, as if, one day, some essence of familial truth would, in the telling of these much told tales, streak into the open like a deer.

Though I was aware of family history around me when I was out in my boat, the way I perceived that history in the landscape was as something ahistorical and mystical, like nature. When I saw Sherrewogue, for example, I did not think that it had once belonged to Grandma's sister Ella. Its meaning had more to do with the way my mother pronounced "Sherrewogue," with a tenderness in the "Sherre" that racked me, and a depth charge of darkness in the "wogue." Its meaning was also in the bend of the reeds in the wind on Sherrewogue Point, their blanched undersides upturned and pleading. It was in the way the current wheeled around the point into the channel, tugging at my boat, and in the contrast between this wildness and the lush green shade at the head of the inlet where Sherrewogue itself—the old Smith homestead—peeked out.

All along the harbor were places that seemed special, that pulsed with meaning. The aborigines of Australia call this kind of energy-in-spots "dreamings," manifestations of the Dreamtime, a quasi-ancestral creative force that underlies the world. They see landscape as the art of the Dreamtime, and consequently every little thing in the landscape is expressive—though the dreamings most powerfully of all. Dreamings are usually located in a specific feature, like an animal or a plant, from which the dreaming takes its name, as in Horseshoe Crab Dreaming at Sherrewogue or Reed Dreaming at Sherrewogue Point. At Rassapeague the incoming tide holds back for a long time, then creeps up fast, fizzing in the dry beach straw and the sand, edging toward acorns and leaves and bracken under the bank. Brimming to full tide, the water becomes black and smooth and rounded with surface tension at the edges, and there it holds and holds and holds. When the tide is holding in this way, one gains access to a silence that is always present though usually inaccessible. High Tide Dreaming at Rassapeague.

The landscape was a map of my spiritual reality. It represented feeling that I could not feel and, as art it expressed what I could not express. It was a substitute for an interior to which I had no other means of approach: it was a map of me.

The windmill was at the center of this map. It stood on the line between the Place—which was meaningful like a text—and the less tame realm of dreamings. It stood on the line between light and the good dark—the dark of the animistic world. It linked historicity with the natural landscape, and it linked society with the solitary adventure of the soul. The windmill was frightening up close but benign from a distance, and from a distance it told me that I was in a safe world in which I was also free. So there I was, finding safety where I was violated, location where I was dislocated, anchorage where I was unmoored from the core of my life. The windmill was an artist of emotional dyslexia, spinning peril into sanctuary, turbulence into peace, and random destruction into order. There, where the moral bearings were scrambled, the windmill faithfully compassed a shapeless sky: North, South; East, West. From the distaff of the troubled air it spun its veils of brightness: a spindle, a wild nun, a merciful witch.

The landscape of the windmill extended to the shore of the Sound on the north and to the Nissequogue River on the west. I'd venture into this farther countryside on a horse or on foot, or sometimes in a canoe on the river. In the direction of the river the spells got thicker, maybe because it was farther from the village, maybe because the cultivated fields, woods, and meadows there had a quality of being just countryside, as if they were unowned. There a feeling of rural antiquity was mixed with a sense of the sea nearby—the river's freshwater sweetness was cut with saltwater that twice a day ran upstream with the incoming tide. Down along the Nissequogue, watercress grew in the terraced pools of an old trout-club hatchery. The club itself, with its round-the-clock stewards and convenient private rooms, was long gone. But I knew only that spring water dribbled down the ruined levels into the brackish river and that tweedy wild geese collected behind bulrushes in a black backwater there. Once, I saw redwing blackbirds riding upriver beyond the bulrushes, unsteady on little rafts of beach straw. I knew they had passed the stubby pony grazing in the sea meadow and the ludicrously noble egret poised on the silvered claw of a drowned tree. Nissequogue dreamings could be so strong I'd get dizzy.

The mood in the landscape of the windmill blurred changes in the lives of those who lived there—even blurred death—but changes in the landscape itself mattered drastically. I felt even small changes—clearing for a house, cutting off a path—somatically. In the second half of the fifties, as I grew toward adolescence, Suffolk County, the county in which St. James is situated, became one of the fastest-growing counties in the country. Big changes first occurred beyond the world of the windmill, inland, where large developments were built and high roads laid down to serve them. These changes were made hastily and haphazardly for the most part, sometimes wiping out whole stretches of topography, so that suddenly you couldn't tell where you were. The destruction seemed to be wrought blindly, in the sense that those who wreaked it had no idea of what it was that they were destroying, or even that they were destroying at all. I quickly learned to respond only to bits and pieces of the old land-scape that were left over—a swatch of field, a tree still standing, a tumbledown barn, from which I would infer a countryside that was whole and, with it, create a sense of wholeness in myself.

For a long time, the landscape of the windmill was left more or less intact, becoming a kind of island in the midst of hellbent change and, in this, ever more insulated and charged. But gradually, inevita-bly, the forces of destruction penetrated there too, never on a large scale but with a kind of surgical fatality, choking off a pathway here, swallowing a meadow there, scarring a hillside—bulldozer blade exposing yellow hardpan in shame to the harbor air. A field falling to houses, the construction of a road through woods were annihila-tions of layers upon layers of meaning, ripping through dreamings, destroying the community of the dead and the connections between the living alike.

As the inner landscape of the windmill became more and more vulnerable too, it became shadowed by impending loss, imbued with prospective grief. Indeed, I can hardly remember knowing the coun-tryside without that intoxicating sweetness of the ordinary when it's doomed. With this came a feeling of helplessness. The forces of destruction could not be stopped, nor was there an ear to listen to a petition. Nor was there even a way to register horror and grief. For though others were bereaved there are no rites of mourning and remembrance for fields and paths. The landscape was the most widely shared thing, yet the community underwent its despoliation without tears and without words.

Meanwhile there were legions of cousins on the Place and big family lunches at Box Hill, with talk under the arbors, talk surging everywhere, particularly Bobby's. Bobby was the king of talk. Nearly always Bobby's talk expressed wonder, and wonder, being God-related, is a great connecting force. And yet my sense of my life at this time is my life in the landscape alone. Certainly my vulnerability to random destruction at home was blocked from my picture of life, and, as I look back, even the presence of my sisters at this stage is elusive to me. I remember the horde of cousins, of which I was a leader, but remember less about my sisters: they were, perhaps, too close to home. I had friends, though I have to push to get to them as well. A reason may be that in seeing myself either with friends or with my sisters I have to sense myself as a child—as I do when I think of myself in our apartment in Rome. As a leader of cousins outdoors I was a giant, but in these other relations I am a little girl in my home. It's always jarring to me to realize that I was a little girl. In contrast, the self I experienced in the landscape was ageless and featureless, like a soul.

However, I remember vividly one incident with a friend that took place when I was twelve. Florence was a year older than I and lived with her parents in half of the Bobby Whites' house. Together we concocted a love letter, purportedly from a male admirer, and left it in the milk box of the two old ladies who were then renting the White Cottage. We did this several times, and the old ladies became frightened and called the police. Ernest, the local cop, whom we knew well, was sent to keep an eye on things, and he sat in his own unmarked car, in plainclothes, with his bulldog, just outside the White Cottage gate. But because Ernest often sat there, albeit in his police car with his bulldog, and in uniform—it was a strategic spot to doze in this sleepy village—we thought nothing of his presence, and were caught, and there was a big scene with a lot of policemen and mention of the District Attorney. The upshot was only that I had to go and apologize to the old ladies—not such an easy task for me at that age. My father stood by me, not only going with me but, when we were there, refusing to endorse the old ladies' more extreme statements about my character and probable future. And then, when we had returned to the Red Cottage, he took me into the laundry and took down my jeans and my underpants and hit me over and over. This may have been the first time since our return from Rome. Certainly, it was the first time in a long time, for I had grown too old to spank; I had pubic hair by this time. The spanking was done at my mother's request, and the attitude that my father adopted was that he was taking orders, and was not responsible himself. I went along with this idea in order to preserve the sense of alliance I had enjoyed on our visit to make my apology, a new kind of collaboration that was degrading in a new way.

One day, soon thereafter, I went down to the windmill and found that my boat was gone. That it could be stolen right out from under the windmill rent the veils, and the bad dark came right in. On another day in the same period I was in the woods with my bow and hunting knife like Bobby's, lying belly down, scanning for pheasants, with a tiny book about the Impressionists in my back pocket. Suddenly there was Bobby. Startled, I turned abruptly so that I was resting on one hip, half rising, embarrassed to be discovered in my dream of the woods. Saying nothing, Bobby reached down and around and snatched the book out of my pocket. "The Impressionists!" he said, and riffled the pages and then handed it back to me with a wryness that made it clear he didn't have to, as a policeman or a customs official would.

When I was thirteen, I went away to Noroton, the convent boarding school on the Connecticut coast which my mother had attended before me. In recognition of longstanding ties between the family and the order—Mama had attended one of the order's schools in Rome and my mother's sister, Elizabeth, had become a Sacred Heart nun—my board and tuition at Noroton were waived. It was a small school; there were only seventy students, all boarders. We used archaic French terms for ordinary features of daily life, learned to perform a deep court curtsy (even on the run), memorized the medieval humors in place of modern psychology, parsed the arguments of Thomas Aquinas, and lived within the seasonal masterwork of the Catholic liturgy. It was a fantastic world, but the rules were consistent. Punishment was by the rules and non-sadistic. I loved this predictability. I became a kind of star of misbehavior.

The central devotion of the order was to the heart of Christ and its human capacity for love and suffering. Hearts were everywhere at Noroton. Soon after being awakened in the morning by a big bell rung up and down the halls, we would meet a nun at the door who would say, "Sacred Heart of Jesus and Immaculate Heart of Mary," and we would reply, "I give you my heart." Embossed on silver crosses that the nuns wore was a heart from which a flame sprouted. The furnishings at Noroton were either stately or severe, but the walls held pictures of Jesus with his heart exposed and pierced by a lance. Drops of blood fell from the wound in the heart, which was also, in some of the pictures, crowned with thorns and sprouting flames. Yet Jesus was otherwise dressed and had a calm expression. Similarly, the nuns were cool yet passionate. One evening in Lent, I walked into the chapel, expecting it to be empty, and was frightened by the sight of a nun kneeling before the altar on the bare parquet floor, her arms painfully outstretched, her head tilted back extravagantly. For a long time, she was unmoving. Then suddenly she threw herself onto the floor, facedown, and in the stretch of her neck and of her arms, still reaching outward, there was a tautness that conveyed feeling so extreme that I had to look away.

At Noroton the adults were adults, and the children were children: we were even called children, as the nuns were called Mothers, and when we wrote notes to them we signed them "Your loving child." At Noroton I was safe for long stretches of my life. These were the years of sexual maturing, and I matured along with everyone else, but we wore uniforms, so there was little opportunity for display. Courtship rituals took place on holidays far away: I only heard about them. Thus I was able to hang back emotionally, being a daredevil in kneesocks and oxfords, mechanically breaking the rules. Though I formed close friendships there which I took with me for life, as I look back, it is as if I did not know how to grow.

Despite my misbehavior, I have a sense of myself at Noroton as solidly in shoes, doing things: winning admission to the literary club early, playing on a field-hockey team. (Barefoot, I would conduct illegal classes in yoga in the library at night.) I felt un-ugly, like a boy, and I even have a sense of myself there as a girl in a way that is entirely wholesome, that does not include my old, terrible companions of borderlessness and shame. But they were there nonetheless. After one of the concerts my parents gave every year to thank the nuns for having me, an upperclassman told me that my parents making music together was the most romantic scene she had ever beheld. She went on to say that during the concert she had looked for me, to complete the picture, but when she found me had been rudely jarred: eyes fixed on my parents, I had been hunched over with my mouth hanging open. I looked like a monkey, she said.

In summers and on holidays, I would be back on the Place, where I attempted to pick up my old life in the landscape. I remember noticing that I had lost a knack I'd had for structuring time and also that it was hard to be Huckleberry Finn with a maturing female body. There were often guests on the Place, at one house or another, people from New York, lots of people sometimes, and often famous people, for in a quiet way, Bobby was successful as a sculptor, and knew people who were successful too. The Bobby Whites would give parties attended by glamorous guests at which Bobby talked of wonders and the guests loved him and everybody drank a lot in rooms that were as serene as Vermeers. For me, as I got older, those parties were the beginning of my becoming a part of the wide world of people, and then Bobby began to kiss me and feel my body in the middle of his parties, with my parents and everybody else present as if there was darkness right there in the light. Bobby was sexy with women out in the open all the time—and in front of his wife, Claire, in front of everybody—and nobody said anything to him; that was "just Bobby." And nobody said anything either when he was sexy with me.

This casual exercise of a kind of droit du seigneur had about it a numbing inevitability. That it went unremarked blanketed whatever protest might have surged in me. I loved the Bobby Whites' house: the serenity of the objects on the walls, the subtle colors of the walls themselves, the wavy wide-planked floors. I loved the field light that in daytime poured in through the tall, narrow windows from the south. Acceptance in that house was important to me, and I particularly treasured Bobby's love—his avuncular love. His acts provoked in me acute discomfort and confusion that every instinct instructed me to conceal. Far from feeling able to resist his advances, my reaction was to do everything I could to make it appear that his behavior was normal. I would smile, and adopt a falsely casual air, as if what was happening were almost humdrum. As I did this, I would feel as if I were partly illusion; had I been photographed, I would, to my mind, have looked two-dimensional, like a paper doll. Then I would feel like a monkey. By the next day, however, or even perhaps as soon as these incidents were over, they would seem ordinary. They neither shocked me nor made me angry; they just were. I accepted what happened with the fatalistic helplessness of a child, though I was fourteen, and fifteen, and sixteen—less and less a child.

Then at one Bobby White party something was said at last, and what was said did shock me. The person who spoke up was Claire, my aunt, whom I loved. What she said—sotto voce, but with people all around us—was that this time I had let things go too far and she was angry. And then my own anger surged out of the dark and I demanded in a blurting way, what did she expect me to do and why didn't she stop him herself? Then, having belatedly realized that she thought I liked what was happening, I said, "Please understand that I do not want this." I packed all the intensity I could muster into this message to propel it across what seemed like an abyss. But Claire stared at me, then turned away as if in disgust.

Claire's rejection hurt badly, but even more painful was what I learned from the exchange. Before she confronted me, my inability to protect myself from Bobby was so profound that it hadn't even occurred to me to try. Claire, however, clearly assumed that I, smiling and casual, had sovereignty over my body. To her it was self-evident that I could say no to Bobby, and for that reason my plea for protection was ridiculous, even contemptible in her eyes. I sensed that this was what she thought, and from this I learned that while I had no power to deny Bobby's wishes, others would assume I did. I saw that because of such assumptions there was no way I could intelligibly ask for help. I was effectively silenced—both undefended and not able to report my undefendedness.

Bobby's predations remained limited to gropings at parties: they ended altogether when I became fully mature. Had he gone farther, however, I would not have been able to protect myself any more effectively. Nor does it seem likely that anyone in the surrounding family would have intervened. I was lucky, therefore, that Bobby was as restrained as he was. Merely lucky.

Decades later, when I asked my mother why she let Bobby carry on as he did, she said, after some thought, that she didn't remember any such thing. First, though, and without thinking she'd answered, "But he did it because you were beautiful." This so surprised me that I felt dazed. It was the first I had heard of being beautiful. Certainly I hadn't felt beautiful. I had felt like a monkey. I did not feel beautiful ever, and least of all at those times.

Despite my consistent misbehavior at Noroton—which ranged from messiness to the almost unthinkable crime of trespassing in the cloister—there was never the slightest hint that my invitation to attend the school gratis might be withdrawn. Indeed, when it came time for me to go to college the nuns, rather than facilitating my application to the nonsectarian college of my choice (I suspect they sabotaged it), arranged for me to be accepted with a nearly full scholarship at Manhattanville, one of their own colleges, to which I had not applied. This was high-handed, and started off my adult life with choicelessness of a new kind, but it was not a rejection.

So there I was at Manhattanville, where I had not chosen to go, and at the center of which stood Ophir Hall, the old Reid mansion with its pink marble interior by Stanford. There I was under the spell of the Place in one sense and, in another sense, for the first time in the ordinary world. For Manhattanville was ordinary. The architecture outside the Reid mansion was contemporary and undistinguished. There was no dense texture of meanings to cocoon me here.

The psychosexual currents in the plainness were charged however. There were currents between students and male professors, between students and students, and between students and nuns—almost immediately in this atmosphere of largely covert sexuality the disturbance inside me became active again. I began to drink. But, whether I was drinking or not, I felt stupefied, weirdly blinded, partly blanked out. I developed back trouble. By the spring of my freshman year I was doubled over, walking to class on the plain concrete paths across the plain grass, unable to straighten.

Half blanked out and uncocooned I found my life making less and less sense as my experience became marked by a severance of cause and effect. Most critically, in my sophomore year I formed a close and valued friendship with a nun who taught philosophy. She had an intensely adoring coterie of the smartest upperclassmen around her: it was flattering that she drew me into her group. She gave me her copy of "Leaves of Grass," and read a paper I had written to an honors seminar for seniors. Then that spring, quite suddenly and for no reason that I could discern, she turned on me, excoriating me in public for tiny infractions, and in private rebuffing with disgust my pleas to tell me what I had done. After this baffling betrayal I went home for the summer, and a few weeks later a dean called to say that, though my marks were very good, my scholarship was withdrawn. As the nuns knew I couldn't attend Manhattanville without the scholarship, they had, in effect, thrown me out. My parents did not question this. They were passive, assuming that I had done something wrong, perhaps, or perhaps that those in power were unaccountable. I travelled to the college to ask the reason for what had happened. We were still in the golden age of nunly lèse majesté: "If you don't know the answer to your question," the dean said, "I can't help you."

That was the first of a number of times in my life when I attempted to get to the bottom of why my scholarship was withdrawn from Manhattanville—once through a psychoanalyst, several times through intermediaries, and once, years later, by again putting the question directly to the guru nun herself. But by that time a revolution had taken place in the Church. She was dressed in street clothes and was teaching in Harlem. She said that she couldn't remember what had happened in another world long ago.

In May of my sophomore year, in the midst of my bewildering trouble, my mother had called to tell me that some vandals had set fire to the windmill the night before and it had burned to the ground. In the infernal ordinariness that Manhattanville was for me that spring, this was unspeakably bleak news. How and to whom could I communicate the depth of my loss? Back in St. James for the summer, I could not bring myself to go to the site of the burning. I did not even go to the harbor: I could not have borne the sight of the emptiness there.

My mother said, "I guess you had better get a job." So I went to speedwriting school and got a job as a secretary. I was nineteen years old and on my own in the city, supporting myself, and in some ways my life made sense, but in truth none of my life was intelligible to me. Fundamentally, I remained in my boat in the middle of the harbor, marooned in family history (known and unknown), cut off from my own experience, cut off from myself—the only footing that would have enabled me to enter the world in a meaningful, effective way.

The first man with whom I had an affair was married, was twenty years my senior, and was an alcoholic. When he drank he became another person, unreachable yet not apparently drunk. Later I found that, as with Bobby, I was unable to reject the sexual advances of any man who had even the slightest parental aura.

Because I could not exercise choice, it was as if I had no sexual morals. Still later, I entered a period in which I tried to reverse my helplessness by ruthlessly and recklessly pursuing men. This was a state as helpless as the former, I can attest. As I look back, the worst aspect of my condition was the unavailability of solid moral ground from which to begin to evaluate what was happening in my life.

When I met the man who later became my husband, he was married though living apart from his wife. He invited me to go horseback riding, but we had to go early, he said. We would have to get up at five. Perhaps I should stay at his place. I could have the bedroom; he would sleep on the couch. I expressed reluctance. I said that I was not ready for an intimate relationship. He said that that was not his plan, that I would sleep alone. And, as he had promised, we went to bed separately, I in the bedroom and he on the couch. Then, when the lights were off and I was almost asleep, the door opened and he came in. I did not resist him. He was nine years my senior, but this time my helplessness had to do with the scene, not with a parental aura. He cannot have known, of course, that for me a man's coming into my bedroom after the lights in the house were out and I was half asleep was a repeat scene. (Even I did not understand that at the time either.) Our affair went on for a long time, and many times I tried to leave him. I would break it off, but then, as if in a trance, I would pick up the phone. It was as if I were bound to him by a spell. Eventually, he divorced his wife, and when I was thirty we married. He was the son of immigrants from Portugal. He had gone to the best college and, as a lawyer, worked for the best firm. In his lowly origins and spectacular achievement he was somewhat like my father. The circumstances of our courtship, while outwardly not so unusual in the late sixties and the seventies, inwardly reflected the choicelessness and moral confusion that were the circumstances of my life. It was as if I lived in a kind of war zone: these conditions of helplessness were the conditions in which I loved. And there was love. There was also my hope for protection in the structure of marriage.

We moved to Lower Fifth Avenue. There was the procession of avenue, arch, and park. There was the flickering joy in the boughs of the trees. There was the brownstone with the sweeping stoop and the Jamesian windows.

When Mama, sitting in the window of that brownstone, saw

Stanford motoring by, his life had been out of control for some time and he was not far from death. He was effulgent still, but the discrepancy between his charm and the destructive forces in his life was at its most extreme. Mama was attracted to that vortex.

So there is Mama, sixteen years old, at her window, and there I am at mine, fourteen stories higher, three-quarters of a century later, at the age of twenty-eight. My husband-to-be and I are painting our apartment. It's winter now and snowing. I am painting near the window, and just outside the window, a street's width away, is the top part of the Gothic tower of the First Presbyterian Church. It's a soot-burned brownish black with thick snow revolving downward in swirling patterns around it. Inside, the paint going on the wall is pale yellow, Eastery and wet—that is the striking thing: the thick wetness of that new-life paint juxtaposed with the texture of falling snow, and the way that the black stone tower within the snow becomes soft, like a dark cloud. The darkness and the softness of the tower seem to be a kind of aperture in the relentlessly resistant surface of the world: a place where one could go *in*. I have an experience of almost painful happiness in that moment, with the snow and the paint, and with a song by Satie that my mother once sang coming on the radio—an experience of convergence, a coming within range of hope, a threshold, the sense of a future.

SILENCE

WHEN, ON JUNE 25, 1906, the sound of gunfire rang out during the performance of "Mamzelle Champagne" at the Roof Garden the refrain of "I Could Love a Million Girls" froze on the singer's lips, and there was dead silence. In that silence, Harry K. Thaw emptied the remaining bullets from his pistol and then held the pistol over his head with the barrel dangling down, seeming, even, to wish that someone would take the pistol away from him as he headed for the exit. Women at nearby tables began screaming as the manager of the show jumped up onto the stage and commanded the show to continue. "Go on playing!" he shouted. "Bring on that chorus!" The chorus girls, however, were unable to respond, though the orchestra did attempt to get the lively tune going again:

it started up several times and then faltered, bringing shouts of protest from other parts of the audience. Just before the murder, there had been a dialogue onstage about a burlesque duel, so many thought the shots were merely part of the show. Meanwhile, a woman in white, who had been seated at a table next to Stanford's, leaned over and kissed his corpse as it lay on the floor.

All this was reported in the New York *Times* the next morning. Also reported was how Harry Thaw finally surrendered his gun to Fireman Paul Brodin, who was on duty near the elevator, and how he was then arrested by Police Officer Debes of the Tenderloin Station, who had also been present. "He deserved it," Thaw said to Officer Debes. "I can prove it. He ruined my wife and then deserted the girl." Evelyn Nesbit Thaw rushed up to Harry and kissed him and said, "My God, you shot him, Harry!" and, "I didn't know you would do it in this way," and then embraced him and frantically kissed him some more. As for Evelyn's relationship to Stanford, the *Times* displayed evenhandedness by quoting George Lederer, producer of "The Wild Rose," a Broadway musical in which Evelyn had starred. Stanford had been a disinterested benefactor, he told the reporter, and had simply gotten Nesbit a part in the musical "Florodora," and later the lead in "The Wild Rose." The *Times* also quoted Mr. Lederer as saying that "from talking many times with Miss Nesbit's mother I am firmly convinced that his friendship for Miss Nesbit and the help he gave her grew out of sheer goodheartedness," and that "she is of frivolous disposition and no doubt refused to break off her friendship for him after marrying young Thaw who is a cigarette fiend and always seemed half crazed to me when I saw him." Lederer did acknowledge that White was "a great rounder." Stanford's affair with Evelyn was indirectly confirmed later on in the *Times* article, Lederer's disclaimers notwithstanding.

As the crowd dispersed, the *Times* went on to report, a great pool of blood spread on the floor. The actors and actresses came down from the stage: "Away from the footlights," it noted, "their painted faces showed strangely in the group of employees and friends of Thaw and the dead man which formed as the last of the audience left.'' The *Times* added that the employees of the Garden, to whom both Stanford and Thaw were well known, ''did not seem greatly surprised at the tragedy.''

On the same morning that this report appeared Papa, having sat outside Grandma's door for hours, finally heard her stirring and went in and told her what had happened. Grandma and Papa were calm, but Nina, Stanford's mother, who was living in the house at the time, became hysterical with grief when she heard the news. As soon as possible Papa and Grandma set off for New York, leaving Nina, who was too upset to come, behind. Upon arriving at the house on Gramercy Park, Papa and Grandma found reporters still camped on the doorstep. Charley McKim joined the family and assumed the position of protector, handling the press and helping to plan the funeral. The *Times* reported that when a newsman had phoned Charley the night before and told him of Stanford's murder he at first was able to say only ''My God—good God,'' and was then ''so overcome by his feelings that he could not speak for a brief time.'' On being told of Thaw's remark about Stanford's having ruined and deserted his wife, Charley said, ''I cannot conceive of any possible ground upon which such a statement could be made.''

Stanford was laid out, amidst his possessions, at the house in Gramercy Park ''almost at the foot of the *Venus Genetrix,* a statue found in the Tiber, which Mr. White purchased and placed in the great drawing room of his Gramercy Park home,'' the New York *World* subsequently reported. ''Living, he placed chaste Diana atop his great work—Madison Square Garden,'' the story continued. ''Dead, he was stretched in the shadow of Venus; she who brought him to the shadow of death.'' The reporter had evidently peered in the window. There were some fifteen papers in New York at this time, and this was the big story for all of them.

Charley informed the press that the funeral would take place at St. Bartholomew's, a large church at Forty-fourth Street and Madison Avenue, which had an entrance porch by Stanford and whose interior had been redone by him too. The *Times* reported that there would be ten pallbearers, their names to be announced. However, as extra editions continued to hit the streets, with ever more scandalous details not just about Evelyn and Stanford but about Stanford's private life in general, it became clear that the story was exploding and that Stanford as a figure of depravity was the gunpowder. Because a crush of sensation seekers was expected, the family decided to cancel the St. Bartholomew's funeral. Charley announced the cancellation and arranged for private services to be held in St. James. The *World* also reported that "the men who constituted Stanford White's intimate friends did not rally to the defense of his memory yesterday." Instead, they disappeared into their clubs or managed not to be found at all—except, of course, for Charley. An additional reason that the St. Bartholomew's funeral was cancelled may well have been that not enough suitable candidates had agreed to take the highly visible position of pallbearer.

On Thursday, June 28th, the morning of the St. James funeral, a hearse was to carry Stanford's body to the Thirty-fourth Street ferry which would take the funeral party to a special train waiting in Queens for the journey to St. James. A crowd, including reporters, gathered at Gramercy Park hoping to see celebrities, but what they saw instead was the Judge John Lawrence Smith family rallying close around Grandma in this crisis. Nearly eighty years later, sitting in the newspaper morgue of the New York Public Library, I was moved to read that the people glimpsed in carriages by reporters were Grandma's brother James and her sister Kate, and even several family members I had known, such as Cousin Charlie Butler, who ran a dairy farm just down the road from Box Hill and poured cream on everything he ate, and Cousin Isabella, who had won the rowing race in the harbor as a girl and was in my time a twinkly old lady who always had Christmas presents for us children. I also learned from the papers that Grandma and Papa drove out to St. James together by car—probably with Charley though he was not mentioned in the press. I knew from relatives that Grandma's sisters Ella and Nellie had stayed out in St. James to comfort Nina. Aunt Ella told Nina that Stanford had been shot by an anarchist. In the

Smith family this also became a handy explanation to give the children when they asked about what had happened to Uncle Stanny.

By the time the funeral train arrived in St. James there were approximately fifty people from the village waiting, and a traffic jam of automobiles and carriages from various parts of Long Island that fell into line to make up a cortège. Nevertheless, given Stanford's stature, the funeral was an obscure one that took place in the privacy of the Smith context. The cortège followed the coffin to the Episcopal church. The church was decked out with flowers, but the undertaker provided the pallbearers. There was no sermon, no eulogy. The absence of most of Stanford's New York pals was conspicuous, but Willie Chanler was there, and so was Jim Breese, Stanford's wealthy photographer friend. After the service, Stanford's body was put in the ground in the graveyard behind the church, among many Smiths, under a Scotch-pine sapling that had been planted there for the occasion. The only other grave nearby was that of Richard Mansfield White, Stanford and Grandma's son who had died at seven months; his pretty miniature tombstone had been designed by Charley McKim.

There was no reception. After the burial, the gathering dispersed, except for Charley and a few others who remained on the steps of the church advising Grandma on how to deal with the scandalous publicity. Grandma told my mother that the course of silence had been decided on then. And so, as my mother observed to me, what was initially a strategy for dealing with a passing storm of publicity became a course that Grandma and Papa stuck to for the rest of their lives.

After the consultation on the church steps, Grandma, Papa, and Charley went back to Box Hill. How strangely quiet that gay house, full of dancing objects, must have seemed to them with Stanford suddenly in the ground. The atmosphere of joy trapped in silence, with catastrophe latent, so familiar to me must have come into being on that day. The abruptness of the change comes through in the McKim, Mead & White correspondence; Stanford's busy letters persist right up to his death. "What would your little Italian ceiling

cost?'' ''I was not at all satisfied with the long rug that you simply
repaired. Where is the small rug?'' ''I was disappointed that the
vendor cannot guarantee more than 20 mph.'' ''[I have had] a heavy
dose of medicine indulged in to cure sciatica.'' ''I can hardly keep
my head above water.'' ''I would like you to make the nude young,
sweet and alluring for what are nudes if not for that?'' ''Might I
carry in my heart the thought that if I ever get on my feet again I
might buy it [a painting] back from you?'' One also reads about the
difference between Blanc de Nîmes versus very pale sienna in a tile,
and about the problem of a grizzly-bear skin that stank, and there
are directions, over several letters, for work on the fancy pergola in
the box garden at Box Hill. After Stanford's death, the office was
writing to contractors about how Mrs. White was anxious to complete the work on the pergola in the box garden according to Mr.
White's original intention. Even before the end of July, Grandma
was urging the office to see that copies of the frieze and the caryat-
ids from a Greek temple were made as Stanford had planned. But in
these letters there is nothing of the same rush as in Stanford's, and
nothing either of that sense of proliferation of business and objects
and relationships and transactions that his letters convey. In the
letters after his death, the items under discussion are few, and one
knows that when they are attended to there will be no more.

Grandma must have been in need of money immediately, because
Charley took charge of selling some exotic trees in tubs from Box
Hill in July: twelve orange trees, a hundred and fifty years old,
imported from a château in France; some pittosporums; several
large, rare bays imported from Bruges; and a Japanese pine. The
office correspondence also indicates that a mounted tiger's head was
sold, and that an ancient Gothic window that had been on loan to
Stanford was returned to its owner. Where once there was a
swirling, inexhaustible inventory, each object has suddenly become
somehow unmoving and singular. There is a polar-bear rug. A marble Greek vase. An antique altar. A large Venetian lantern consisting
of three lamps standing on top of carved wooden horses. Soon the
only remaining concern is Stanford's tombstone—a stela with a

scrolling shell on top, designed by Charley. Matters at issue in the correspondence about the tombstone are the type of marble to be used and, once that point is settled, various delays in the execution of the work.

After the tombstone was in place beside the stripling pine in the Episcopal graveyard, Stanford's name disappeared from the McKim, Mead & White correspondence. Reading the correspondence in Avery Library, at Columbia, I saw the Place sinking into a kind, restoring oblivion, the waters of ongoing time closing over it in a healing way as life at the office boomed on with other people's business under categories such as boilers, garages, and gymnasiums.

In fact, however, the noise about Stanford went on in the world in a way that deeply affected the family. For months, it was on the front page of the *Times* nearly every day, and the tabloids and some periodicals gave it even shriller prominence. A typical tabloid headline, over a story accompanied by a photograph of Madison Square Garden featuring the tower, was "RETREAT OF GOTHAM SYBARITES; *Aphrodites and Sapphos Crowded the Caves.*" "STANFORD WHITE, VOLUPTUARY AND PERVERT, DIES THE DEATH OF A DOG" was the title of an article in *Vanity Fair*. Another tabloid headline was "THAW FULFILLED A LAW AS OLD AS THE WORLD SAID DR. GREGORY: *Writer and Clergyman Strongly Defends the Deed of Young Husband Who Took Life of Stanford White.*" A follow-up story on the murder described Stanford as going up to the manager of "Mamzelle Champagne" and saying, of the lead actress, Maud Fulton, "Give me an introduction to little Fulton, she looks good to me," and then saying, "Give all the girls a drink: you know I got a couple of babies in this bunch." Another article stated, "Nothing in the world seemed to please him better than to catch a girl just starting into her teens in his ever working net." According to still another, "Irate fathers and mothers of children just budding into girlhood who have fallen into his clutches have sought assistance from the Gerry Society and the Police." (The Gerry Society was an advocacy group for victims of various kinds of abuse.) One columnist wrote, "Thaw merely gave his enemy a new sensation—something he had sought in vain, probably, for twenty years."

The *Evening Journal* ran a serial called "The Girl in the Pie," about Susie Johnson, who had jumped out of the pie with twenty-four canaries at the infamous stag dinner. The serial claimed that after she married, her husband discovered her past and kicked her out of their home, and that she ended up in potter's field. In other articles, young women who had come forward with testimony were quoted. Miss Katherine Pilon, for example, one of the few who agreed to be named, said that "the stories of Stanford White and the men around him only state half the truth," that she had witnessed scenes aboard a yacht that "baffled description," and that she could point to a hundred similar instances. Stanford was defended by a member of the "Mamzelle Champagne" chorus: she said, "Temptations? Nonsense! . . . Every girl knew what his attentions meant and most of us would have given a year's salary to get those attentions." An unnamed friend of Stanford's was quoted as saying, "What if poor White did play around with stage-girls? They were nothing but little butterflies to him. Why make such a fuss because a few of them fell by the wayside? They were gay, brief playthings. That sort of thing is to be expected." The preachers, of course, disagreed. John D. Rockefeller's pastor said, "It would be a good thing if there was a little more shooting in cases like this."

In the meantime Thaw's defense team got organized, generating another tier of publicity. Harry K. Thaw came from a very wealthy Pittsburgh family that was known locally for its philanthropy. Harry's father, William Thaw, was a self-made coal-and-railroad multimillionaire, and the Thaws were still social aspirants in the larger world. One of Harry's sisters had married a Carnegie. Another had married the Earl of Yarmouth, no matter that he was in fact a penniless actor in New York; no matter that on the very morning of the wedding he had been arrested for debts and on the spot had extorted an extra million from the Thaws. The Thaws also had ambitions for Harry, their only son, although he had been a worry to them from an early age. He had difficulties in the many schools that he attended. For one thing, he would without provocation throw himself on the floor in a screaming rage. As a young man, he had embarrassed the family with shenanigans such as driving his automobile through a shopwindow in revenge for inadequate service, and, for no known reason, flogging a bellboy in his hotel room and then rubbing salt in the wounds. By 1901, when Harry became interested in Evelyn, he was thirty years old and his father was dead. He was an heir to forty million dollars, making him far, far richer than anyone in the White family circle—so much richer as to put him beyond comparison. However, because of his erratic behavior his money was controlled by his mother. At first Mrs. Thaw was appalled by his liaison with Evelyn, but as Harry's behavior continued to be worrying (at some point in this period he was convicted in Pittsburgh for enticing a minor) eventually she went as far as encouraging him to marry Evelyn in the hope that doing so would calm him down.

Mrs. Thaw was an ardent Presbyterian, a do-gooder with austere tastes and the looks of a grand dowager. When her son shot Stanford she was on an ocean voyage, on a cattle boat, to visit one of her daughters, the Countess of Yarmouth, in Europe. As soon as she arrived, she caught a boat back and on her return mobilized her considerable resources for Harry's defense. Since there was no doubt that Harry had pulled the trigger, only two courses were open to the defense: to plead either insanity or extreme provocation. In order to bolster the provocation defense, Mrs. Thaw hired a platoon of detectives to dig up dirt about Stanford. "Many actresses scamper to avoid subpoenas," one paper reported. Mrs. Thaw also hired a publicist who not only planted news stories about Stanford but also arranged for three plays and a book, all depicting Harry as an avenger of virtue, to be written and produced. These efforts rode a groundswell of popular opinion that favored Harry, and they supported Harry's publicly proclaimed belief that he had served as an instrument of Providence in killing Stanford. Mrs. Thaw also hired a former Pittsburgh police commissioner to clear up the matter of Harry's trial and conviction in Pittsburgh for enticing a minor. Subsequently, the ledger that contained the record of this trial disappeared and then mysteriously reappeared with the page about the trial cut out.

A subsidiary theme in the newspapers was how a man of Thaw's background fared in jail. Headlines read, "THAW DINES ON SQUAB HOT FROM DELMONICO'S OVEN," "HARRY THAW PASSES UP TURKEY," "THAW ORDERS FIVE NEW SUITS." Still another theme of the Harry Thaw story concerned Evelyn, who had to be protected from adoring mobs by a cordon of policemen when she visited him. Mrs. Thaw's relationship with Evelyn was also a topic. Mrs. Thaw had foolishly snubbed Evelyn one day when their paths crossed at the Tombs, where Harry was imprisoned. Counsel quickly pointed out to her that both Evelyn's popularity and her potential as a witness were assets for Harry, and Mrs. Thaw changed her ways. During this time circulation was way up for all the New York papers and for others as well. The Hearst chain is said to have risen on the back of the story.

Mrs. Thaw was quoted as saying, "While I am prepared to spend the last dollar I have in Harry's defense, I do not think that the whole trial will cost more than a million." That summer she decided to sell her family home and all her Pittsburgh property, and told the press that she had decided never to return to Pittsburgh but, rather, to "live near Harry if he is in prison, to go to England if he is executed, to take him to Europe if he is acquitted." (Other Thaws were also reported to be leaving "costly residences" in Pittsburgh because of "unpleasant notoriety.") Mrs. Thaw's enormous fortune contributed significantly to ruining Stanford's reputation, and hence to Papa and Grandma's nightmare. Mama, in whom I never detected the slightest trace of paranoia in any other connection, wondered to the end of her life whether stories about the murder and the scandal that continued to surface in the press as the decades rolled by were not financed by the Thaws.

In August, the house on Gramercy Park was rented out, and Charley McKim arranged for tickets abroad for Grandma, Papa, and himself. On the liner Charley and Papa shared a cabin next to Grandma's. The three toured Scotland together, but then Charley fell ill and had to stay in London while Grandma and Papa went on to Paris; soon, however, he joined up with them again, and they all took a tour of Normandy and the Touraine. "McKim preaches architecture to Larry by the hour," Grandma wrote to Saint-Gaudens, and Larry was "in heaven." But to her sister Nellie she wrote:

> As for myself—nothing could be more than what I have already been through—I fear nothing—anymore—and am laying in a good stock of strength and courage to be ready for the winter which is bound to be a hard one no matter where I am.
>
> Where Larry goes I go.

On their return in late October, she moved to Cambridge and lived there in a rented house with Papa while he went to Harvard. Papa took great care that she never saw a newspaper, and also kept from her the gravity of the financial situation in which Stanford had left them. In New York, McKim coped with the details of tidying up Stanford's life—details having largely to do with objects: objects mixed up with other people's things, objects lent out, objects borrowed, and objects promised to others. And then there were collateralized objects, and the extraordinarily tangled matter of Stanford's debts.

In October trial preparations got under way, pouring kerosene on a newspaper story that had never died. Because of the difficulty of finding an impartial jury, the trial itself didn't start until January 23, 1907, seven months after the murder. The prosecutor was one of New York's great district attorneys, William Travers Jerome, a stocky, forceful man, reminiscent of Teddy Roosevelt. Thaw had five lawyers, led by Michael Delmas, a short, fat, lion-headed celebrity attorney from California, who was said to be the illegitimate son of Napoleon III and was often dubbed "the Napoleon of the Western Bar." Large crowds gathered daily outside the courtroom, requiring a police cordon to enable the principals to enter. (Evelyn's entrances nearly caused riots.) A telegraph office was set up in the main hall of the Criminal Court Building for the convenience of reporters, and extra seats for reporters had also been installed in the courtroom. More than a hundred reporters covered the trial. The rest of the seats were taken up by the Thaw family and friends, including two of Harry's sisters, Mrs. George Carnegie and the Countess of Yarmouth. One of Stanford's secretaries, Charles Harnett, attended. Aside from Harnett, however, once Papa had opened the trial with his brief testimony and then gone home, there was no one in the courtroom associated with Stanford other than Evelyn.

In the end there were two trials, both centering on the issue of Harry's sanity, for Harry had eventually been persuaded by his lawyers to plead not guilty by reason of insanity, a novel concept at the time. In return for this capitulation, the lawyers agreed to introduce into his defense the idea that he had done only what honor would require of a husband—that Stanford's behavior had driven Harry insane, as it would have driven any honorable man. Delmas put it this way in his summation: "If Thaw is insane, it is with a species of insanity known from the Canadian border to the Gulf. If you expert gentlemen ask me to give it a name, I suggest that you label it *Dementia Americana*. It is that species of insanity that inspires every American to believe his home is sacred. It is that species of insanity that persuades an American that whoever violates the sanctity of his home or the purity of his wife or daughter has forfeited the protection of the laws of this state or any other state." The *Dementia Americana* aspect of the defense turned the trial into a trial of Stanford.

William Travers Jerome pressed the case that Harry was sane and that the murder had been premeditated. Since Harry had for weeks walked around New York with a gun declaring that he wanted to kill Stanford, this case was not hard to press. Then Evelyn took the stand. She made her appearance dressed in schoolgirl clothes, with a demure hat that had been carefully chosen by Delmas. According to newspaper reports, her voice was high, like a child's, and though she was twenty-two by this time, she looked sixteen. She looked helpless and small. Irvin Cobb, a reporter for the *Evening World*, wrote that she was "the most exquisitely lovely human being I ever looked at" and described her as having "the slim quick grace of a fawn, a head that sat on her faultless throat as a lily on its stem, eyes that were the color of blue-brown pansies and the size of half-dollars, a mouth made of rumpled rose petals."

As it happened, the prosecutor, Jerome, was himself having an illicit affair with a very young woman at the time, a fact that could have ruined his career had it been known. Evelyn, who in effect was telling on *her* lover at the trial, infuriated him. He lost his temper at her several times, and so appeared to be bullying a frail creature; he missed important chances to press his case when others were on the stand; and at times he even undermined his case because he was so intent on trying to elicit testimony that would blacken Evelyn.

He won a victory, however, when Stanford's behavior outside his relationship to Evelyn was ruled out of order. This was a mercy for the family, because Mrs. Thaw's detectives had amassed a formidable arsenal of tales. Jerome would probably have been able to get Evelyn's relationship with Stanford ruled out as well, but Delmas circumvented this by having Evelyn testify not about her relationship with Stanford directly but about what she had told Harry about the relationship.

That Evelyn had consistently stoked Harry's jealous rage at Stanford had been widely reported. Wherever they might be, if Stanford turned up Evelyn had made sure that Harry noticed him. In fact, on the night of the murder Stanford had arrived at a restaurant where Evelyn and Harry were dining, whereupon Evelyn passed Harry a note (later produced in court) that said "That B——— is here." ("B———," she testified, stood for "Blackguard.") What had not been reported was Evelyn's story of her affair with Stanford, six years earlier, when she was sixteen. Before this part of her testimony, Evelyn insisted that court stenographers be male, because what she had to say was too shocking for a young woman to hear. This got the court, and then the nation—including the President and Congress—into an uproar. If it had not already been made clear that Stanford was the real defendant in the trial, there was no question about it from this point on.

Evelyn told of being befriended by Stanford, of being invited to parties with other chorus girls, and of being given gifts. Then one evening when her mother was out of town, she went to what she had expected would be an after-theatre supper for four but had turned out to be a supper for two. Stanford, who up to that time had limited her to one drink, gave her many drinks that night. As Delmas summarized her testimony, she then said that

he finally took her to a room where there was a small table upon which stood a single glass and a small bottle of champagne; that while her attention was attracted by a picture, Stanford White filled the glass with champagne and insisted upon her drinking; that she did drink and in a minute or two a pounding began in her ears, a thumping and a pounding and then the whole room seemed to go round and everything got very black and she lost consciousness; that when she regained consciousness she was in bed with nothing on but a little shirt and Stanford White was in bed with her nude, and that there were mirrors all around the bed; that she was alarmed and screamed and Stanford White tried to quiet her; that when she got out of bed to reclothe herself she saw large blotches of blood all over everything and thereupon she began to scream more than ever, and Stanford White came back into the room and tried to quiet her; that after she was dressed Stanford White took her home to her hotel and left her and that she sat up all night and continued to sit up until the afternoon of the next day when Stanford White appeared at the hotel; that Stanford White then kneeled beside her and picked up and kissed the edge of her dress and that she would not look at him, and that he said to her that she should not be worried or upset; that she had the most beautiful head he had ever seen, and he would do a great many things for her, and that every-body did these things and that that was all people were born for and lived for and that she was so nice-looking and slim that he couldn't help it, and that only very young girls were nice, and the thinner they were the prettier they were; that nothing was so loathsome as a stout or fat woman; that everybody was doing these things and that she must be very clever and not be found out and made her swear not to tell her mother about it.

Delmas's brilliant and persuasive summation lasted eight hours, and at the heart of it was a description of what was, at the very least, a statutory rape, as the age of consent at the time was eigh-teen. Jerome, in his summation for the prosecution, said, "Will you acquit a cold-blooded, deliberate, cowardly murderer because his lying wife has a pretty girl's face?"

After two days of deliberation the jury remained deadlocked, seven finding Harry guilty and five finding him insane. The judge dismissed them and ordered another trial. That one began a year after the first and was comparatively swift. Harry K. Thaw was found not guilty by reason of insanity and was committed to Mat-teawan, a mental institution in Fishkill, New York. A large approv-ing crowd attended his passage—in his own car, accompanied only by two of his lawyers—from the Criminal Court Building to Grand Central Station, where he boarded a train for Fishkill. He had hired a private railroad car, well stocked with whiskey for the trip, and had invited a large group of friends to celebrate with him.

During the second trial Grandma and Papa were in Paris, where Papa, having graduated from Harvard, was studying architecture at the École des Beaux-Arts. Charley stayed in close touch, taking an intense interest in the details of Larry's schooling at the École, and daydreaming about his future. To Larry he wrote:

When you get through with your work on the other side and come home ready to build, you will find opportunities awaiting you that no other country has offered in modern times. The call is Roman, and it will have to be sustained. . . . There is no danger of falling back into the degenerate order of things which has heretofore always existed. [The way is now being paved for the next generation] who are to come home and design the *really great works*.

Charley was at the height of his influence as an architect, and his letters to Paris were full of encouragement; but his health had been fragile for years, and Stanford's death, the trials, and the publicity precipitated an irreversible nervous decline. He lost his ability to concentrate, became melancholy and fearful, and began to take extended leaves from the office. As the years passed, his distress only worsened. Eventually he had to have an attendant with him at all times.

In this period of mourning and decline, Charley's long attachment to Smithtown and to the Judge John Lawrence Smith family's vision of life came to the fore again. Before sailing for Paris, Grandma had sent him a painting of St. James and Charley had written back:

Thank you for the picture; I love to have it as your gift—and for all the memories it calls up. For nearly twenty-five years I have associated it with so much in my life that has smoothed the way and helped to make existence more worth living that I should be helpless now if I were to try to tell you my affection for the soil of the Smiths.

In sickness and in health, through many years which seem such a little way back, they have endeared it to me by everlasting kindness. Is it any wonder that Crane Neck and the Sound rejoice my soul as well as theirs?

Ella was not over fifteen years old, nor you very long out of short frocks when we landed, Prescott and I, one very hot summer morning after an eventful night on the Sound and arrived twelve hours late at his new cottage by the harbour.

I can see Cornelia [Nellie] now, meeting us at the door, young and handsome, full of concern—ministering to our wants and sending us to bed immediately after breakfast! Those were halcyon days of pioneering, when the old "cord-wood" path was good enough, and the sky blue enough, and [Bessie's brother] James' axe cleared the way. Your grandmother used to drive over then to see the "improvements" and I was called in to explain to the Judge the beauties of one of my first efforts in Architecture.

As I look back, from then till now seems only yesterday. Nothing is changed. Winter has taken the place of summer, the country is as beautiful as ever.

In another letter to Grandma he wrote, "You alone have made life worth living."

When Grandma and Papa came back from Paris in 1909, Charley could no longer tolerate the stresses of the city at all. So Grandma fixed up the Red Cottage for him. She put in gateposts adorned with beskirted bronze horses that had been figureheads for gondolas in Venice. She put in little gravel paths, held in by strips of iron that also kept out the weeds. And she furnished the house with, among other things, a five-foot-high Tyrolean chest with a big iron key in the lock; a Swiss gaming table, with a slate top for keeping score; and a corner cabinet that Stanford had improvised out of some ornamentally painted wooden panels from a Bavarian church. These were still fixtures of the Red Cottage in my time. Charley lived there for only a few months, however. In September of 1909, just as Pennsylvania Station was nearing completion, he died in the Red Cottage. Stanford had died wearing a heavy gold ring depicting the nude figures of a man and two women. Charley died wearing a ring on which two hearts were entwined.

WINDMILL

SEVEN YEARS AFTER I moved into the apartment on Lower
Fifth Avenue, I found myself on the Place on a wet November day,
crouching in the woods just below the point where the Rhododendron Drive burst out into the fields on its way up to Box Hill. The
drive cut through a rise here, wooded on the northern side where I
was crouching, and with a swaying, gently descending pasture on the
other. In the nineteen-sixties, Mama had divided up the Place
among her children, and this pasture was a part of Johnny's share. It
had, consequently, come to be known on the Place as Johnny's field.
The far side of the pasture was defined by the hedges of the Privet
Path and in summer, the sun on the meadow grass, against the
darkness of the hedge behind, stopped time: had something of

Heaven. But even in rainy November the contrast was pleasing, as was the offbeat lilt of the descending land.

After his lobotomy (twenty-five years in the past by this time) Johnny had been impaired but not to the degree that one would expect after so drastic an operation. He was perhaps calmer than his former self, but a sometimes frightening energy still surged in him and his predicament continued to be an infernal combination of vigor and ineffectuality. He had remained physically superb—tall and fit and tan, with a wonderfully rich way of speaking: he was both an attractive man and, to anyone who looked closely, an invalid. Since the lobotomy, he had lived much of the time in Vermont—for a long stretch on a farm with a distant relative—though periodically he would be on the Place for extended visits. On one such visit he met an otherworldly poet, whom I will call Wendy, at one of the parties at the Bobby Whites'. To everyone's astonishment the two married, and went to live on the west coast of Ireland. The marriage lasted for less than a year, but in that time Wendy conceived a child. Because of Johnny's condition these developments were worrisome, but they also generated explosive feelings in the family, especially in Mama, that went far beyond the scope of normal worry. It was as if in stepping out of the role of invalid and becoming sexual and fertile, Johnny had stirred some deep, unbearable family pain. Nevertheless, after the separation Wendy came to stay with Mama in the White Cottage until she had her baby, while Johnny returned to Vermont. Pregnancies made Mama edgy under the best of circumstances.

Then one December morning, when Wendy was nine months pregnant and there was snow on the ground, Mama turned up at the Red Cottage dressed in a coat and hat of black Persian lamb that my mother had never seen before, and announced that she was going to New York for the day and that Wendy had better be out of her house by the time she got back. Later in the day, Mama called from New York and told my mother that Wendy couldn't stay in the Red Cottage either, because it was too near. So my mother arranged for Wendy to move to the Smithtown House, which happened to be empty at the time. As it turned out, Wendy went into labor that very night. My mother drove her to the hospital in the middle of a cracking freeze, with accidents happening right and left, but they got there without incident, and a little girl, whom I will call Pamela, was safely born.

By the time I was crouching in the rain in the woods across from Johnny's field, Pamela was ten years old. In the years since her birth, Johnny had deteriorated greatly. Only his brute health was unaffected, seemingly impervious to the inroads of time, accentuating his interior decline and the absence of happiness in his life. As time went on, his physical splendor seemed to become a form of torture, as if aging were a relief that he was being denied. By 1979—the year in question—he was living in a tiny apartment in the cow barn, and eating at Mama's twice a day. He yelled at her. He breathed in a seething way. He ate enormous amounts very slowly: there was no fat on him; the calories just burned. Because epilepsy had resulted from the shock treatments, he had never got a driver's license, so his mode of transportation was an orange moped. Rain or shine, he wore a voluminous yellow waterproof poncho, and a motorcycle helmet with a green-tinted face guard. He was a big man for a moped, and he sat on it in a posture that conveyed ferocious speed.

Johnny's deterioration, sad enough in itself, was additionally painful to observe because it made the sadness in our family plain. One had to work to be patient and good-tempered around him—for he could be very difficult—while also fighting against the feeling of hopelessness that his state could engender. The obviousness of his pain was hard to tolerate: one could endure Johnny-sadness more calmly when he wasn't there. I transferred my deeper feelings about him to his field, for example, which was in no way spectacular, although there was something superb about it in the same *echt* way that Johnny was superb. Others saw to it that the taxes were paid and the land was to some degree maintained. And so of all the parts of the subdivided Place Johnny's field was the part that was most communal. Johnny's field, being in a way just the Place and not owned by anyone in particular, was the field of the excellence and the sorrow of what was shared.

The spot where I was crouching, on the other hand, had never had any meaning in my time. It was a nowhere. In the era of the cow-barn landscape, it had been pasture, and probably called something, but whatever that name was had been long lost. All that was left was an ancient oak, a remnant of the virgin forest, that stood a little behind me and to my right. One could see that the oak had given the erstwhile pasture its character. The double bole was nearly four feet in diameter at the base, and it towered over second-growth trees. The oak created a problem, because it was directly opposite the higher part of Johnny's field. The lower part had become grown up with a jungle of vines and briars. My problem was that when I moved even twenty feet to the left, I would be opposite meaningless jungle, but when I moved right I crowded the oak. The task was to find exactly the right site for my house.

My life on Lower Fifth Avenue had, by this time, withered in ways that were baffling to me. A promising writing career had been throttled by frustration. A highly valued network of friendships had frayed. Above all, my marriage, which had started out full of hope, had become painful and empty as even the home I had worked to create with such joy had become a place without sanctuary. There was no reason for any of these developments that I could discern. For no reason, when I heard my husband's key turn in the lock I would, invariably, experience a stab of fear. For no reason it had become more and more difficult for me to be a part of the world outside my home either, to have a life with colleagues. I had failed to develop an adult context for myself. As the years went by, the pentimento of isolation had pushed up through the surface of my life in much the same way as the spectre of the Place pushed up through contemporary environments, though I did not understand this at the time.

Then I had a dream in which the procession of avenue, arch, and

the circular area around the fountain in Washington Square overlapped with the formation of the Rhododendron Drive, the Propylon, and the Rond Point. After that I became more conscious of the
interpenetration of my present and my past. I noted as Stanford's
the Italianate tower of Judson Church, on the south side of the park,
with its logical little loggias rising story upon story to a flatly peaked
roof, watching over the ancient men and women who sat on benches
like shoulder-to-shoulder Daumiers along the symmetrical walks.
Especially on weekends, the park would be roiling with a diverse
mixture of humanity. At these times the symmetrical layout made
the humanity seem to me like so much flotsam and jetsam, washed
in by one tide only to be washed out by the next. At another time
the symmetries might seem flimsy and wishful, like childish fantasies, like doodles on the sky. Once as I was walking through the
surging, crashing noise of the Square, a lull occurred, and into this
silence rose three or four uninterrupted measures of Elizabethan
music played by a brass quintet. The music was stalwart, humble,
sensual, festive, and also structured. The fragment of musical structure seemed to beckon like a golden room.

It is a part of the character of Manhattan that interior and exterior realities mingle recklessly. In Manhattan, anyone can slip into a
vulnerable, thin-skinned state in which a few notes of music can
suddenly become a longed-for home. My longing in this period,
however, when awakened, was shattering, and nowhere was it more
easily awakened than in the neighborhood of Lower Fifth Avenue.

Ghostly overlappings of history that undermine the primacy of
the present are also common in New York. Half-built buildings and
buildings in a state of demolition are a part of the cityscape always,
so that what is there and what is not there can easily get mixed up.
On a walk one mild winter afternoon I came across a site, not far
from my apartment, where a historic church that had burned to the
ground was being rebuilt exactly as it had been—a time-scrambling
endeavor in itself, in a way. The frame was up, but the roof was
open to the sky and the floor was not yet in place over the deep
foundation. Gray steel bars descended from the rafters right on

down, past where the floor would eventually be, into the subterranean darkness. The gray bars looked like rain that came through the roof and did not stop at the floor, or even at the ground, but rained through all barriers including that of the earth itself.

In the midst of this period, news of unexpected death exploded in the already tentative solidity of my world. In July of 1976, my cousin Natalie, the youngest of the Bobby White children, was killed in an automobile accident just a few weeks shy of her eighteenth birthday. The accident happened at an oversized, directionless intersection in the destroyed countryside of greater Long Island that surrounded the Place. It was more or less a random event: a hurtling garbage truck, its driver blinded by turning cars, hit her car sidewise as she, also blinded, was turning to cross the traffic in the other direction. I had last seen Natalie running out of her parents' yard in a blue dress that left her shoulders bare and swung loosely around the middle of her calves, her figure on the very edge of womanliness, her blond hair in the sultry light near-phosphorescent. In my grief, but especially in my terror, I was inconsolable and was also unable to re-consolidate the world.

On the day after Natalie's funeral, a group of us, including Natalie's sister, Stephanie, and her two brothers, Sebastian and Christian, all in their twenties, spent the day together—playing tennis, walking, swimming, but never speaking of Natalie, or of death. Those were the primary thoughts in our mind, but with respect to them we could not speak. The July sky was cobalt and the green of the trees was emerald. We swam in the Sound in the morning and on the western shore of the harbor in the evening. Many years had passed since the windmill burned, yet the place where the windmill had stood still ached. Now the landscape had become disorganized all over again, and in our inability to speak it seemed to me that language had become disorganized too.

Just before the sun set, the air became hot and still. The tide came brimming in through the reeds and creeping over the short salt grass that grew behind them. Sebastian suggested that we lie down in the salt grass, where the water was only a few inches deep. The feeling of the grass against my back was both soft and prickly. The water on the back of my head, down my back, and on the underside of my legs was cold. But the sun made the dry half of my body hot enough to sweat. It was a confusing sensation: wet, dry; soft, prickly; hot, cold. The subject of the windmill arose, and also the burning.

Stephanie seemed almost assaulted by this topic. She lay there with one hand on her chest, her mouth open, wordlessly working the air. Then, in a wavering little voice, she began to tell of the day she overheard her classmates snickering gleefully about the burning, in the hall of the local junior high school. That was how she found out the windmill had burned, and it was clear from the snickering that it had been kids from her school who had set the fire. Stephanie said the information was so horrifying to her that she could barely absorb it, and at the same time she could say nothing of her devastation. Who there would understand the meaning of the windmill? As the arsonists were viewed as heroes, she would only be jeered at. So for her there was only horror and silent rage.

As Stephanie told us this, I felt us all drawn closer: the windmill was a symbol freighted with our deepest feelings. And yet its relevance to our present situation seemed inexpressible. That, surely, was more than language could manage. Indeed, Stephanie was speechless again there on the beach—with her hand on her chest, and looking at the sky. I felt us all drifting apart in that silence, each into a separate universe of unspeakable experience. Then with tremendous satisfaction, with a kind of combustion, Stephanie said: "The burning of the windmill was my first experience of death."

Instantly we were connected on the level of our deepest feelings about a common experience and the world became coherent again. As Natalie had shared in that experience, she was connected to us too—hence snatched back from chaos into a realm of meaning. Dear windmill, returned from ashes to save us through the very image of your own annihilation. In this, you proved more powerful than the mindless violence that destroyed you! You were always ingenious. But this, surely, was the most ingenious thing.

In retrospect, my decision to build a house on the Place seems so strongly fated that almost any strand in my life would lead to that conclusion. The impact of Natalie's death, as captured in Stephanie's remark about the windmill, was just one of the strands, but it is the one that belongs in the story here, for I know of no better way to explain why I built the house than that I was attempting to recapture the alchemy of the windmill in my life, to protect myself from death. By setting myself down in the landscape of my childhood I was paradoxically hoping that the meaningfulness through connection, and with it a sense of protection, would be restored.

Another death was a more immediate factor. In 1977, Gil, my husband's oldest child by his first marriage, developed bone cancer. He was twelve at the time. For two years Gil struggled through desperate and draconian treatments and then, in December of 1979, he died. It was a month before his death that I was crouching in the woods on the Place looking for anchorage, you could say—a way of tying us to the earth.

There had been no major construction on the Place for three generations; even repairs were habitually made not with new materials but with whatever might happen to be lying around. In keeping with this aesthetic, we decided to move an old house to the Place, rather than to build a new one. We chose an eighteenth-century shingled cottage in the New England style that was sitting on a commercial strip about twenty-five miles east of St. James. The house was owned by a contractor who was eager to put up a commercial building on the lot. It had a long, sloping shingled roof, with deep eaves. It had been built by a cabinetmaker and the interior was exquisite in an austere way. It was a delicate house with very fine points, but you had to look closely to see that: it was, at first glance, unassuming.

Because the tiniest feature of the Place was invested with meaning and feeling, I knew that it was important to cause as little disturbance as possible in intruding my house. I chose the spot opposite Johnny's field both because it was close to the heart of the Place and because, with the exception of the oak, the actual spot was insignificant. It was a little nowhere of unnamed woods, into which I would slip this invisible old house that was the color of whatever was lying around.

Gil died in December, and by January I knew that I was pregnant. My husband, unable to speak of his grief either before or after Gil's death, was also unable to respond to the staggering prospect of a new arrival. He was withdrawn but we had agreed, in any event, that the house was my job. I became fanatical about the siting. Eventually I figured out a way to keep the oak yet also have a view of Johnny's field.

In May the clearing began. Chain saws tore into tall second-growth oaks and hickories and they crashed down with earth-shaking thuds. This bit of woods, it seemed, was not so undistinguished after all. One day my mother reported to me that my aunt Lizzie—the Sacred Heart nun, who was visiting—had rushed into Mama's house in distress, saying that they were cutting down the dogwoods *in bloom*. But no one could have been more shocked by what was happening than I. After the trees were cut down and chopped up and the roots hauled out, the bulldozer dug a hole in the cleared space, the hardpan, stripped of its thin mantle of woodland topsoil, exposed to the sky.

In order to make it possible for my house to enter the Place, one of the massive stone posts that flanked the South Gate by the White Cottage had to be demolished. As the route would then pass through an outer pasture to Johnny's field, a section of the Privet Path also had to be removed, scooped up by the bulldozer and set to one side, the privet bushes listing over in a sickening way with their roots poking out from the clumps of earth that bound them. I was able to postpone the worst of the violations, the closing off of the Rhododendron Drive, which was a part of our lot. Because the drive ran so close to the site of our house, my husband made closing the drive a condition of our choice of that particular lot. This became an issue between my husband and myself that to him represented whether our property was our own or a hostage of the extended family.

In the meantime, my house was still standing on its original site. In June, the carpenters took down the roof. The body was then cut in half—the long way, from side to side—and jacked up, giving the structure the disreputable look of buildings that are half demolished. The magnificent central chimney was steadied with odd scraps of wood stuck every which way between the aged bricks. Most nerve-racking, the interior was now protected from rain only by haphazardly arranged plastic sheets. A moving date in mid-June was allowed to go by because the concrete of the foundation had not had sufficient time to set properly, and later another date passed, because of a rainstorm so ferocious that ordinary traffic did not move at all. Then, in July, the movers became unavailable because they were transporting some portable classrooms for the schools. The delays were stressful because our way of financing the house was fragile and depended upon a swift completion of the project.

I was living at Mama's in this period while my baby grew inside me. It was a lively house: the phone ringing, the kettle boiling on the stove, the cat chasing a mouse. One day, Bobby's dog Pindar dragged a live quail in and dropped it behind the chaise longue in Mama's bedroom. It hurtled about and battered itself blindly until Mama caught it and, calmly commenting on the beauty of its plumage, put it out. At lunch and supper Johnny ate with us, seething.

That June, the rhododendrons bloomed prolifically. They bloomed first in front of the site of my house and then, like a wave splash-leaping, reaching over, and sequentially unfurling, they bloomed successively down the drive, bursting out in profusion—like a wave crashing and swirling—in the Rond Point. From May through July there were violent thunderstorms. The heavy rains threatened our house, sitting by the side of a commercial road, in pieces, under flimsy wraps. Still, I heard in the thunder—as I felt in my baby's kicking—my life knocking in a vigorous way.

Meanwhile, I began to sense ambivalence to my project in the larger community of the family. There were no invitations to dinner. If I encountered an aunt or uncle at Mama's, the visitor was apt to act surprised to see me and then carry on as if I were not there. I began to understand that the building of my house created destabilizing shifts in a complicated distribution of power. As this chilliness deepened, my endeavor began to feel less and less like a kind of coming home and more and more like an act of aggression.

One day in July, a part of the house arrived suddenly—a small kitchen that had been added on to the back of the main house in the nineteenth century. The kitchen came lickety-split, with no warning, and was small enough to be driven on its trailer right up the driveway to the site. The movers left it jacked up above the foundation, hovering—an apparition from Tobacco Road. By the time the kitchen arrived, I knew the idea of building a house on the Place had been a mistake.

A week later, news came that the house itself would be coming that day. Mama had her cook bring out some lemonade on a tray into the rough pasture by the South Gate—now deformed by the demolition of one of its stone piers—where she and two of my aunts sat on chairs. Then two long half-demolished trailerlike structures arrived with a police escort, each one half of my house with the roof taken down, each wrapped in foggy plastic and mounted on a large trundle of rough-hewn timbers pulled by a truck. Almost immediately the first trundle got stuck in the mud of the outer pasture, creating deep ruts, then eventually was pulled on its way, very slowly, leaving tracks deeply disruptive of the fragile and complex field floor. Finally, the contraption crept through the gap in the Privet Path, where the two removed sections of hedge were upended, and into Johnny's field. There it was, left on the edge of the steep bank down to the Rhododendron Drive. The second trundle followed, and was placed beside the first. The next step was to build up a trestle of railroad ties in the declivity of the drive, lubricate the top ties with detergent, and slide the two halves of the house across onto the foundation. But by then it was four o'clock. Everybody went home. The next day the movers did not return nor was there an appearance by them for weeks thereafter.

It was mid-July. The baby rabbits were half size, though still a little slow; the trumpet vines were in flower, the trees had become heavy; and I was very pregnant. My husband remained in New York during the week, but even when he came on the weekends he remained distant from the problems caused by the delay. Violent thunderstorms with torrential rains continued. After each one, I would go over to my dismantled house, hoist my great weight up onto the trundles, and attempt to draw back the plastic sheets so that moisture trapped inside could escape. By this time, the only position in which I was truly comfortable was prone in the water. Weather permitting, I swam every day in the Sound, usually off a beach on Nissequogue Point, three miles from the Place.

Driving to the beach, I would often get caught behind concrete mixers or pieces of heavy construction equipment far too large for the road, on their way to one of the many construction sites in the area. In fields pyramidal mounds of excavated earth sat next to stacks of cesspool fittings. Swimming at midday, I would hear the guttural, uneasy tempo of bulldozers slaughtering land in the vicinity and feel it as violence, and the old sorrow would arise. But one evening, as I walked from the car park down to the beach through a jungly place, I heard a woodpecker rapping on a tree, *rat-a-tat-tat,* and then, while I was swimming, the sound of a hammer travelled over the water from a place where a house was being built by the shore. It rang out sharp, with a quick little echo pure and joyful. And then a family came down from the construction site to the beach and sat together on the sand in the evening light in still attitudes that conveyed full hearts and awe.

In late July, Johnny's daughter, Pamela, who was by this time nine, came to visit for a week as she had done since she was five. These visits set off dangerous vibrations on the Place, like a low chord out of range of hearing but felt in one's bones. Pamela would stay in the Red Cottage with my mother—my parents were divorced by this time—and expeditions with Johnny would be arranged. She had Johnny's good looks in a strawberry-blond palette, and very white skin. I watched her that July as she flew around from house to house, stumbling a little as if she were in high heels, her hair a triangle of red-gold light.

By the end of July—perhaps because of old troubling feelings stirred by Pamela's visit, or maybe because of the heat—Mama had become distant and turned-away. Looking into her eyes was like looking into an aquarium, and though I worked hard to engage her in conversations that might be interesting to her, she often forgot we had spoken at all. Or perhaps the progression of my pregnancy disturbed Mama. Pregnancy always made her strange, but gripped by anxiety about my own affairs I did not think to spare her distress by moving out. In early August, it seemed that Mama's house was encircled by a current of oblivion within which I too was forgotten.

One Friday in mid-August, I took a chance that the movers would not come (they never informed me of their schedule) and went into New York for the weekend. Though my due date was two weeks off, that night I went into labor, and at dawn my son came suddenly and fast, so fast that the nurses had not even moved me into the labor room; so fast that my obstetrician got there after the birth was well under way. So fast that his heart stopped: the doctor on duty feared he was dying, but he and my own doctor concluded later that his heart stopped because of the speed. The very next day, the house was slid across the drive on the lubricated trestle. The maneuver went off without a hitch. The old house fitted perfectly on the new foundation.

My husband and I named our son Julian. He had an angular jaw and a tidy, straight nose. He had two looks: a sharp, mischievous look, lupine and laughing, as when a dog looks as if it were laughing, and a dreaming look in which he was like a sharp-nosed little mouse with bright eyes. In his dreaming mode he would make a whistling formation with his mouth. I could hold him, but he was in a way as unreachable as a star. He made me think of Mama when she was lost in her solitude on the very hot days just past in St. James. At those times, she had seemed to slide away from us into the distance, facing the other way like an ocean liner heading out to sea.

In our first days together Julian was distant too, but he soon threw out lines and we hooked up. He developed a great shout—a kind of "Hey!"—and, as if recalled by that "Hey!," Mama swung around and sailed into New York with the grandeur of a whole regatta in a merry breeze. She brought a blanket for Julian and ordered diaper service and once again became the practical, energetic person she had been in her sixties.

By October, Julian had turned from an apple blossom into an apple, and I moved back to Mama's house with him, to oversee the construction. By the time I got there the new roof was up, and though the earth all around was yellow and raw, the house looked as if it had been there for centuries. I became involved in matters like types of insulation and showerheads, copper pipe versus lead, electrical outlets, overhead lighting fixtures, and the angles at which a staircase can be turned. I concentrated on these details as if there were just one right answer, as if minuscule shades of difference in a stain or the difference between eggshell whites could spell the difference between getting my life right and getting it wrong.

For the first time in many years, I watched the slow fire of a Long Island autumn take hold slowly and then blaze. On warm October days, the rich sun on lawns that were still deep green matched a sapphire sky with a Grecian brilliance that was blinding. Then the blaze fell away. There was a pasture behind the barns which had grown up with jungle, and through it Bobby had cleared a labyrinthine network of little paths. I often took Julian there on his afternoon outing, pushing him in his pram, where he lay on his back looking at the different kinds of leaves and vines and branches passing close overhead. Being in this orchestrated little wilderness was like being in a mind. The paths' merging and circling back on themselves and the terrain itself were at one moment as familiar as the palm of my hand and, at another moment, transformed by jungly growth. From the unexpected angle of a turn in a path, or because of the way a big grapevine had weighed down and smothered an old tree, suddenly, unbelievably, I momentarily wouldn't know where I was.

In the meantime, the costs of reconstructing the house were streaking past the original estimate. It became obvious that we would have to rent the house out in order to pay for it, but in order to be able to do this we would have to bring the house up to suburban standards of comfort, thus driving costs even further upward. The time that it was taking to complete the job was another murderous factor: we had borrowed at a prime rate of nineteen per cent until the day we got a mortgage, and we could not get a mortgage until the house was complete. In order to hurry things along, I started doing whatever work I could myself. More and more, I felt myself helpless in a situation that was spiralling out of control.

A moment came when I was up on a ladder painting some outdoor trim and I suddenly saw myself in a detached way—up on the ladder in the middle of my family past, with disaster massing around me. I saw how far the mire extended, how deep it was, how impossible escape was for me. I saw how futile my little brushstrokes were, a barely measurable attempt to make progress in an endeavor that, even if successful, seemed now to be a mistake. And yet, despite everything, I did not regret having made the decision to do this. When I asked myself why, what came to mind was a sense of the great, groaning novel of the family, an unfolding story of which I was irrevocably a part and to which I was committed. Being committed meant believing in the humanity of the participants, and believing that there was a truthful way to know the story that would restore meaning and reveal love. Up on my ladder, I sensed the story in a subverbal form, embodied in a kind of inscape all around me. At that moment, I could see the inscape in the mass and roofline of the barns silhouetted in the setting sun; in the soft, light-absorbent marble of the fountain in front of Box Hill; in the pouring, weeping lines of the swamp maple behind the fountain, towering over the house; and, of course, in the gabled mass of Box Hill as well. My sense was like the sense of a novel that one has years after reading it, when one has forgotten the plot and even most of the characters, yet retains an essence that is strong and moving nonetheless. I saw that I had plunged myself into the heart of the novel; that I might, in having done this, lose my life, but that without taking this risk I might never gain my life either.

Shortly thereafter, Johnny had an accident on his moped (he'd lost consciousness briefly: it could have been epilepsy), which nearly killed him. The accident broke his health, broke the extraordinary physique that for so long had seemed to mock him. After that his expressive slowness became accentuated. He would be late for lunch, and Mama would scold him in a frigid way and he would bellow at her, "I've apologized! What else do you want me to do—commit suicide?" And then he would sit down at the table. When I went one morning to the apartment in the cow barn to take him to an appointment, I found him just sitting down to a breakfast that he had prepared though it was eleven o'clock. As I stood there he ate very slowly—as was his wont—and the time of his appointment came and went. His rage seemed to be initiated in every cell and to extend outward taking in the entire earth.

Similarly, when Mama and I watched the *CBS Evening News* on television, we heard, night after night, that the hostages were still captive in Iran—heard of the paralysis of our powerful country, itself held hostage by its own world-destroying weapons—and I saw the world as gripped in a cold rage that reached to a cellular level. I saw a zombie world, embalmed in rage. I began to have the sense that either I was dead or everyone else was dead or that the world was dead. Late one afternoon toward the end of October, when I was pushing Julian in his pram, I saw the rhododendron leaves reflecting a dull pewter light, hanging down and flickering like fish lures, and in this look of theirs I felt the separation between me and the world. Then there was a fierce gust of wind, and my mother appeared, and looked seeingly at my son, sitting up now in his pram with ruddy cheeks and very much alive. My mother said it was turning nasty and I had better get Julian in.

In early November, Aunt Alida's son Tommy came over to Mama's to watch the results of the Carter-Reagan election. Tommy and Mama exchanged some bad old Black Roman gossip, which made Mama bright-eyed. Then she went to bed, and the country went to Reagan, state by state, like the old domino theory, while Tommy got drunk and said many times, in a theatrical enunciation mixed with a German "r," "The Florodora girls went to *Flori*da."

A few days later, a backhoe digging a trench from my house to the road in order to lay water pipe broke into the old clay conduit that had carried spring water from the tower to the White Cottage, part of the system that had been presumed long dry since the fifties when it was discontinued and drained. Yet water flooded out of the old pipe, and continued flooding, spreading into wider and wider pools that, in the wan November light, looked black and thick, spreading across the driveway and on to the White Cottage grounds. Workmen struggled for several days to cap the shattered pipe that was hemorrhaging water from the past.

By the end of November, no leaves were left on the trees, and the ground was so hard that it was easy to push the pram along the old woods road that ran down the steep slope behind my house, where the land fell rapidly to the harbor. Through the bare woods I could see the shape of my house silhouetted clearly at the top of the hill, and from it there came the sound of one hammer only, desultory and very lone—one carpenter on a large job. In December my contractor and all his crew went shooting in the Adirondacks—as, the contractor informed me, they did every year. There were crows among abandoned pumpkins in the fields. Bobby's wood was leafless now too, so that instead of being in an enclosed universe there, you could see right through to the public road. One afternoon when I was pushing Julian, I plainly saw a big yellow school bus as it came to a clattery halt, and some children got off, noisy and unself-conscious. The bus seemed large and top-heavy, old-fashioned in its boxiness; in the deadness and the discontinuity that I was experiencing, I was amazed that this orderliness, this pact with the future, was continuing—that the world was going on.

When the crew got back from the Adirondacks it was Christmas, and then it was too cold to work at all. This happened every year, the contractor told me; it was routine for construction to stop in midwinter.

The house was not completed until February of 1982, two years after we had started. We were by that time more or less ruined, financially and in other ways as well. Our marriage was gutted, though it did not actually collapse for eight more years. My relationship with the extended family had deteriorated too. When the house was done, I put two fat logs upended in the middle of the Rhododendron Drive to indicate that it was now closed. One day, I came home to find the tree rounds split by an axe into very small pieces. One night, I dreamed of a cousin running across my lawn, his face black in a gangrenous way with rage. One morning, I woke up to find a brightly painted sentry box equipped with a field telephone and a papal flag standing on the crossroads that marked the border between my property and Box Hill. Speech failed me, and seemed to be useless in any event. I became fearful of approaching my relatives' houses.

And yet there were moments of joy. One winter afternoon after the house was finished, I went up to Diana with Julian. The ground was in shade already, and the wind pressed against my cheek like the flat of a steel blade, but the trees were shot through with the crazy amber of a theatrical gel, and the Sound was a hot, summery blue. My uncle Peter's dog, Rosie, had picked up the scent of a mole and was digging a little trench in the field in front of Diana, snuffling deeply in it with her nose while my mother's dog, Melly, watched with outraged interest. Suddenly I too could smell the earth.

One late February, three years after the house was completed, I took a walk down through the woods to the harbor. There was a warm southerly storm going, but in the woods it was calm. The wind blew in the treetops in long exhalations. The path that I followed was a circuitous one laid out in recent years by the Smithtown Hunt to get every possible bit of footage out of this scrap of open land. Because of houses that had been built in the woods near the harbor, the path eventually circled back to the top of the hill. I trespassed the rest of the way, slipping past new houses and then past what had once been Grandma's sister Kate's house and coming out on the shore. The harbor there is protected from weather from the south. The water was nickel, and the leafless trees along the shores were charcoal, except for wedges of pine that were dense and slate-colored.

After passing the spring that had once served Box Hill, and then a small beach, I headed up an old trail along the high bank that runs along the shore there. This property—Grandma's sister Nellie's old land—was now owned by strangers. There was a chain-link gate and a "No Trespassing" sign, but bypassing it was easy, and I felt no qualms as I did. In places, the trail along the top was worn so deep into the sandy soil that the sides were hip high, with mossy overhangs and with tree roots protruding. The water directly below, in contrast, was dark and smooth except for the pocking raindrops. The trail led to the place where the windmill had once stood, a spot I had avoided since the burning.

I had expected to find at most a clearing in the woods, healed over by time and identifiable only to one who knew what to look for. Instead I found a vivid scene of disaster: massive charred timbers piled on one another topsy-turvy, machinery, long steel cables twisted by heat, huge bolts that had held timbers together—all an almost living record of the violence of the fire. Obviously, the vanes had come crashing down through the flames. At the site of the windmill the ground was bare and had a raw look. Not much had grown. This was a catastrophe that showed.

On the way home I passed Diana in a driving blue rain.

BEAUTY

Evelyn Nesbit was born in Tarentum, a suburb of Pittsburgh, on Christmas Day in 1884. Her father, Winfield Scott Nesbit, was a lawyer. It was a matter of pride with his wife, Elizabeth, that he was successful enough to have offices on Pittsburgh's Diamond Street, and to commute to work. Their daughter was christened Florence; "Evelyn" was a stage name she adopted in her teens, but I will use it here for her early years as well, to avoid confusion. A neighbor who lived across the street from the Nesbits described Evelyn as "a sweet and winsome little thing and divinely beautiful, affectionate, and lovable." Two years after Evelyn, her brother, Howard, was born.

In 1893, when Howard was six and Evelyn was eight, Winfield

Nesbit died, leaving the family penniless. Elizabeth Nesbit, a gentle-woman with no experience of the working world, which in any event was largely closed to women, tried to make a living by taking in boarders at a series of rooming houses that she rented. She did the cooking, washing, ironing, and cleaning for her guests, and Evelyn helped her with the workload, but she could not make ends meet. They moved from a bad neighborhood to a worse one, by the Pittsburgh coal mills; she sold whatever personal possessions she had and was finally reduced to begging alms at the mansions of million-aires. In 1899, she moved the family to Philadelphia, and they all got jobs at Wanamaker's, a department store, though Evelyn was four-teen and Howard was only twelve. In this period they were boarders themselves for a brief spell in a relatively decent rooming house, but then Howard got sick and was sent to live with an aunt in Tarentum and without that extra income they started to slide downhill again.

It was at a lesser boarding house that Evelyn was noticed by John Storm, an elderly, courtly artist who was visiting his brother there. Storm was staggered by Evelyn's beauty and asked her to pose for him. Through Storm she also got work posing as an angel for Violet Oakley, a stained-glass artist, and for some illustrators, for whom she often modelled fairy-tale costumes. Then in late 1900, Mrs. Nesbit decided to move, with Evelyn, to New York, where she hoped to get work as a seamstress. She failed at this, but Evelyn had a letter of introduction to New York artists, with whom she soon got work. She posed for the Hudson River School master Frederick Church, who adopted a grandfatherly attitude toward her—he was eighty-four—and for Charles Dana Gibson, who drew her in profile with her hair forming a question mark—a drawing that he called "The Eternal Question" that was used as a cover on Collier's maga-zine. Evelyn loved romances and fairy tales and read them whenever she could. "I began to see myself as the fairy tale characters I loved so well," she wrote in "Prodigal Days," one of two memoirs. She also loved a fantasy in which she imagined herself being soothed by her father as she sat on his knee.

At fifteen, Evelyn got work modelling fashions too: it seems that in New York she became the sole support of the family, though she was not yet physically mature. In her short dresses, she appeared to be, if anything, younger than she was. In mid-1901, when she was sixteen, she met a theatrical agent, and he arranged an audition with Fisher & Riley, the producers of "Florodora," a Broadway musical. It is an indication of how young Evelyn looked that, when she turned up with her mother for the audition, the producers assumed that it was Mrs. Nesbit who was applying for the job—that Evelyn was her little girl just tagging along. When they realized that it was Evelyn who wanted to audition, Fisher said to Mrs. Nesbit, "Madam, I'm running a theatre and not a baby farm." The "baby" then began to cry, and in the end she was cast as a Spanish dancer in "Florodora." She learned the routines in a week.

Backstage, Evelyn was known as Baby and the Kid, and she wrote in her memoir that the other dancers automatically stopped talking about their love affairs when she was around. She observed that her older colleagues went off in carriages after the show, and she knew that the carriages were sent by gentlemen, but because she knew nothing of the facts of life she didn't understand the nature of these relationships. "A girl my age *had* to possess the virtue of sex ignorance or she was not respectable," she wrote in her memoir.

Evelyn's word on her innocence at this point has almost invariably been doubted in accounts of the story of Stanford and Evelyn. In most accounts it is assumed that she had to be sophisticated in sexual matters because she had frequented "artists' studios." Yet it is equally imaginable that a girl in her early teens, who looked even younger, and who had been posing as shepherdesses and fairy princesses, was not being violated by men like John Storm and Frederick Church. One might ask why interpreters of the story of Stanford and Evelyn would need to insist on her lack of innocence. One answer would be in order to preserve the story as a romance, for if Evelyn was as innocent as she claims one can only see what happened to her with Stanford as monstrous.

Evelyn became friendly with two members of the Florodora sextette, Nell King and Edna Goodrich, who were mother and daugh-

ter, though Nell was often taken for Edna's sister. In fact, in theatrical circles they were known as the "Goodrich sisters." It was
through Edna that Evelyn would meet Stanford White. Indeed, it is
clear from other sources that Edna was having an affair with Stanford, but Evelyn knew nothing of that. All she knew was that one
day in August of 1901 Edna suggested that Evelyn come along with
her to lunch with some gentlemen, and that Nell, as one mother to
another, had convinced Mrs. Nesbit that it would be fine for her to
go. "Mama dressed me in a little homemade black and white
dress," she wrote. "I wore my best hat, my copper brown curls
hanging down my back tied with black taffeta ribbon." She looked
so young that she and Edna were sure that passersby would assume
she was Edna's daughter.

To Evelyn's surprise, they went to a dingy doorway, next to the
early F.A.O. Schwarz on West Twenty-fourth Street. The door
opened automatically when they rang. They climbed several flights
of stairs, at the top of which stood the large, charismatic figure of
Stanford White, forty-seven years old and showing signs of wear
beyond his years. He took them into a softly illuminated room that
was painted in different shades of red and had heavy red velvet
curtains shutting out the daylight. There were tapestries on the
walls, and paintings, including a painting of a nude. This startled
Evelyn. The table was set for four, and another man was there, who
seemed to Evelyn even older than White. The men made a fuss over
Evelyn, and their admiration and frank gazes made her feel grown-
up. They served themselves a delicious lunch from a portable cabinet, and poured champagne, although Evelyn was allowed only one
glass.

After lunch, the other gentleman left and Stanford took Edna and
Evelyn up another set of stairs to a studio that was two stories high,
with etchings of nudes on the walls, and a swing. (The joke about
inviting a girl up "to see one's etchings" had its origin in Stanford's
loft.) "Let's put this little kid in the swing first," Stanford said, and
he pushed Evelyn until she swung high enough to kick a hole in a
paper parasol that was hanging near the ceiling.

It was four o'clock by the time Evelyn and Edna left. As they were putting on their hats and coats, Stanford told Evelyn that she should visit his dentist. He gave Edna the address, and instructed her to take Evelyn there that very afternoon. "My dentist will fix your tooth," he said to Evelyn. "It's your only defect. It spoils your smile." Edna, whom he had sent to the dentist some time earlier, knew what this meant, and decided not to follow up on Stanford's request that she get Evelyn to the dentist too.

Evelyn's second lunch at Stanford's loft was with Elsie Ferguson, an actress who was in "The Strollers" at the Knickerbocker Theatre, and Thomas Clarke, the art collector and dealer whose house on Thirty-sixth Street Stanford was designing at the time. Clarke had white hair and walked with a cane. Evelyn told Stanford, whom she called Mr. White, that Mr. Clarke looked as old as Methuselah, which made Stanford laugh. Stanford was annoyed, however, that Evelyn's tooth had not been fixed, but he reassured her that this was a "purely aesthetic urgency." After she'd had another session on the swing, he wrote down an address on a card, and asked Evelyn to have her mother come to see him at his office, to make arrangements for getting her to the dentist.

Mrs. Nesbit didn't comply, but shortly thereafter she received a letter from Mr. White requesting a meeting. She agreed, met him, and was charmed. Within a week of their meeting, the fortunes of the Nesbit family took a sudden turn. Not only did Evelyn go to the dentist but, at Stanford White's expense, they moved out of their rooming house and into the Hotel Audubon, just opposite the theatre where "Florodora" was playing. Stanford also paid all their bills and in addition opened a bank account for them into which he deposited a weekly allowance of twenty-five dollars, the equivalent of approximately a thousand dollars in 1996 currency. He went on to make arrangements for Howard to attend a military academy in Philadelphia, and he paid for that as well.

The Nesbits were more comfortable in their new quarters than they had been at any time since Tarentum. Stanford sent flowers regularly, while Mr. Clarke called daily and sent huge baskets of fruit. "What fine men they are!" Mrs. Nesbit said to Evelyn. "And how wonderful it is to live in New York!" But above all she admired Stanford, whom she found "so kind, so thoughtful and above all so safe," as Evelyn wrote in her memoir. Mr. White bought Evelyn a long red cloak with flowing lines and a boyish satin collar in which he and Mrs. Nesbit agreed that she looked like Little Red Riding-Hood.

A few weeks after the Nesbits had moved into the Audubon, Mrs. Nesbit wanted to visit Howard at his new school in Philadelphia, and her old friend Charles Holman, in Pittsburgh, but she confided to Stanford that she was worried about leaving Evelyn alone. Stanford assured her that she needn't worry—he would look after Evelyn for her. Stanford and Evelyn went together to see Mrs. Nesbit off on the train.

While Mrs. Nesbit was away, Stanford sent a carriage to the stage door for Evelyn every night to take her back to her hotel, though the hotel was right across the street. The other members of the cast, however, did not know the destination of the carriage, and from this time forward they no longer called Evelyn the Kid. The Goodrich sisters, Edna and Nell, stopped speaking to Evelyn altogether.

One day after a matinée, the driver of Evelyn's carriage told her that he had instructions to take her to McKim, Mead & White at 160 Fifth Avenue. As Stanford was showing Evelyn around the office, they ran into Charley McKim. Stanford introduced Evelyn, saying, "This little girl's mother has gone to Pittsburgh and left her in my care." "My God!" said Charley. That night when Evelyn got into the carriage after the show, the driver gave her a note from Stanford instructing her to meet him at the loft over F.A.O. Schwarz. This was the first time she had gone there at night. It was late September. She was wearing her Little Red Riding-Hood cloak.

According to Evelyn, the table was set for two this time, and this time Stanford poured several glasses of champagne for her. Then, after supper, he took her to a room she had never seen—a room that was about ten feet square and had walls and ceilings of mirrors, and a floor like glass. There was an immense couch in the room, and

Stanford, whom she still called Mr. White, left her sitting there on it and then came back with a yellow satin kimono and some more champagne. She drank the champagne and tried on the kimono, looking at herself in the mirrors. When she sat down next to Mr. White on the couch he was trembling.

Then he took her to a bedroom, which she had also never seen, and in which there was a fire burning low in a fireplace, and a big fourposter bed with heavy velvet curtains that hung from a canopy. Stanford showed Evelyn how the curtains could be opened and closed with a cord, and Evelyn tried it. The headboard and the inside of the canopy were of mirrors, as was the wall next to the bed; concealed around the interior of the canopy were tiny electric bulbs. Mr. White showed how the color of the lighting could be changed by turning a knob: you could have rose, or amber, or blue, according to your whim. Stanford gave her some more champagne, and then she must have passed out, or blacked out, or simply blocked from consciousness what happened next, because the next thing she knew she was coming to, naked on the bed with Stanford beside her, naked too. She saw blood on the sheets.

Another reason Evelyn's testimony is often doubted is that her memories of this moment are contradictory. Especially if she didn't in truth know the facts of life—but even if she did—it's hard to see how she might have experienced this moment in a way that was *not* fragmented. In one version, she says that she began to cry, and that Stanford petted her and said, "Don't cry, kittens. Don't. Please don't. It's all over. Now you belong to me." In another version, she says she screamed many times, and he told her not to make so much noise. And in still another version she says that she managed to scream only once. Of course, she could be lying about everything: she could have been fully conscious and consensual throughout. But where there is such a difference in age and power the issue of consent is almost beside the point. In any event, the part of her story that is consistent is that after she either screamed or cried Stanford removed the bloody sheets and took her on his knee in an armchair and soothed her until she quieted.

Evelyn wrote in a memoir that she didn't remember how she got her clothes on or how she got home: for this she has also been disbelieved over all. But she did remember how, once back at the hotel and by herself, she felt utterly confused, dizzy, and embarrassed. She also felt excited. She thought, This is what people make such a fuss about. This is what love means. As she had not known the "big stunning facts of life," she could not tell the difference between what was a violation and what was an act of love. She was also afraid. Assailed by these contradictory emotions, she sat up all night and into the next afternoon in a chair, most of the time stock-still.

When Stanford came to see her the next afternoon, she would not look at him. He kissed her, trembling violently again. What Evelyn said when she finally did speak to him reveals how confused and naïve she was. "Does everybody you know do these things?" she asked. "Did the sextettes, in 'Florodora'?" And, she wrote in her memoir, he laughed and laughed and laughed.

If Evelyn were to invent a story to provoke sympathy and protect her reputation, I doubt that this would be the story she would choose. But whether Evelyn's account is true or not, and whether she, a sixteen-year-old in precarious economic straits with no real parental protection, was an estimable character, are gratuitous questions. Regardless of how one constructs this tale, what happened that night was a rape: unquestionably it was a statutory rape because the age of consent was eighteen, and it was morally a rape because Stanford was immeasurably more powerful than she was, and a benefactor on whom she and her entire family were dependent. What is striking to me is how thinly the exploitation of Evelyn is disguised by the romantic gloss that has been put on the story. The interpretation of those events as romantic cannot stand up to even light examination so implicit is predation in the basic facts of the case.

After that night, Stanford moved the Nesbits into the Wellington, a new hotel at Seventh Avenue and Fifty-sixth Street, which was swankier than the Audubon. He decorated their suite for them, down to the toothbrushes in the bathroom. Evelyn's room had white satin on the walls, red wool carpets and a white bearskin on the floor, ivory-white furniture, and a bed with an ivory-white satin-and-lace cover and a white satin canopy crowned with white ostrich plumes. There were white planters around the suite, shaped like swans; there was a white piano too, and Mr. White informed Evelyn that a piano teacher had been hired, with whom she would learn how to play Beethoven for him.

Evelyn had two choices. She could repudiate Stanford, on whom her family depended, or she could gloss over the violative aspects of what had happened. Who, in her life, might reinforce repudiation? Surely not her respectable mother, who had in effect delivered her to Stanford, and surely not her backstage pals. What footing did this sixteen-year-old have from which to reject one of the most powerful men in New York? Evelyn chose to fall "head over heels in love" with Mr. White. She began to see what had happened to her as a manifestation of her power. "As the weeks passed, I couldn't help but marvel at the strange effect I had upon him," she later wrote. "Whether at his office or in the intimacy of his rooms, always when he first put his arms around me—or only touched me—he would start trembling. I was the type he adored and fell slave to; I was a constant thrill."

For Christmas—which was also her seventeenth birthday—he gave her a large pearl hung on a platinum chain, a set of white-fox furs, a ruby-and-diamond ring, and two solitaire-diamond rings. Their affair was about four months old at this point. Sometimes when she and Stanford were in the loft with the red velvet swing Stanford would dress up in a toga and put Evelyn naked on his shoulder, pick up a big bunch of grapes, and then, looking at their image in the mirrors, march around the loft, singing at the top of his lungs. Sometimes she went to parties that he gave in the Madison Square Garden tower suite, and she would stay on after the guests left. Often they drank heavily together. Sometimes they climbed to the top of the tower, held hands beneath Diana, and looked out over the city. At other times, after his guests had left the tower Stanford would begin designing at a drawing table, and when he did that she would wrap herself in an animal skin and go to sleep. In the morning a messenger from the office would tiptoe in through a snowfield of crumpled paper to pick up the designs he had left on the table. Stanford would be asleep in his opera clothes. Mrs. Nesbit would be home alone at the Hotel Wellington, apparently unalarmed.

Others admired Evelyn. Flowers and jewelry arrived in quantity backstage, and men tried to ambush her at the stage door. In addition, there were eligible young men, known as the Racquet Club boys, whom she met at Stanford's parties, several of whom were millionaires, and several of whom fell in love with her. Indeed, six millionaires proposed to her, including Bobby Collier, the heir to *Collier's* magazine, who thought that Evelyn was talented as an artist and urged her repeatedly to go to Paris to study art. But Evelyn remained besotted by Stanford. Furthermore, she had convinced herself that he was in love with her and that she was the only girl in his life—even that he would leave his wife and marry her.

Once, she saw a photograph in his loft that jarred her. It was of a nude on a bear rug—the same bear rug on which she herself had been photographed nude by the same photographer. She discovered a little book in which Stanford had written down the birthdays of all the beautiful women he knew. When a gala reception was put on at the Metropolitan Opera for the King of Prussia, Stanford got a seat for Evelyn in the uppermost balcony, while he and Bessie sat in the dress circle. She must also have heard in the talk backstage that Edna Goodrich had sued Stanford for breach of promise on the basis of some letters he had written to her, and that Stanford had settled out of court for the hefty sum of five thousand dollars—or two hundred and fifty thousand 1996 dollars. A tension set in between what was obvious and what she chose to believe. The tension still existed when she wrote her memoir ten years later. In it she both claims she was the only one in Stanford's life and admits to how painfully jealous she was.

When, in January of 1902, "Florodora" came to the end of its run, Stanford arranged for Evelyn to audition for George Lederer

for a part in his new show, "The Wild Rose." She got the part and
was a hit. But Stanford, meanwhile, was not around very much, and
probably, if his pattern was holding, was around less and less as the
affair became less fresh. In the summer of 1902, when the affair was
not yet a year old, he went to Canada for a month, with Bessie; then
he was back for two weeks and then gone again, overseas. At this
point, the question was not only whether there were other women
in his life but whether Evelyn would continue to be one of them. An
essential aspect of the story of Stanford and Evelyn is that, long after
the fiction of Stanford's love for her could not possibly be maintained, Evelyn continued to be obsessed with him. The quarry continued to be bound to the predator after the predator had moved on
to other prey.

Also in the summer of 1902, Evelyn encountered the extraordinarily handsome actor John Barrymore, who was then twenty-two.
He later became an alcoholic and a terrible womanizer, but in 1902
he might have seemed to Evelyn to offer a way to break the obsession that bound her to Stanford. Barrymore worked as a cartoonist
on the *Evening Journal*, and lived in a cold-water railroad flat in the
East Village. They met at one of Stanford's tower parties. While
Stanford was out of the room he said, "Quick, your address and
telephone number," and she gave them to him. During Stanford's
extended absences that summer, and in the probable context of his
waning interest, Evelyn and Barrymore became romantically involved. They also spent at least one evening together after Stanford
came back in the fall, during which they both drank too much red
wine and, as a result, decided that it would be better for Evelyn to
go back to Barrymore's apartment to sleep it off before going
home.

At the flat, Barrymore wrapped Evelyn in a cape in which his
father, Maurice Barrymore, had played Romeo, and they both went
to sleep, with the intention of waking up in a few hours and getting
Evelyn home. However, they slept right through until eleven
o'clock the next morning. Evelyn was panic-stricken when she woke

up, because "Mother would be wild and the first person she would call would be Stanford." She went on:

When I walked in, at home, Mama met me with a face of stone. She took it for granted that I had sinned and did not accept any explanation. She summoned Stanford and I told them both the truth, but disbelief was written large in their countenances. Still nauseated from the red wine, I badly wanted to go to bed and rest. But there they stood: he white and tight lipped, she shaking like an aspen, weeping and wringing her hands. "Oh Florence Nesbit! How could you forget your mother, your name, your future! Your reputation is ruined."

Mrs. Nesbit sank down onto the divan, and covered her face. Then she abruptly switched tack. "Suddenly she looked up, her gentle face distorted by an expression of hatred I had never seen before," Evelyn wrote. "But it's not you I blame," her mother said to her. "It is that Barrymore." This spelled trouble for Stanford, because if Mrs. Nesbit took action against Barrymore, Barrymore might reveal what he knew about Evelyn and Stanford. With this turn of events, Stanford's anger at Evelyn vanished, and he became intent on managing Mrs. Nesbit. He had to ensure that she would leave this matter in his fatherly hands. Evelyn wrote:

Stanford bent over her solicitously and assured her every-thing would be cleared up, that no future harm would befall me. She looked up at him trustingly as he spoke, and nodded her silent consent to anything he might deem it best to do. "Come along, Evelyn," he said. And taking me by the arm I obeyed submissively.

Stanford took Evelyn to his friend Dr. Nathaniel Potter, for a gynecological examination. As Stanford knew that Evelyn was not a virgin, he must have done this to determine whether she was telling the truth about not having slept with Barrymore. At Dr. Potter's even deeper confusion set in. I speculate the truth was that Evelyn did have an affair with Barrymore but had not slept with him specifically the night before, because Evelyn is so unequivocal in her memoir about *that*. What Dr. Potter would have found in that case was that she was not a virgin but that there was no evidence of recent intercourse. He gave her all sorts of tests, then questioned her, and locked her in a room. She banged on the door, but to no avail. Finally, at the end of the day, he came in and said:

> "You must tell me the truth, Evelyn. Is it true? Did Barrymore seduce you as your mother believes? Do you know your mother threatens to make a terrible scandal?" "Good heavens No!" I exclaimed. "That's impossible." "What do you mean impossible?" he asked quickly. Having almost let my secret slip out, I refused to talk further. "You had better send for Mr. White. If there is to be any talking let him do it."

Clearly, Stanford had withheld information from Dr. Potter. So Evelyn had to cover up for Stanford again, even though he had, in effect, made her a prisoner and the person she had to deceive was her warden. After interrogating her, Dr. Potter left, turning the key in the lock. "For heaven's sake, send me something to eat. A glass of water, at least. I'm famished," Evelyn shouted through the door.

Eventually, Stanford arrived and confided to Evelyn that Mrs. Nesbit was intent on punishing John Barrymore, and that this was causing him a lot of anxiety. "For what?" asked Evelyn, "and why do you keep me locked up?" "Because I'm afraid of your mother. She is liable to do something that will get into the newspapers. I'm to blame for all this," Stanford said, in a moment of honesty which was swiftly followed by extraordinary dishonesty: "You are the only girl in the world who can point a finger at me."

After this declaration, Stanford drove Evelyn to the Madison Square Garden tower where he sent for Barrymore and called him on the carpet, again as if he were Evelyn's father. It emerged that

John had already taken Evelyn to a doctor to find out if she was pregnant and it seems *that* test had been positive. This startling information came out right then. (Dr. Potter could have failed to spot pregnancy at such an early stage, especially as pregnancy was not what he was looking for.) Ironically, John Barrymore seems to have thought the pregnancy was what the whole confrontation was about:

> "Will you marry me, Eve," he said.
> "Good Lord, no!" Stanford remonstrated. "You two kids couldn't marry. What would you live on?"
> "Love," said John with an impish grin.

Evelyn turned Barrymore down, however, because she was still fixated on the possibility of a future with Stanford. "I was still obsessed with a fanciful notion that a man who loved a girl ought willingly to give up all others," she wrote in her memoir.

From the tower Stanford took Evelyn home to her mother, and reassured Mrs. Nesbit that nothing had happened—as Dr. Potter already had. Soon thereafter, Stanford arranged for Evelyn to go away to a boarding school for the next nine months. The school was the Pamlico School in Pompton Lakes, New Jersey, run by Mrs. Mathilda Beatrice De Mille, the mother of movie mogul Cecil B. De Mille. (Cecil was in his early twenties and just starting out.) After Evelyn's departure for boarding school, Mrs. Nesbit moved to the less swanky Algonquin Hotel.

Evelyn loved the Pamlico School. She was one of fifteen girls there. Circumstances suggest she was pregnant, but, if so, she did not allow her condition to interfere with her enjoyment:

> What a sublimely happy time I spent at the school! Here indeed was my lost girlhood regained. I couldn't absorb enough . . . studied music, English literature, philosophy, psychology. How I slaved to make up all the preparatory work I hadn't done in the past few years.

She had a. roommate called Prunes, with whom she played pranks. She went skating with a young man named Robert Fulton, in an outfit her mother sent her—a fuzzy gray sweater with a cap to match and angora gloves. At another time, she nearly fell through the ice, causing a great tumult among her classmates: "Doggone the luck! Everything always happens to Evelyn!" She was, for the most part, by her own account, "industrious; a model scholar, obedient."

John Barrymore left love notes around on the grounds of the school, but she didn't respond to them. She continued to struggle over Stanford: it seems as if she were still struggling twelve years later as she wrote these contradictory sentences about her feelings for him in her memoir:

> When I was robbed of my illusions by Stanford's continued interest in other women, love had died in my heart. And I did resolutely put him out of my mind too. I went on adoring Stanford for his kindness, his thoughtfulness, no more.

At this point, Harry Thaw began pursuing Evelyn in earnest, as he pursued other women with whom Stanford was involved. The origin of his fixation on Stanford appears to have been Stanford's response to something Harry did at one of the tower parties. Whatever it was, Harry was struck from Stanford's guest list. Stanford also blackballed him at a club. Furthermore, right before taking up with Evelyn, Harry had suffered fresh humiliation at Stanford's hands. A group of actresses from "Florodora," whom he had invited to a party at Sherry's with dinner, orchestra, and champagne, stood him up and went to a party at Stanford's instead. The incident was publicized in *Town Topics:* "Florodora beauties sing for their supper in White's studio, while Thaw's orchestra fiddles to an empty room at Sherry's." In addition to chasing women who had been seduced by Stanford, Harry devoted himself to exposing Stanford's immoral deeds, all the while fending off troubles that arose from his own behavior. He was being sued, for example, by a young woman whom he had brought to his apartment and lashed with a dog whip until her clothes hung from her in tatters.

Because of his unsavory reputation Harry at first sent flowers backstage to Evelyn under a pseudonym. Then he contrived to meet her in a restaurant through a chorus girl whom they both knew. At this very first meeting, he launched into an inquisition about her relationship to Stanford, demanding to know how her mother could permit her to go out with "that beast." Evelyn got up and left, and vowed to have no more to do with him, but he pursued her nonetheless. Even after she had gone off to the Pamlico School he pursued her, inundating Mrs. De Mille with flowers and gifts until she finally interceded for him with Evelyn. "This wealthy young man is madly in love with you, Evelyn," she said. "He tells me he wants to marry you." Evelyn told her that Harry K. Thaw "almost scares me to death."

Harry also managed to ingratiate himself with Mrs. Nesbit. When, approximately eight months after Evelyn's enrollment at the Pamlico School, Mrs. Nesbit was suddenly informed that her daughter was "ill"—the first symptoms were sharp abdominal pains—she tried to reach Stanford, but when she failed she called Harry, who took her out to the school right away. Mrs. De Mille, however, succeeded in reaching Stanford, who immediately dispatched Dr. Potter and a colleague, one Dr. John Walker. Dr. Potter diagnosed appendicitis so acute that Evelyn could not be moved to a hospital. It was necessary, he said, to operate immediately. All the other girls were sent away from the school, while Evelyn underwent some sort of medical procedure in a classroom. Of course it might have been appendicitis, but, given the timing, it is possible that Evelyn gave birth that day, though I can find no record of this. As the ether was administered Evelyn saw her mother, Mrs. De Mille, and the doctors and nurses standing around her bed and Harry Thaw "on his knees beside the operating table kissing my limp hands." When she woke up, Harry was gone, and Stanford was standing there saying, "Poor kiddie. Poor little kiddie."

That was the end of school for Evelyn: another indication that the real purpose of her sojourn at Pamlico was not education. Whatever the medical procedure was, in any event, there were complications, for afterward Stanford sent her to a private sanatorium in New York City, run by Dr. Walker. Dr. Potter's orders were "no dancing, no strenuous walking, no parties, no theatrical work for six months." While she was at the sanatorium, Harry Thaw continued to shower her with flowers and gifts. He also retained Oscar Tschuerke, the famous chef at the Waldorf Hotel, to cook whatever she asked for, whenever she wished, and send it over to her. Stanford visited too (scrupulously avoiding Thaw) and had a telephone installed in her room—a great novelty at the time. But he no longer expressed a romantic interest in Evelyn. She began to respond to Harry's overtures, and let Stanford know about it, but Stanford merely warned her about Harry. That must have been a devastating moment for her: to realize that he wasn't in the least jealous. When she was deemed well enough to leave the sanatorium, she agreed to go to Europe with Harry and with her mother as chaperon. Evelyn, who had her pick of suitors, now chose to put herself in the hands of a scorned man who was mentally unbalanced and scared her but, like her, was fixated on Stanford White—though in his case fixated with hatred.

Evelyn's mother disapproved of the European trip. She thought they ought to remain associated with Stanford, but Evelyn said, "What difference does it make, Mama. We'll stay in Europe till I'm well again. Then we can come back to New York, and I will get a job in some show." They sailed for Europe in May of 1903. Evelyn was eighteen now, an adult who had been raped and possibly had gone through pregnancy and childbirth, but now had as a chaperon the mother who had failed to protect her when she was a minor. Just before they left, Stanford gave Evelyn a letter of credit in case of emergency.

In Paris, Harry rented an apartment for the three of them. Mrs. Nesbit was upset by this: she didn't think it proper, even though Harry's bedroom was separated from hers and Evelyn's by an enormous drawing room. She felt that Stanford had been like a father to

Evelyn, and that Evelyn, in going to Europe with Harry, was being ungrateful to Stanford. Evelyn humored her, though, and eventually Mrs. Nesbit was more accepting. Harry took them on shopping sprees and introduced them to society where they met royalty and where Evelyn became known as La Bébé. Harry could be unsettling, however. If a waiter brushed the crumbs off their tablecloth in a restaurant he would fly into a rage, screaming *"Imbécile! Arrêtez! Arrêtez!"* Once, when an American friend, passing their table, asked Evelyn if she ever heard from Stanford, Harry overturned their table with everything on it.

Harry first proposed to Evelyn in Paris, soon after they arrived. She turned him down, on the ground that she wanted to devote her life to a career on the stage. Harry wept and flew into a rage. He refused to leave the apartment for days yet would not allow Evelyn and her mother to leave without him. Mrs. Nesbit decided that it was time to go home, but Evelyn didn't want to give up the chance to see London, Vienna, and Berlin. When they began to go out again, Harry's moodiness continued. He would sit in a chair for hours, biting his nails and staring off into space, and then fly into a rage after which he would fall to his knees and apologize, kissing Evelyn's hand and saying, "I'm sorry, boofuls. Her so boofuls. Please forgive." There were more marriage proposals, and at night, after Mrs. Nesbit had gone to bed, there were long, long inquisitions into whether Evelyn was a virgin.

One summer evening when Evelyn had become exhausted by such an inquisition, she finally told Harry the story of the night in Stanford's loft. As soon as she started to tell it, she saw it excited him; Harry later wrote that as she told that story for the first time "her eyes were sable and soft as death." That night, he made her tell the story over and over until dawn: "A sixteen-year-old girl. The beast. That filthy beast," Harry said, weeping and wringing his hands. But he also said he had known all along that she spent whole nights in the loft and at the tower because he'd had her followed by detectives.

Thenceforth Harry made Evelyn tell him the story of herself and

Stanford every night, dragging new details out of her. She would feign reluctance until he was pacing and wringing his hands with frustration and then she would gratify him. One night, she varied the routine by telling him that he should not call Stanford White a beast, because Stanford was above other men. Harry flew into "an incredible rage," not only then but whenever he happened to remember what she had said. They might be in a restaurant, and something, anything, might trigger the memory, whereupon he would begin turning over tables—their own and other people's too—and smashing dishes.

Harry assumed that the Nesbits had no money of their own and therefore could not go out on their own. But when he travelled ahead of them to London, they cashed Stanford's letter of credit and bought some fancy Parisian underwear. In London, Harry spotted the new lingerie and, knowing that he had not paid for it, demanded to know how they had acquired it. In this way Harry learned of the money from Stanford, and this time he flew into such a grand rage that Mrs. Nesbit developed the habit of going to bed whenever he was around.

In London the Nesbits stayed in one hotel and Harry in another. After a few days of Mrs. Nesbit's strike, Harry offered to pay her way home, promising to find a chaperon to replace her. Mrs. Nesbit accepted the offer but insisted that Evelyn return with her. Evelyn, however, packed her bags and moved in with Harry Thaw. Mrs. Nesbit went back to New York alone.

Another mysterious aspect of Evelyn's medical history is that in Paris her beautiful, thick auburn hair started to fall out. She comments on this in her memoir only by saying Harry took her to a well-known doctor who said that the hair loss was a result of her operation for appendicitis, and that the remedy was for her to shave her head. This she did, getting herself fitted out with "a gorgeous blond wig." Later in the summer she went, in her wig, to the Tyrol with Harry, who rented a castle, the Schloss Katzenstein, that was situated above a fairyland alpine valley and so remote that it could be reached only on foot. An old caretaker and his wife came to serve Evelyn and Harry in the daytime, but at night the two were alone.

In the Schloss, Evelyn slept in an ancient bed that stood high off the floor and had carved bedposts—like "a princess' bed," she thought. One night, the covers were suddenly swept off her, and she woke to see Harry standing over her stark naked. She screamed, and he covered her mouth, hissing, "Be quiet." He tore off her night-gown; she fought him; he became more violent; he managed to tie her hands behind her back; and then he whipped her with a dog whip. Evelyn screamed and screamed, and eventually he stopped trying to make her be quiet, because, after all, there was no one nearby. Evelyn had thought that she could manage Harry and see the world, but here she was, bald and naked, being beaten in a fairyland setting where no one could hear.

The beating lasted a long time. Occasionally, Harry would pause and then start up again, and eventually Evelyn stopped screaming and just sobbed. Then she began to make promises to him if only he would stop. He liked this, and asked her to beg him for things. She did, and then suddenly he became deflated, stopped beating her, and left the room, saying, "Stay there. Don't move. Don't move," and she lay there terrified of what would come next. But Harry returned dressed in his pajamas and a robe and slippers. His mood was calm and compassionate. He untied her hands and gave her brandy and spoke as if nothing had happened. He drew the bedcovers gently over her bleeding body. It took her a week to recover, and after that, she wrote later, she could not figure out a way to escape.

Harry had a black bag with a lock on it, in which he kept some hypodermic syringes and drugs, and also different kinds of whips and some reproductions of Persian and Turkish slave girls on the auction block. Even before the whipping, he had liked to show these to Evelyn and say, "If we were living in ancient times you would be my slave." After the first whipping a game evolved in which Harry asked Evelyn if she detested him for beating her and she said yes and he got down on his knees and begged her to forgive him, saying, "Please, boofuls, please." But every so often he would whip her again, telling her that she had been "too impudent." He would tie her hands and stuff a napkin into her mouth to silence her and would use a rattan cane on the backs of her calves as well as a dog whip. The cane beatings were by far the most painful.

There was cocaine in the black bag too. He took it and compelled her to take it, letting her know that he would regard her as "impudent" if she didn't. She enjoyed the effect of the cocaine, but the drug's effect on Harry terrified her; she felt she lost control of him when he fell under its influence.

After three weeks at the Schloss Harry and Evelyn returned to Paris. There they lunched at Robinson's, a restaurant with tables set on platforms in the lower branches of a huge elm, where Gypsies sang love songs to Evelyn from below. The routines with the black bag continued in the evenings. After they had been there awhile they had tea with two American ladies who were about to sail for America, and Evelyn told Harry she would like to join them alone. He agreed casually, and inexplicably; he had, until then, kept Evelyn on a very tight leash. But now he would allow her to go with her new friends, he said, and would follow shortly. So Evelyn escaped. Three days after she got back to New York, there was the sound of a rippling of fingers across her hotel door—a signal that she recognized. When she opened the door, there was Stanford White.

"Oh Kittens," he said. "Oh Kittens, where have you been?" And then he hugged her; after Harry, that must have felt like paradise.

But though Stanford drew Evelyn back into his gravitational range, that was all he did. He invited her to parties at the tower, but she had so little time alone with him that it was weeks before she had a chance to tell him what had happened at the Schloss Katzenstein. When he did at last hear it, he "boiled over," according to Evelyn's memoir. But the story didn't give her any power over him, as the story of Stanford had done with Harry. He responded merely by arranging to have her hear other stories of Thaw's atrocities—of how Harry had whipped this one and poured scalding water on that one—as if Evelyn didn't know enough about these tendencies in Harry.

Stanford also sent Evelyn to Howe & Hummell, and asked that she take with her a young woman named Edna McClure, who had recently been photographed by Rudolf Eickemeyer for Stanford. Howe & Hummell drew up an affidavit of the atrocities in the Tyrol—Stanford had hoped that hearing Evelyn's testimony about life with Harry K. Thaw would serve as a warning to Edna, who was being courted by Harry (now just back from Europe). Edna, it would seem, had been on a course almost identical to Evelyn's.

Howe & Hummell informed Harry of the existence of the affidavit, enjoining him to stay away from Evelyn. Harry ignored the warning, however, and, his courtship of Edna notwithstanding, bombarded her with flowers, gifts, and billets-doux throughout the fall, addressing her as "angels, her tumtums, her tweetums, her boofuls." When Evelyn did not get one of the coveted invitations to a Christmas Eve party Stanford gave in the tower every year, she accepted an invitation from Harry to celebrate at Rector's, the restaurant where he had examined her about Stanford the very first time they had met. She began to see Harry regularly again after that. Harry, for his part, hired detectives to follow Stanford and also put Anthony Comstock, the president of the Society for the Suppression of Vice, on Stanford's tail.

In June of 1904, Evelyn, now nineteen, went to Europe with Harry for the second time. On their return, in early 1905, she had another attack of "appendicitis" from which she required six weeks to recuperate. Mrs. William Thaw, Harry's mother, had long opposed her son's association with Evelyn, but over time Harry's behavior had been so publicly embarrassing that she now saw Evelyn as her best hope. Not long after Harry and Evelyn's return from Europe, she made a trip to New York and begged Evelyn to marry Harry and come to live at the family mansion in Pittsburgh. The meeting had the character of a negotiation, with Evelyn raising the matter of Harry's oddities and Mrs. Thaw averring that once he had settled down with a woman he loved he would be all right. On April

4, 1905, Evelyn and Harry were married. Evelyn's mother, who in the interim had married her Pittsburgh friend Charles Holman, received a hundred thousand dollars for her consent.

Life at Lyndhurst, the Thaw family mansion, was dreary. Evelyn and Harry lived in a separate wing but dined always with Mrs. Thaw, who was a dominating personality. There were always more servants than persons to be served, and what guests there were made strenuous efforts to pander to Mrs. Thaw's Presbyterianism.

That fall Harry began to take trips to New York, and then the household would consist of Evelyn and Mrs. Thaw alone. A certain warmth developed between them. One night at Lyndhurst when Harry was home, Evelyn woke up screaming from a bad dream. Mrs. Thaw appeared within moments in her nightgown and nightcap to demand of Harry, "Did you strike her?" When Evelyn explained that she'd only had a nightmare, Mrs. Thaw turned to Harry and said, "If you ever lay a hand on her, I'll cut you off without a penny." This moment, in which a parental figure actually protected Evelyn, stands out in her recorded life story.

Already by the end of that summer Harry had begun biting his nails, staring into space, and seething again. Evelyn suggested as a change that they go to New York together. One evening there, they were dining at the St. Regis with a friend, a Mrs. Caine, when Stanford and Bessie appeared and sat down at a table facing them. Harry's mouth became a thin, hard line as he stared at Stanford, while Stanford acted as if he hadn't noticed Harry and Evelyn at all. Mrs. Caine leaned over and whispered to Evelyn, "What's the matter with Harry, Evelyn? He has a revolver on his lap under his napkin." Evelyn felt suddenly debilitated by terror. Then she pulled herself together and said to Harry, "If you don't put that gun away, I'll leave the table." Harry looked as if he were about to spring like an animal, but she threatened him again and he suddenly flip-flopped, relaxing and smiling. "It's all right, angels, don't her worry," he said, and put the gun in his pocket. Evelyn became angry then and they left, with Harry apologizing all the way back to their hotel. They returned to Pittsburgh the next day.

Harry's rages resumed in earnest now. Whips were discovered by a maid. A flatiron sailed through a window and narrowly missed a gardener working in the flower beds below. After such incidents Mrs. Thaw would lecture Harry, and he would be "meek as a kitten for days," but then his mood would build up again. It was a long, hard winter. In June of 1906, Mrs. Thaw decided that they all ought to sail to England to visit her daughter Alice, the Countess of Yarmouth. Mrs. Thaw would go by cattle boat; Harry and Evelyn would follow on a German liner.

Harry and Evelyn moved into the Hotel Lorraine in New York for a two-week stay prior to their departure. As usual, Harry was having Evelyn followed by detectives. On the morning of Monday, June 25th, Evelyn went to a doctor because she had a sore throat, and she ran into Stanford there. They hugged and chatted and parted. Because Evelyn knew she was being followed, she told Harry that she had seen Stanford, but when he subjected her to an inquisition she claimed that they hadn't even spoken.

That evening, Harry expressed a desire to see "Mamzelle Champagne," opening at the Roof Garden theatre of Madison Square Garden. Evelyn agreed: the plan was that they would dine with two old friends of Harry's first at a restaurant called Café Martin. Harry went ahead without Evelyn because he wanted to stop for a drink on the way. He was dressed in an overcoat, though the weather was hot, and he had three drinks in a bar which he paid for with a hundred-dollar bill. Then he joined Evelyn and his friends at the restaurant. One of these friends was Truxton Beale, who had been acquitted of shooting a man in California for reasons having to do with a woman. The acquittal was based on an "unwritten law" that in certain circumstances murderous jealousy was justified. Harry had celebrated Beale's triumph at many previous dinners during his friend's visit.

The Stanford White issue was very much in the forefront that day, as Evelyn must have been keenly aware. At Café Martin, she took a seat that allowed her to survey the room while Harry could not, so that Harry didn't notice when, in the middle of dinner,

Stanford White passed through. Harry could tell from Evelyn's face that something had happened, however, and when he asked what was wrong she wrote him a note: "That B—— is here." By the time Harry turned around, Stanford was out of sight, but he began biting his nails, and Evelyn, anticipating one of his restaurant scenes, hurried them out.

At the Roof Garden, they were seated at a table in the back, and Evelyn observed Harry glancing in an ominous way at the tower that loomed over them. Then Harry left the table and wandered. There was a sound of gunfire. Many people in the theatre thought the gunfire was part of the show, but Evelyn, though she could not see anything of what had happened, said, "My God, he's shot him." Later, when Harry was in the custody of the police she kissed him frantically and repeatedly, saying, "My God, Harry, you killed him," and, "Kiss me."

District Attorney William Travers Jerome wanted to bring an indictment for murder against Evelyn as well as against Harry. He refrained from doing so only because public sympathy for Evelyn had made it impossible. His grounds would have been that Evelyn knew Harry was unstable and in a murderous rage at Stanford, and knew furthermore that Harry was carrying a gun, yet fanned Harry's hatred nevertheless, and had done so specifically and recklessly on the evening of the murder. Some of Evelyn's friends—May Mackenzie, for example, who was at Evelyn's side throughout the trial and had been worried enough to warn Stanford about Harry—also thought that Evelyn was at least as guilty as Harry. I'm inclined to agree with May and District Attorney Jerome. Evelyn was enslaved to Stanford, who had used her and then insouciantly moved on. A way to free herself was to kill him, using Harry K. Thaw as her weapon. With Stanford dead and Harry arrested for murder, she was rid of them both in one play.

When Evelyn left the stand after testifying for Harry, her legs could barely carry her. When, at the end of the second trial, Harry was declared not guilty by reason of insanity, her teeth started chattering uncontrollably.

Mrs. Nesbit did not come to her daughter's side after the murder but instead defended Stanford in statements to the press. Indeed, she planned to testify in defense of Stanford's character at the trial, directly contradicting her daughter's testimony. She agreed not to testify only after the Thaws bought her off: newsmen estimated that the price was fifty thousand dollars. Despite the payoff, during the second trial Evelyn's mother met with Jerome in the evenings to pick Evelyn's testimony apart.

Mrs. Thaw promised Evelyn a million dollars in a divorce settlement if she testified in Harry's defense—that is, testified that he was crazy. The insanity plea was his only real hope of avoiding jail, although he would have to go to an asylum nonetheless. One of the Thaw attorneys privately warned Evelyn that she should not trust Mrs. Thaw and should get the promise in writing, but Evelyn did not listen to him. "I'm sure Mother Thaw will do the right thing," she said.

After the second trial, however, Evelyn was informed by Thaw's legal counsel that Harry couldn't be divorced because, thanks to her own testimony, he had been declared insane. On the other hand, if she had the marriage annulled she would have no claim on his estate whatsoever. Because she still might be needed to testify at sanity hearings for Harry's release from the asylum—this time testifying that he was *not* insane—Mrs. Thaw agreed to give her a modest retainer.

Depleted by the trials, by the betrayals of her mother and Mrs. Thaw, and by having lived in a kind of extreme danger for a long time—managing it, manipulating it, surviving—Evelyn became listless and dependent, evidently without resources of her own, and unable or unwilling to pursue her old ambitions. When she had gone through Mrs. Thaw's retainer, she was informed by the Thaws' attorney that she was no longer needed. "No more money will be paid you by your husband or his family." The attorney also told Evelyn that Mrs. Thaw's strategy was that "without money from the Thaws you will land in the gutter and thereby gain sympathy for her son."

Evelyn had learned to drink heavily with Stanford, and the profile of her life in the aftermath of the trial is characteristic of a drinker's. She sank to worse and worse accommodations, wheedling pittances out of Harry when she could, and—what is most telling— was no longer courted by men. Sometimes she gave little parties, and her old admirers, the Racquet Club boys, would come; but she would not be their girl. She would invite girls for them, and grill the steaks.

In 1912, when she was twenty-seven and living in a cheap apartment on 112th Street with no prospects at all, Evelyn suddenly rallied. She made a connection with some theatrical luminaries, and starred at the London Hippodrome in a smash hit called "Hello Ragtime." The show was brought to New York by Oscar Hammerstein—and Evelyn with it—and then went across the country, breaking box-office records in city after city. (Mrs. Thaw tried to get an injunction against the show in Pittsburgh on the ground that it was immoral, but she failed.) Often crowds of fans became so unruly that Evelyn had to be secluded. There was a European tour, then another American tour, and then Evelyn fell to morphine addiction. She was evidently seduced into it by a fellow-actress who trafficked in drugs and initially proffered the morphine to relieve Evelyn's pain from neuralgia. There were other comebacks in which Evelyn temporarily overcame her addiction, but the over-all trajectory of her life was one of decline. By the time she was thirty-nine, she weighed less than a hundred pounds and could not rouse herself out of inertia. The last of her theatrical comebacks ended when she was forty-five, at the Kelly Ritz, a whorehouse in Panama City, where she was booked to perform a cabaret act she had developed. The run was cut short when she was arrested for gambling.

In 1955, when "The Girl in the Red Velvet Swing" was released, Evelyn was seventy-four years old. There was a wave of publicity about her, and the picture that emerges from it is not one of a person in an advanced stage of morphine dependency. True, she was then living in Los Angeles in a bare little studio that shook when trucks passed on the Hollywood Freeway above. But she sculpted there and she taught sculpture at a school nearby. She was healthy and coherent. Evelyn, who had, Houdini-like, escaped from the trap of Stanford and Harry, had somewhere along the line freed herself from the beartrap of morphine addiction as well.

"Most of my life I've been dressed in fancy clothes like a horse," she said in a newspaper interview she gave at the time. "I like to wear just a tunic and sandals now." She did, however, wear what she called her Go-to-Hell Hat on a publicity trip to New York. It was a tiny blue hat with pearl wings. According to the newspapers, she said that she stayed young because "I never bear a grudge." She also said, "A really beautiful woman suffers many, many more handicaps than a plain woman. Beauty can bring her—as it did to me—great confusion and sorrow. You must be wiser than most women and wealthier than most women if you are beautiful. For there is no way to avoid danger if you are beautiful." So there is Evelyn, in her Go-to-Hell Hat, still taking the blame.

GRACE

I N   T H E   S E V E N T I E S and eighties it was a custom in the family to have a summer party, with dancing, in the carriage house. Family parties at Box Hill sometimes had an upper-crust ambiance, albeit a faded and eccentric one, but the events in the barn were frankly bohemian. The character of the family on these occasions was that of a community of artists, somewhat bibulous, with a new generation of babies coming up but life going on much as before: with Bobby kissing the girls, for example. In the summer of 1985, three years after my house was completed, he was kissing my cousin Pamela, Johnny's daughter. She was sixteen by then: it had been her turn for a while. Pamela visited every summer, but this was the first time her visit had overlapped with a barn party.

One of the charms of these gatherings was that no distinction was made between the mad and the unmad—all family members were included and accepted—but in retrospect it seems that there was mass madness in the failure to distinguish between the mad and the menacing. As if there were a genetic virus travelling in the family line, William, one of my younger cousins, had for many years been preoccupied with sex in a frightening way. In his teens, William also became obsessed with guns. By the time he was twenty-five, he drank excessively. By then he was a strong young man (stronger even than Johnny had ever been), well over six feet tall.

By the mid-eighties the women in the family—especially the very young women—were afraid to be alone with William. And yet for those of us who had been around in the days when Johnny roamed the Place with his shotgun, it was easy to tolerate that fear without ever speaking about it to one another, much less doing anything to restore safety. At a family party one thought of William as just another element in the mixed bag that included the sometimes deranged cousin who talked his head off and, indeed, Johnny in his greatly deteriorated and harmless condition.

And so at this barn party, as at others, William would be there dancing with his cousins, who weren't always thrilled but put up with him, just as they endured partners like the neighbor with famously big feet, or were amused by the portly relative who came dressed as the Pope and ended up after a polka flat on his back, his face as puce as papal silks, and gaping like a blowfish. Halfway through the party, a small owl appeared on a rafter, from which it looked down on all of us like a minor deity—the deity of the whimsical blessedness of our tribe in its giftedness and its drunkenness, its glories and its failures, its charming idiosyncrasy and terrible disturbance. Even as late as that summer, when my sense of the world as a zombie planet had become entrenched, I was still capable of being touched by an occasion like this, in which the mad and the unmad danced in our ancestral barn among our houses great and small, cradled in our landscape of sacred spots that held our love for one another in trust.

With Johnny as her father, and her mother an otherworldly poet-ess unsuited for motherhood, Pamela was in effect without parents: a convent boarding school in England had been her actual home. The family world was therefore to her a magnetic one to which she felt she had only a tenuous admission. Above all, Pamela longed to be accepted. At the party in the barn, she got tipsy, and she met William for the first time. "Oh, another cousin," she said. Because the fear of William was like an animal fear, existing in silence, no one had warned her about him. So Pamela danced with William, as others did, and went outside with him—as others did not—and he took her arm in a strong grip, propelled her behind the barn, and, after discharging a stream of filthy language, raped her. Between ten and ten-thirty in the evening on July 13, 1985, a Saturday, William was raping Pamela behind the barn while in the barn people danced. The light in the barn was mellow, but behind the barn it was dark.

In the midst of being raped, Pamela became aware of the beam of a flashlight sweeping back and forth across her assailant and her-self—across the rape—and then a male voice called, "William!" Whoever this was, perhaps he had noticed William leaving with Pamela and become concerned. (Indeed, my mother had noticed the disappearance and was out in the dark, shouting for Pamela, though in the wrong places.) When his name was called, William got up abruptly and left. Whoever it was who had come with the flashlight did not then go to Pamela. The flashlight went away. She was left lying there in the dark.

Later Pamela could not remember how long she had lain there, but eventually she got up and tried to straighten her clothes and brush herself off so no one could tell that anything had happened. That was her first concern after the rape, and it remained her primary concern. She found her way to a bathroom in an apartment in the upper part of the barn and fixed herself up some more, and then got herself back to the Red Cottage.

In the morning she lay in bed in the Red Cottage, listening to a cousin talking to my mother downstairs in the kitchen, and she became gripped with terror that someone might find out. The terror was that if it was known in the family she would be rejected definitively. Accordingly, she told no one until she returned to school in the fall. Then, fearful that she was pregnant, she confided in some friends. With their help, she was tested and was found not to be pregnant. Six months or so later she told her mother about the rape. Her mother wasn't sure whether to believe her, but she did, eventually, tell my mother in passing on the telephone. My mother knew that what Pamela had said was well within the range of possibility, and told Pamela's mother that that was so, and then spoke to Pamela. Pamela's chief concern was still that no one know. She swore my mother to secrecy.

My mother nevertheless told me, and Isabella and Trudi, each separately, and passed on Pamela's fervent wish that the information be kept secret. And there communication stopped. We did not tell others. I rarely spoke to my sisters in any event. We did not relate to each other: we spoke to our mother. It was as if it was not safe for us to talk to each other, and when we did—especially if there were several of us—we fell back on a style of truncated girlishness that guaranteed that no interchange of emotional significance could take place. Certainly, our relationship with each other was not one that could bear discussion of this rape.

I did not even see the rape as an event that had happened in a family, whether the subgrouping of myself and my sisters or the larger family as embodied by the Place. I did not see it in a context of any kind. Certainly, I had no thought of confronting William, or bringing him to account, either within a family forum or a court of law. Indeed I hardly thought of it at all. I would not think of the rape when I encountered William, or even when I saw William and Pamela in the same room at a family event. It's not that it disappeared from consciousness altogether, but, like a fox killing rabbits in the woods, it was somehow not a part of history. My knowledge of it disappeared into the old family silence, in which the world appeared unchanged in a nitroglycerine air.

Ironically, the only person able to speak of the rape with impunity was William himself. As Pamela later recounted, the next time he saw her he flirted with her and offered to give her a ride into the city, and when she refused he laughed and said, "Don't worry. I won't rape you again." This remark is a measure of how lost William was. He had no gauge of the meaning of his act.

As I look back and see myself in my forgetfulness, making no effort to avert a repetition of what had happened to Pamela, I see myself at an advanced stage of separateness from self and well into the despair that this brings on. I also see myself—though I had no sense of this at the time—as, like William, a part of a family history that in some ways had devolved down from Stanford with the same mechanical predictability and hopelessness as had governed Stanford's own life. There is no force that I know of that can reach into this kind of dead momentum and effect lasting change other than grace.

The grace of the quotidian that was celebrated on the Place, however, is a conservative kind of grace that enriches and thus reinforces the texture of the status quo. It says nothing need be changed, because the miraculous is close at hand. To break the iron grip of an unconscious mechanical progression, a revolutionary grace that disrupts the status quo is required. Revolutionary grace strikes at a given moment after which nothing is ever again the same—Saul on the way to Damascus, for example, though it need not be so dramatic and can happen to a group of people as well as to an individual. It is, in other words, a historical kind of grace. Revolutionary grace did come to me and my sisters, but as I look back I see in my own life a third kind of grace that is neither conservative nor able to effect lasting change, but is a premonition of that possibility and perhaps prepared me for it. This third kind of grace comes in the form of moments of perception, a deep layer of being that is always there in the world but usually imperceptible. It's very different from quotidian grace in that it's eerie, conveying a sense of different realms of reality lying alongside.

In the years surrounding Pamela's rape, the beauty of the world seemed to me to be a lie, a kind of shellac sealing over a horrific emptiness. Yet I might see a cock pheasant in a clearing, looking a little ridiculous, a little off balance in his gaudy getup, and there it would be all around him—the old world, a world that was true. My son's vocabulary could do it. He called the outdoors "outie," and one day when we were already outdoors he said he wanted to go "outie." I said, "You can't get any more outie than this," and then it struck me, with the world seeming a lie under shellac, that you could get more outie than this: that there was something *inside* the outside world—something more real, more exposing, that was hidden from us. I'd slice open a beet, and there was the undiscovered planet in the beetroot. I'd take a walk and, for no reason at all, there it would be, the world hidden in the world breaking through the shellac like the back of a whale.

Sometimes I could see the world hidden in the world, too, when my grandmother was in it—when, for example, Mama appeared coming through the rhododendrons on her afternoon walk, debonair in a woolly hat, with her cane, the thinness of her ankles revealed beneath the wide cuffs of her slacks, and the narrow length of her feet full of gesture. In great old age, Mama had become exaggerated, her shins sharp, her long nose longer yet, long with inquiring into the world, with savoring this little spot of Long Island for which she'd had such contempt for so long but which from the perspective of great old age was now just the world and, in that, international—as good as Italy.

In January of 1984—the year before the rape—quite suddenly, at the age of ninety-six, Mama began to die. A light flu precipitated it: having been quite well, she simply started to go. Snow was on the ground. Julian was three. I was living on Lower Fifth Avenue. The dying took several weeks. Hers was not a passive fading away; it was active—the hardest thing she had ever done, she said. In the first part of her dying, she had my mother read to her from a technical book about battles in the Revolutionary War. She'd lie in her bed with her eyes scrunched tight, listening intently, and if she didn't understand a passage she would peremptorily instruct my mother to read it again. She was alert and aware of her surroundings. One day

she bewildered the young Italian-American doctor who was attending her by saying to him, *"Io sono Romana."* ("I am a Roman.")

Then she went into a two-week period in which her dying
seemed to require an entirely absorbing interior form of concentration, though occasionally she would open her eyes and say something. Once, she held her big, handsome hands in front of her face
and said, "I don't need these anymore." Another time, when my
mother was sitting with her at two in the morning, sipping a glass of
whiskey for fortification, Mama opened her eyes suddenly and said,
"Man does not live by bread alone." My mother asked her what she
meant, and Mama said, "Sometimes he eats his hat." My mother
then said, "Mama, do you want to eat your hat?" and Mama
thought for a few minutes and then laughed and said, "No, it would
be much too tough," and then asked my mother what she was doing
drinking whiskey at two in the morning. Mama was one hundred
per cent up for the challenge of dying and she did it not in the
manner of someone on whom fate was closing in but in the manner
of someone who was breaking out.

I would go to St. James on the train from New York to sit with
Mama and hold one of her hands, as family members did in turn.
On one hand she wore her wedding ring together with a diamond
engagement ring, and the other hand was bare. Her ringed hand
brought to my mind a vision derived from an ancient Chinese poem:
A nobleman is being carried along a riverbank in a sedan chair,
surrounded by courtiers of varying ranks, who are dressed in rich
fabrics embroidered with symbolic designs. Along the river is a
carefully arranged, cultivated landscape, but in the background there
are snowy peaks. When I held her ringed hand she was a part of the
scene on the riverbank, but when I held her ringless hand, I had a
sense of her as already half out of the world—up in the snowy peaks
where, stripped of her worldly definitions, she was becoming her
essential self. I too had a wedding ring on one hand and another that
was bare. When I held her ringed hand with my ringed hand my
sense of the texture of society around us became so dense that I
could not imagine a world outside it at all. But when I held her bare

hand with my bare hand there it was: the mystery and namelessness of identity, how exposed we are, the fatality of how we conduct our lives, and our irreplaceableness to each other.

One day when I was sitting with Mama, I accepted my aunt Claire's offer of relief and went out in the snow for a walk. I walked up the Privet Path, and since it was leafless I could see right through to Johnny's field, more grown up now, with beards of leafless vines weeping from stunted trees, and to my house in plain sight beyond. I wished to reinforce Mama in her passage, and the only way that I could think to do this was to say a prayer. So, not having said a prayer in a very long time, I now said the Our Father. This was as earnest and open an attempt at prayer as could be, yet phrase after phrase fell meaningless to the ground. "Our Father." Who was that? "Who art in Heaven." What meaning was there in that? There in the providential landscape of my childhood, life seemed haphazard, and without significance, as if Providence had once again fallen away like a deceiving scrim. There was only myself, and the violence within me. Yet there can be a kind of opening in the falling away of significance. Perhaps it's required, even, in order to break through to connection, that one become able to sustain all that one feels in an atmosphere of abandonment by God: that one be willing to undergo that; to be present to oneself, alone. Standing in that bare place, I knew only that Mama was dying and that I loved her.

I was not there when she died—no one in the family was—but the caretaker with her reported that she opened her eyes and made the little *ciao* sign with her fist, to signal goodbye, as Roman children do, and then she was off. Looking back on Mama's life, it sometimes appears to me to have been, in so many ways, like the party in the barn with a rape occurring on the other side of the barn wall. In other ways it had the simple depth and perfection of her little *ciao* sign on leaving the earth. It is as if these two parts of her lived alongside. During her dying I felt as if, as always, she had taken me to the edge of a territory that she herself had not been able or willing to enter: but she could show it to me. It was as if out of a concealing darkness that was right there in the light she had slipped me a golden apple, without a word, without a look.

The full textural panoply was rolled out for her funeral, my father on the organ, the Noroton graduates singing her out to the Gregorian "In Paradisum," gorgeous texts read by her children gorgeously, and our family priest—our exquisite cousin—presiding, saying from the pulpit that Mama had once told him that good manners were no more than a manifestation of charity. The larger family was drawn in by Mama's death, from the farther reaches of the Chanler cousinage and from the nearer reaches of descendants of her six brothers and sisters: a family sensing yet one more time its continuing existence as an entity. At the end of the funeral that ecumenical entity joined in a triumphant rendition of "The Battle Hymn of the Republic," composed by Julia Ward Howe, Mama's great aunt on her mother's side. Then Mama was buried in the graveyard behind the Episcopal church—with Stanford and Grandma, Papa, Natalie, and little Richard Mansfield White, Stanford and Grandma's baby: the ground had been selectively blessed by a priest for the Catholics. Later her name was chiselled on the slab of pink marble under Papa's, so that the whole slab read:

LAWRENCE GRANT WHITE
Architect
1887–1956
and his wife
LAURA CHANLER WHITE
1887–1984

Almost from the start, but more and more as time went on, the name on her gravestone seemed like a snare from which the quarry had slipped.

The family had configured itself in a pattern around Mama, and that pattern became somewhat disorganized after her death: in retrospect, it seems that perhaps this condition of incoherence was propitious for the disrupting power of revolutionary grace. But I have learned that grace is not dependent on conditions of any kind and can lightly, at any point, reverse the chronology of a hundred years. It's independent of the sequential, evolutionary ways in which our earthly stories normally unfold. Thus grace, while it creates narrative where there was none, also creates unusual narrative structures, for in ordinary narratives the outcome arises out of character, out of preceding events, and in good time whereas a story that turns on grace turns on an unprecedented factor that is inherently lawless and unpredictable, an unconditional transforming force that flashes suddenly like lightning.

Our moment of grace in the Red Cottage family happened in the Christmas season four years after Mama's death. In the context of the Place, so dense with charm and poetry, the event was extraordinarily plain. Madeleine, who lived in Europe, called each of us sisters before she arrived for the holidays and asked that we meet by ourselves. She wanted to talk to us about something having to do with our childhood, she said. The suggestion of our meeting by ourselves was in itself revolutionary. Years later Beatrice told me that the mere proposal of the meeting filled her with an overwhelming sense of danger. At an ordinary time, resistance would have intensified until the plan fell apart. Instead—this was the first sign of the presence of grace—the plan went forward easily, seeming almost to fall into place by itself.

On New Year's Day, 1989, Beatrice, Madeleine, Isabella, and I—Felicity was not able to be there and Trudi came later—met in a room in my house that we called the studio, a room that was not part of the eighteenth-century house but newly built. We bracketed eighteen years—I was forty-four and Trudi was twenty-five. The room was large and square, with a pine floor and a tray ceiling, the walls white with rough wainscoting. The furniture was a wooden table with benches for dining, a library table, a sofa, and an armchair, and a sofa bed in one of two bay windows that flanked the door and looked south across Johnny's field. Now, in winter, we could also see right through the trees to the peak of the cow barn, embedded in its hill, with its large top window for Bobby's studio. In the west wall were three windows set together through which, to the left, one could see the carriage house, the stables, and the water tower, all together a continuous shape, an inscape or kind of sub-form that paintings sometimes bring out, in this case embodying the essence of what was deeply loved on the Place.

It was midafternoon when we gathered: the sun was already low and fierce, its rays piercing like spears through black trees and into the room. We sat tentatively, a little awkwardly, gathered around Madeleine, who sat on the sofa with the bank of three windows behind her. As we had no precedent for talking together in a serious way, it was one of those moments in which there was no illusion of translucence between present and future. No preliminary chatting, no preamble, no warming up seemed possible and, in the vacuum that developed, Madeleine had no alternative but to come out immediately with what she had on her mind.

She had been seeing a psychoanalyst in France, she said, and had mentioned to her that she had been sexually fondled by our father at night in the Red Cottage when she was a child. She had told her doctor that she had always known this, but that the knowledge had been drained of feeling and seemed insignificant. The psychoanalyst, however, thought what had happened was very significant, and also that it was important for Madeleine to talk to her sisters about it. Her plain words were spoken calmly. But as she spoke I had a sense of something like a sound barrier breaking, a psychic reverberation that reached to the edge of the cosmos and down to the subcellular level at the same time. With it, the world cracked open. And inside was the world.

Beatrice instantly, explosively, burst into tears, and then said that she too had been visited by our father in the night. When she was fifteen he had gotten into her bed and lain on top of her, his body hot and sweaty, she said, and then, after a time, had gone away. Later, she had told herself that this was *not* a sexual act, an account that allowed her to preserve the idea that her childhood was safe. I told about the cellar stairs, the exploding airplane, and another memory, far firmer, of a sexual embrace by my father, in pajamas, with an erection, when I was about fifteen. Except for Isabella, each of us had one clear documentary memory. Isabella, nevertheless, was in tears as well. She said that she didn't have such memories, but then again she remembered almost nothing of her childhood. Trudi arrived, and sat down, and we told her what had transpired. She said, almost offhandedly, Oh yes, that had happened to her too, but it was nothing. We said it wasn't nothing, and she, in her turn, burst explosively into tears. In her case, our father had had her masturbate him when she was five years old. Beatrice had continued to vacillate between crying hysterically and anguished attempts to continue to downplay her experience. Trudi's account broke down her last reserves of hope that a vision of our childhood as safe could be maintained.

We remembered how it was a story about Dad that he walked in his sleep as a child, and the idea was—perhaps from our mother—that he walked in his sleep in the Red Cottage too. As adults we knew that alcohol was a likelier cause for what had happened. But the idea that our father had walked in his sleep had helped put these incidents out of the realm of consciousness—not only his but ours too—and thus we all became somnambulists ourselves. Each of us had lived with her memories for a long time by herself. None of us had had any idea that such things were happening to anyone else. Where, by themselves, our memories had seemed isolated and in that somehow bloodless and irrelevant and easy to downplay, when put together it was clear that sexual violation was a condition of life in the Red Cottage. That danger had been in the atmosphere we breathed though ahistorical, without acknowledgment. Now the danger was in the picture. It was a part of history now.

There was a kind of involuntary combustion to the way these terse factual statements shot out, accompanied by explosions of tears. But the air, in contrast, was no longer explosive. The air had become stable and calm. I was sitting in a chair which was the height of a child's chair from the ground but was built for an adult, with a wide rush bottom and ample, curved wooden arms. I felt myself sitting in this chair with my knees apart, my hands cupping the curved ends of the wooden arms, my chest open, my breath easy and deep, my back light against the back of the chair, my weight even in my buttocks, and my feet evenly and comfortably on the floor. I felt very calm, as if I could sit there forever. I felt connected to my sisters, calm with my sisters, *with* them—a true familial connectedness. I saw them in the context of our history together, not only the history we had just uncovered but all of it, a whole picture. I *saw* them, in a sense for the first time.

Beatrice, who follows me in age, sat next to Madeleine on the sofa, the rays of the sun creating a coppery halo of her dark-brown hair. Thirty-nine at this time, she was wiry and fit from having made her living fishing for cod off Nova Scotia, as well as apple and tobacco picking, though now she was a professor of law. In ordinary times, Beatrice had an air about her of deploying rationality as a peacekeeping force in an emotional environment that threatened, at any moment, to go out of control. Mixed with this was an intuitive artistic nature that showed especially in her hands and the way she used them. Her hands were the big beautiful hands that run in the family—Mama's hands—and she painted with them, as Mama did, and used them expressively when deploying rationality as well as in more creative modes. In the moments after the breaking of the sound barrier, however, one hand was in her lap and one was hanging over the arm of the sofa, at rest. The peacekeeping force had vanished. There was something very full, very occupied, very calm about her presence, though she said that she was having an experience in which her childhood seemed to be erasing itself like a movie.

Madeleine, next to her, also with a coppery halo from the sunset, was olive-skinned with brown eyes, hair that was blond when she was a child but nearly black in her adulthood—as black as our mother's. I mention the blondness because, for us who grew up with her, Madeleine will always have a nimbus of light around her head. The fourth-born, she is pretty in a fine-boned way—probably the prettiest, though there might be some disagreement about that. There is a softness about her and yet a highly intense vibration as well, and both the softness and the intensity are often present in her eyes at the same time. A dancer, her body lithely strong, she usually seemed active even in repose, often taking difficult positions and holding them as if they were entirely normal. But now she was leaning back, sinking into the sofa, relieved, almost smiling. Her age showed in her face from the strain, but she was relaxed: we were all, for us, extraordinarily relaxed, but Madeleine, who had taken the initiative—who had known in advance what was to come—was exhausted as well.

Isabella, the fifth one, long legged and slim, with straight, long light-brown hair, our father's winged jaw, and long, nimble fingers that played the classical guitar, was, of us all, the gentlest, the most quiet, and the most hidden. She was also the best clown. Isabella could be very funny, and being funny was her most assertive mode. Indeed, for some years she had pursued the circus arts before becoming a musician. A difficult marriage, however, and motherhood under those circumstances, had made for a hard life that had begun to show through both her gentleness and her humorous take on life. Gifted but modest, rangy yet feminine, and pretty in a cozy way, she was now slumped in her chair, her face wet with tears and upsetness still showing in her features—upsetness for us, upsetness at information that required a drastic revision of the picture of what our childhood was like. Ordinarily her expression was veiled, but not now. She looked her age, which was one day short of thirty. Her posture was easeful, conveying a sense of connection that did not need to be artificially sustained.

Sitting in a chair beyond Isabella was Trudi, the youngest, and the athlete among us, with the physicality of a horsewoman, a quality that she later turned to a relationship with metals and gems and the minute engineering problems that arise in the making of classical jewelry. She had always been the difficult one, the black sheep, the one who fought with our mother where we protected her, and who later didn't bother disguising what had gone wrong in her life.

Trudi, like Isabella, had straight hair, long and light brown. Her eyes were green, and at this moment they were bright. She too was slumped, relaxed, in a cocoon of privacy, inspecting her hands— another edition of Mama's hands. Her face was flushed, with the sense of release and connection, but with turbulence too—we all felt much, much grief in this moment. I saw Trudi for the first time as a full-fledged adult. There were no truncated girls here.

There were women in the room.

ARCHITECTURE

F OR A PERIOD we attempted to work as a family to understand the information that came out that New Year's Day. Our mother and even our father participated, although he said he had no recollection of what we reported. In the end we could not cohere as a family in this endeavor and set off, each on her own road, to find a resolution within herself.

Over the next twelve months, we five sisters who had met each experienced drastic changes in our lives. I left my marriage, but this was not an altogether unexpected development. A far more surprising and clearly direct consequence of our meeting was that the very next day a paralysis that had crippled my writing for years disappeared. Soon I embarked on the narrative that has come to fruition here. Another paradox of a story that turns on grace is that the moment of grace is what makes it possible to tell the story at all. Without that moment there would be no consciousness, no under-standing—no story therefore, because there would be no one to tell it.

A year or so after our meeting, when I was well along in this work, I designed a tour for myself of Stanford's architecture. My cousin Pamela was interested too, and joined me. With a little over a quarter century separating us, we were the oldest and the youn-gest of Stanford's great-granddaughters. As it happened, we both had red hair, as Stanford did, though mine was partially gray by this time and Pamela's was a strawberry blond, quite unlike Stanford's chestnut. Even so, this redness underscored the cat's cradle of inter-generational connection: the tightness of it and the physical reality of it.

We started on a June morning in the area of small streets in downtown Manhattan where Chinatown and Little Italy intermingle. On Grand Street, a modest thoroughfare with narrow sidewalks further narrowed by stands of fruit and exotic vegetables, we came upon the magnificent and monumental neoclassical façade of the Bowery Savings Bank. The bank, completed in 1895, was the first of the firm's neoclassical works to come primarily from Stanford's hand.

The central feature of the façade was a high pediment containing statuary with a big clock in the middle and a frieze running under-neath, the whole supported by four massive Corinthian columns. Behind the columns were four windows, one and a half stories high, set in complex, protruding frames, which broke the façade regu-larly, casting deep shadows and creating a dramatically inflected surface. The windows flanked a handsome door, also one and a half stories high; running across the top were small rectilinear windows covered with iron grillwork in a comely pattern based on squares. The Bowery Savings Bank is a great cube. Its pleasure is that of the stabilized symmetry of a cube. Squares show up all over in its decorative details, along with Stanford's signature of scrolling, leafy shells, and spiky lanterns.

Inside, the bank was a world in itself. The gilded and coffered ceiling had a skylight at its center, with panes of deep-yellow glass. There were Corinthian columns all around, both freestanding ones and pilasters along the walls—all the free wall space was put to work, either flanking or framing or being framed. The freestanding columns were of ochre marble with red and black veins, and in combination with the skylight they gave the room a sombre golden glow. The volume of the cubical interior was made semisolid by that glow. There was an area in the middle of the floor where people leaning over desks generated rustles and small echoes under a ceiling so high that it was a kind of sky.

After we had taken in the attributes of the building, Pamela remembered that she needed money. Looking around, we spotted a cash machine against a far wall, and she set out toward it. As I watched her walking away from me across the mosaic floor, I shifted my weight from foot to foot, no longer paying close attention to the aesthetic features of the architecture. In a sense, I was off guard and, suddenly, the old fear set in. That quality in Stanford's interiors which had caused me to avoid them in the past enveloped me, like a perfume triggering an allergic reaction: a swelling in the chest near the throat, a pressure of tears behind the eyes—and, above all, fear. The source of the fear was the very geniality of the architecture; its delicacy, its glow, its enspelling seductiveness.

Immediately, Pamela's vulnerability was appallingly apparent. She looked so white, soft, and trusting as she performed her pedestrian chore. In an emotional reflex of aversion I mentally pushed her away. Horrified by my impulse I then searched for its source. At first there was blankness only, erasing even the bank. Then, out of the depths of forgetfulness rose the scene in the dark behind the barn. It was not really even a scene: there was no mental image— just a visceral acknowledgment of something very bad happening in the dark. With this acknowledgment my aversion left me and instead I found myself working strenuously to bring that scene out of darkness into the bank—to have in one world the disparate realities of our family life.

Within the magnificent enclosure of the bank the scene behind the barn seemed almost nonexistent. Even the space behind the barn seemed two-dimensional, paper-thin, conceptual. It was difficult to conjure particulars of a moment in a place—leaves stirring, clouds passing in front of a moon—or to sense the solidity and contours of the ground, much less to see the spot as a part of geography, as a location coextensive with other locations that could be pinpointed on a map. It was difficult to see it as a spot that existed in continuous time, so that you could say of it the next day, "This is the spot where such-and-such happened last night." In that two-dimensionality, it was especially difficult to imagine a whole body, lungs rising and falling, much less two bodies and violence.

So unreal in the family environment had the event behind the barn been that William could confidently laugh and say, "Don't worry. I won't rape you again." The dense texture of the family was, for him, no more constricting than the beam of moving light that had fleetingly passed over him and his crime. But there in the bank the image of that moving beam turned, in my mind, into bars that caged the event like a beast. The bars of light gave me a purchase on the scene that allowed me to pull it out of the place of forgetfulness into the solidified golden light of the Bowery Savings Bank, where the bars dissolved and the scene in its three-dimensional reality was present—a rape.

Every aspect of the bank interior—the sure proportions, the sensuous, well-chosen marbles, the pilasters, the columns—was working toward the effect of the whole, an effect of elegance, strength, and authority. This was an architecture of stability and security, of lawfulness, of institutional justice. The scene behind the barn was unlawful and uninstitutional, without justice, without any kind of elegance or aesthetic: it was the whirlwind. So there it was: The whirlwind in the calm—the very quality that I had felt in Stanford's architecture for so long, brought out of its lair. The familiar serenely beautiful environment in which there was terrifying danger, except that now the danger was seen. And the fright felt.

Afraid, I walked across the mosaic floor toward Pamela. It was a transformative passage, though one I had made before—in the meeting with my sisters—and one I would make again. This is a journey that is made in increments. One cannot easily break the habit of looking for protection to that which is powerful. One cannot in one motion cast one's lot with the unprotected. One cannot in one day learn to see sanctuary and strength in *that*.

There was, I knew, a word for every little turn and variation in the highly articulated environment of the Bowery Savings Bank. The realm of experience that linked Pamela and myself, in contrast, has for most of human time been outside the architecture of civilization as we understand it. But our experience is not, in fact, outside the architecture. It is in it, and always has been. It is embedded in the materials of the shelter that we have made for ourselves. We therefore cannot know ourselves truly without seeing when there is terror in harmony; without registering in our marrow a coldness that may feel like warmth, or violence that presents as lust for life. We try to see these things not to demolish but to strive toward a whole world, because an unwhole world is ghostly: no matter how beautiful it might be, no connection is possible there. We do this not to place blame but to make connection possible. We do this to live.

ENVOI

A T THE END of our day of looking at our great-grandfather's buildings in New York, Pamela and I drove up to Newport to have a look at the Gilded Age palaces in which Stanford had had a hand—principally Rosecliff, the white confection that he built for Tessie Oelrichs. We arrived in Newport late at night and made our pilgrimage to Rosecliff the next morning. It was a beautiful summery day. There were roses and Saint-Gaudens statues in the gardens around the house, and swallows swooping around the delicate Renaissance façade. There were carvings of musical instruments in bunches on the façade, conveying conviviality and happiness. Through large, arched windows we could see through to the blue ocean on the other side of the house.

Pamela ran toward this pretty little palace, her arms stretched down, her hands out flat, and her strawberry-blond hair bouncing. I saw how different the meaning of the pilgrimage was for her from what it was for me. She had not grown up on the Place, and, even if she had, being so many years younger, her sense of Stanford would have been much more remote than mine. She was only proud of her great-grandfather, eager to honor him for his achievement and to bask in the reflection of his fame. I watched her go, and with her Grandpa and Grandma White, Mama and Papa, my mother and father, my sisters, my cousins, my uncles and aunts, my once husband, and, most beloved of all, my son—each in their impenetrable mystery, each in the passion of their life. Each one would write a history different from this one—some so different that it might be hard to connect them at all. I myself would write differently if I took on the task ten years hence—it would already be slightly altered if I started tomorrow. We live as irrevocably subjective in a changing perspective of time. This history, like all histories, can only be fathomed definitively by the true architect of desire, whose intentions, even in constructing infernal predicaments at the heart of our most tender relations, are, we have to trust, to serve love.

CREDITS AND ACKNOWLEDGMENTS

Deep personal thanks are owed to David Soeiro who endured the frustrations of the earlier years and extended financial support at crucial times. To Lynne Adams boundless gratitude for unbounded emotional and editorial support on the long home stretch. Thanks as well to my son, Julian, for whom the writing of this book was a condition of life from the beginning and who grew with it to be a source of support as well.

I thank my sisters and the person identified as Pamela in this text for their love, loyalty, and patience, and my mother for her extraordinary and unwavering support. I thank my father for our long discussion of aesthetics. I thank my parents together because in the end I owe everything to them.

ACKNOWLEDGMENTS

Because this book evolved over a period of almost two decades, the people who have helped me along the way are almost beyond accounting. I expect that for years hence, names will come to mind that should have been in these acknowledgments. Those that follow should, therefore, be regarded as little more than a rough indication of my indebtedness.

For help in my research I thank J. Winthrop Aldrich, Anya Aldrich, Richard Aldrich, Louis Auchincloss, Mosette Broderick, Paul Baker, Gertrude Chanler, John Chanler, Robert White, Claire Nicolas White, Peter White, Jehanne White, Edwin Morgan, Mrs. Brian DeMott, William Alfred, and Ann Buttrick.

For moral and editorial support I thank Mindy Aloff, Maureen Brady, Honor Moore, Susan Chace, Caryn Leland, Jody Procter, Carol Southern, and Charles McGrath. I thank Linda Steinman for her sensitive legal scrutiny of my work and Schellie Hagan for her meticulous fact-checking. My gratitude to my caring, exacting, incisive, persevering editor, Susan Kamil, is beyond words. Special thanks to Eleanor Gould for her unseduceably logical pencil, and to Elizabeth Macklin for her rigorous literary mind and full-hearted commitment to this text. And a salute to Vincent Virga for his awesomely perceptive work as photography editor.

For financial support and encouragement I thank Robert Gottlieb, Tina Brown, and the Whiting Foundation. Thanks also to Georges Borchardt and Andrew Wylie. This book is dedicated to William Shawn because without his support and encouragement it would not exist.

Deep personal thanks are owed to David Soeiro who endured the frustrations of the earlier years and extended financial support at crucial times. To Lynne Adams boundless gratitude for unbounded emotional and editorial support on the long home stretch. Thanks as well to my son, Julian, for whom the writing of this book was a condition of life from the beginning and who grew with it to be a source of support as well.

I thank my sisters and the person identified as Pamela in this text for their love, loyalty, and patience, and my mother for her extraordinary and unwavering support. I thank my father for our long discussion of aesthetics. I thank my parents together because in the end I owe everything to them.

PHOTOGRAPHS

PHOTO CREDITS

ABOUT THE AUTHOR

Suzannah Lessard, recipient of a 1995 Whiting Award, was an editor and staff writer for *The Washington Monthly* for three years. She remains a contributing editor there and is also a contributing editor at *Mirabella*. For twenty years she was a staff writer for *The New Yorker,* which she left in 1995. She now lives in New York City with her son, Julian, and is at work on her next book.